MEN WHO LEFT THE MOVEMENT

JOHN HENRY NEWMAN, THOMAS W. ALLIES,
HENRY EDWARD MANNING, BASIL WILLIAM MATURIN

By

GERTRUDE DONALD

Essay Index Reprint Series

BOOKS FOR LIBRARIES PRESS, INC.

FREEPORT, NEW YORK

First Published 1933
Reprinted 1967

NIHIL OBSTAT:

GEORGIUS D. SMITH S.Th.D., Ph.D.,

Censor deputatus

IMPRIMATUR:

✠ JOSEPHUS BUTT,

Vicarius generalis.

WESTMONASTERII,
die 2*a* *Januarii*, 1933.

To my pastors and teachers;

and especially

in most grateful and affectionate memory

to

G. H. P.

INTRODUCTORY NOTE

THE writer begs to be allowed to offer her most sincere gratitude to Messrs. Longmans, Green & Co. for their kind and generous permission to use the extract from Miss Mozley's *Letters and Correspondence of J. H. Newman* which form the basis of the first chapter of her book; to Messrs. Burns, Oates & Washbourne Ltd. for similar kindness with regard to the use of *A Life's Decision* in the second chapter; to Messrs. Macmillan & Co. Ltd. for allowing her to draw so freely upon Purcell's *Life of Cardinal Manning* in the third chapter; and again to Messrs. Longmans, Green & Co. and Mrs. F. J. Sheed for permission to use so many of the letters contained in the latter's *Father Maturin—a Memoir and Selected Letters.* She desires also to thank Messrs. Hutchinson for their kindness in authorizing her to quote the extracts from *Letters of the late Father B. N. Maturin to Lady Euan Smith* which, with those taken from Mrs. Sheed's *Father Maturin*, form the main part of the fourth chapter.

PREFACE

Those responsible for the celebrations in honour of the Oxford Movement centenary are publishing a series of short pamphlets on the leaders of the Tractarian party. Keble, Newman, and Pusey, of course, with Hurrell Froude and one or two others, are included ; but many of the men who helped to start the Revival a hundred years ago are not mentioned in the list of tracts published or promised.

As several of them, with Newman at their head, left the Oxford Movement within a few years of its founding, the omission of their names helps to obscure one of its characteristics which seems so far to have escaped notice. Among the many powerful forces which comprised it, there was one, latent in it from the very first, which manifested itself six years after it started ; gathered strength as time went on ; and remains unimpaired to-day. That force, which is inherent in every subdivision of non-Catholic Christianity, is a centrifugal force.

Newman was driven by it to leave the Movement in 1845, as all interested in it know. But many have no idea that though he was almost the first, and by far the greatest, who did so, a long list of men followed him in the path to Rome. The Tractarian desire for Unity and Authority in the Church awakened a want in their hearts which no revival in the Church of England could supply ; and their successors still find the same lack, and take steps to fulfil their desire in the same way, as the Oxford converts did.

Pius IX foresaw this when, in 1849, he spoke to Allies of the 'great good' Dr. Pusey had done towards the conversion of England by spreading abroad this ideal of a Church and causing his countrymen to desire it. It was, as the Pope said, the first step in 'preparing the way for Catholicism.'

Recent Anglican accounts of the Movement give very little prominence to the names of most of the men who left it. When, as sometimes happens, they are mentioned, the fact of their subsequent conversions is usually omitted. This method was lately employed in a paper describing the part taken in the Movement by Dodsworth and Oakeley. In the case of Newman and Manning, of course, it is equally impossible to avoid mentioning them in connection with the Movement and to ignore the fact that they left it; but few who read of their conversions realise that they were less than one-sixtieth of those which took place amongst the English clergy between 1845 and 1855.

Six years after Newman went, Manning also left the Movement; to those who remained his going was almost as great a blow as the loss of Newman. Ward and Dodsworth went; Robert and Henry Wilberforce; Dalgairns, Faber, Maskell, Allies, Coleridge, Laprimaudaye; the time would fail me to tell that long list of names. Amongst the laity the tide of conversions was equally strong; it is reckoned that several hundreds accompanied the one hundred and thirty Tractarian clergy who left the Movement for Rome during those ten years.

Its centrifugal force remains unspent. If the statistics provided some time ago by the Church Association, which represents the militant Protestant section of the Church of England, be correct, the English Church Union, founded in 1859 'to defend and maintain unimpaired ' Tractarian ideals, has provided a steady stream of converts to the Church annually since that date till the present day. And in a Catholic list, published in 1929, of about seven hundred and fifty English clergymen who have been received into the Church since the Movement began, a large proportion of those mentioned have come from Tractarian and Anglo-Catholic surroundings.

It is interesting to compare the reasons given by the first Tractarian converts for their respective conversions with those of Father Maturin fifty years later, and with the accounts of a similar experience written by men, formerly Anglican, who have become Catholics within the last few years. Partly for this reason, and partly because their motives are sometimes misrepresented, it seemed worth while to take four of the men who left the Movement—Newman, Allies, Manning, and Maturin—in chronological order, as typical in their different ways of their contemporaries; and to base a short study of each man's conversion on the letters and diaries written to and by him in the years which immediately preceded it.

The choice of Newman and Manning needs no explanation. Allies gives a very clear and detailed account of his progress towards the truth, and much that he says of his difficulties then applies to men who stand now where he stood during his last years as an Anglican. His correspondence with Newman, soon after the latter's conversion, shows how typically eclectic his ' churchmanship ' was at that time; and Newman's rebukes (which he seems never quite to have understood or considered justified) point a moral for some who are attempting to square the circle now in the same way as he was doing then. Father Maturin's letters give ample proof that no ' Catholic Revival ' which stops short of the Unity and rejects the Authority of the One Church can usurp that Church's place. His sympathetic understanding of certain difficulties which had not arisen in the 'fifties makes his experience useful to those whom they confront to-day.

In the course of the first three studies several names appear whose owners played their part in the Movement in a greater or less degree. Some, like Keble, Pusey, and Gladstone remained in it; and their opinions of the action of those who did not are set forth in letters written by and about them. But by far the greater number of the names mentioned in these pages belong to men who left the Movement; whose own words have been used, as far as possible, to show the reasons which forced them to leave it. Every one of them did so against his natural inclination, in obedience to the vision of the Truth vouchsafed to him. Each of them entered into the inheritance waiting for him to claim it; that inheritance lost to him by the action of his forefathers but now restored to him by the grace of God.

For when the men who left the Movement (founded, in all good faith and sincerity, in order to make the Church of England Catholic) had the courage to shut the door which they discovered led only to a blind alley, another opened. And by that door they entered the Church, One, Holy, Catholic, and Apostolic, whose 'doctrines unchanged and power always exercised' date back to the first Whitsunday; the One Fold; under one Shepherd.

In vain the surge's angry shock
In vain the shifting sands—
Unharmed upon the eternal Rock
The eternal City stands.

May 29, 1932.

CONTENTS

MEN WHO LEFT THE MOVEMENT

CHAPTER I

JOHN HENRY NEWMAN

NEXT year[1] the centenary of the Oxford Movement will be celebrated by those who attribute to it 'the restoration of the Sacraments, the recovery of the practice of confession, and revival of the religious life, of belief in the Church and, above all, the restoration of worship to its right place' in the Church of England. Great preparations are on foot to create an appropriate atmosphere in which those who honestly believe it has accomplished what Lord Irwin (in the words just quoted) claims for it may worthily give thanks for God's blessing on it and do honour to the memory of its leaders.

By common consent, three men stand out preeminently amongst the first Tractarians, and of those three Newman was by far the greatest. At his death *The Guardian* acknowledged the debt owed to him not only by the High Church party, but by the whole Church of England, in the following passage:

'He was the founder we may almost say of the Church of England as we see it. What the Church of England would have become without the Tractarian

[1] The reckoning here, and in similar instances throughout the book, is from the year in which it was written, 1932.

Movement we can faintly guess, and of the Tractarian Movement Newman was the living soul and inspiring genius. . . . Whatever solid success the High Church party have obtained *since Cardinal Newman's departure* (italics mine) has been due to their fidelity to his method and spirit.'

Much water has run under the arches of the 'Bridge Church' since that obituary notice was written forty-two years ago, and much of the fidelity it speaks of seems to have been washed away, if the teaching of certain Anglo-Catholic leaders to-day is any criterion of their beliefs as a party.

'Since Cardinal Newman's departure.' Like Banquo's ghost at the feast, the thoughts those words conjure up can never be banished from the minds of those about to celebrate the Movement's centenary. The greatest of its leaders, 'its living soul and inspiring genius, without whose sermons,' Dean Church writes, 'the Movement would never have been what it was,' left it soon after its first decade had passed; and those responsible for its due celebration are on the horns of a painful dilemma.

For the enthusiastic love inspired by Keble and Pusey is only a faint memory to the descendants of those who felt their personal influence; and their writings, even *The Christian Year*, have little power over the minds of the present generation. An attempt to circulate a reprint of Keble's once famous sermon has fallen flat; while 'Cor ad cor loquitur,' seems eternally true of all that Newman wrote. It will be impossible to rouse interest in the Centenary of the Movement without causing intelligent and independent minds to study its history at first hand; and it will be hard for those who do so without prejudice to avoid asking themselves: 'If Newman, for the reasons given by himself, came to distrust the Movement he inspired, why should we believe in it ? '

The promoters of the Centenary celebrations are naturally aware of this difficulty, and have already begun to take steps to meet it. The methods they adopt differ according to the degrees of generosity and fairness possessed by each individual writer, but all agree in one particular. The many who have already attempted to answer the old question ' What then does Father Newman mean ? ' have all carefully avoided giving the clear, full, and easily accessible reply he himself made to it.

Some prefer to speak of him as ' a great heart led astray ' ; or say that he left the Movement ' disheartened and hopeless, to end his chequered life in the Roman Communion,' as if his disillusionment followed him into the Church. They claim that ' no greater tribute can be paid to the enduring power of his work than this, that he spent the last forty-five years of his life in trying to destroy the edifice he had raised, and failed.' If they are right, how can the edifice raised by John Henry Newman, and impervious to his subsequent attempts to destroy it, have any claim to be called Catholic ? ' Quod semper ' cannot apply to the work of a man born anno Domini 1801. The great Tractarian leaders, who in all good faith believed they were restoring their ancient Catholic heritage, would have been horrified at such a tribute to the work Newman began with them, but abandoned as soon as he saw that its foundations were in reality but of man's devising.

Another way out of the difficulty is taken by others who acknowledge Newman's greatness with generous enthusiasm, and do not attempt to suggest that any tinge of self-love or any personal element whatever caused him to leave the Anglican Communion. Unlike the creators of the Newman legend, they have read the whole of the account he gives of 'the three great blows' which shook him, and they therefore realise why the condemnation of Tract 90 affected him so deeply. Not because the Bishops disagreed with him, but because they disagreed with the Catholic Church, of which he earnestly believed the Church of England was a 'Branch.' So the line of defence taken is to ask: 'If Newman were alive to-day, in the Church of England as it is to-day, would he leave it as he did eighty-five years ago?' and to answer it as the questioner, Lord Irwin, did in the words quoted in my opening paragraph.

But there is another aspect of Anglicanism of which Lord Irwin seems unaware; yet 'if Newman were alive to-day' it would seem to him fully as dark and menacing as that which was forced upon his notice eighty-five years ago. For the lack of Authority, and therefore of Unity, in the Church of England is as great, and the symptoms of that lack as plain as when Newman left it in 1845 for the only Church which possesses both.

Is there any difference in the spirit which tolerated mutually exclusive beliefs on Baptismal Regeneration then, and that which allowed the late Archbishop of Canterbury in 1928 to pronounce two completely opposed views on Our Lord's Eucharistic Presence to be equally orthodox in the Anglican Communion?

Would Newman have had his faith in the Church of England strengthened by hearing Bishop Barnes speak of the Blessed Sacrament in the Tabernacle, or Dean Inge on the Virgin Birth and Bodily Resurrection of Our Lord, in words I cannot bring myself to quote?

Would he have approved Canon Raven's views on the Priesthood of Women or gone to hear him preach in a Unitarian chapel, or have endorsed the teaching of Dr. Major, Principal of one of her Theological Colleges, on the Divine Humanity of Our Blessed Lord ?

What would he have said to the sermon preached in Westminster Abbey by the late Archdeacon of Westminster, in which Dr. Charles spoke to a congregation which included the boys of Westminster School of the *legend* of the Empty Tomb ?

What would have been his attitude to the resolution of the Lambeth Conference in 1930 to the effect that ' a baptised communicant member of a Church *not in communion with our own* ' (italics mine) should, ' if cut off by distance from the ministrations of his own church . . . be welcomed to Communion,' or to the Bishops' desire that the privilege should be extended to those of similar status ' in school or college chapels where the Anglican rite is used ? '

And finally, what would he have done if he had been at Evensong on Sunday, July 13, 1930, in All Saints, Margaret Street, when the Apostles' Creed was set aside, and a dignitary of the Greek Church was authorised to recite the Nicene Creed, without the Filioque, in its place ?

The incident is thus described by the Vicar, Prebendary of S. Paul's and a leading Anglo-Catholic.

' At the point where the Apostles' Creed is recited in our Office, the Patriarch recited the corresponding Eastern Creed, which is our Nicene Creed without the clause " and from the Son," after which the Clergy and Choir sang the same Creed in English as an act of Unity in Faith.'

It is not clear whether ' the Clergy and Choir ' restored the clause omitted by the Metropolitan of Thyatira when they sang the Nicene Creed in their turn ; or whether they followed Mgr. Germanos in the same omission as that which caused the first great Schism in the Church of God nearly a thousand years ago. If they restored it, where was their unity with him? If they did not, what becomes of their claim to be 'Catholics of the Western obedience?'

And as to the possibility of Newman's acquiescence or approval as regards the foregoing, let him answer for himself:

'Whereas the Church of England has a claim on the allegiance of Catholic believers only on the ground of her own claim to be considered a branch of the Catholic Church.

And whereas the recognition of heresy, direct or indirect, goes far to destroy such a claim in the case of any religious body.

And whereas to admit maintainers of heresy to communion without formal renunciation of their errors goes far to recognising the same . . .

And whereas the dioceses of England are connected together by so close an intercommunion that what is done by authority in one immediately affects the rest.

On these grounds, I, in my place, being a Priest of the English Church and Vicar of St. Mary's, Oxford, by way of relieving my conscience, do hereby solemnly protest against the measure aforesaid, and disown it, as removing our Church from her present ground, and tending to her disorganisation.'

His voice was heard crying in the wilderness of the Church of England in 1841, in protest against the intercommunion with Lutherans which the Jerusalem Bishopric entailed. 'In the Church of England as it is to-day' Modernist Churchmen, maintainers of heresies quite as much opposed to Anglican doctrine as the Lutheran, are freely admitted to communion. Soon, if Convocation carries out the Bishops' proposals, members of schismatic bodies who left the Church of England on account of their sacramental beliefs will have a right to receive communion in her churches if prevented by distance from attending their own. And a prelate of a Church whom her Articles declare to have erred has been allowed to recite his Creed, the very form of words which embodies that error, in a church which has lately figured in a book on London churches as 'The Church Catholic.' How can anyone who knows what Newman stood for in 1841 imagine he would be silent now ?

> 'Oh to love so, be so loved, yet so mistaken !
> What had I on earth to do
> With the slothful, with the mawkish, the unmanly ?
> Like the aimless, helpless, hopeless, did I drivel ?
> Being, *who ?*'

The third method is to write with admiring gratitude of the Vicar of S. Mary's the Virgin, to acknowledge and extol his genius and the part he played in the Movement, and then to credit him with reasons for leaving it which could not possibly lead anyone reading them to follow him. They let the curtain fall on Father Newman of the Oratory, they speak pityingly of his tardy recognition by Leo XIII, and they give the impression that his happiness and his usefulness came to an abrupt end on October 9, 1845. But if ever any man gave proof that he changed 'cœlum non animum,' in the sense that his powers and his genius were in no way less fruitful under the sun which shone from a different heaven, it was John Henry Newman.

It seems therefore worth while to try to show the motives which inspired him to make that change, and incidentally his real character, by collecting some of the many passages bearing on the step he took which are to be found in a number of contemporary letters, scattered up and down large volumes of biography, in which he explained it to his friends. For in these scattered letters, even more perhaps than in the *Apologia* and *Certain Difficulties of Anglicans*, the true Newman is to be seen.

Before beginning this attempt to study him as he really was, it may be well to consider for a moment the legendary Newman, who, as pictured by his creators, is almost as difficult to fathom as Hamlet in his inconsistency.

He did not become a Catholic for the only valid reason in existence, the reason which the Newman of history gave to his sister just before his reception into the Church : ' My motive simply is that I believe the Roman Church to be true.' No, he ' seceded to Rome ' because he was disappointed at the slow progress of the Movement ; discouraged by the treatment he met with from the University authorities and his own Bishop ; from a sort of pique at being undervalued ; even, they imply, because Rome could drug his mind into a sort of stupefied assent to doctrines he longed to hold, but could not while the bracing air of Canterbury freshened his brain. For any reason, in fact, except the true one.

Yet the creators of the legend acknowledge this man, weak in faith and in purpose, dependent mentally and morally on the support and approval of the majority, swayed by pique and self-pity, daunted by rebuff, as the mainspring of the Oxford Movement during the first twelve years of its existence ; and having drawn their portrait of this paradoxical character go on to complain that ' the Roman Church in this country does not know how to use the best sons of Canterbury,' and ' wasted Newman ' ; or as another complaint runs, ' they did not know how to use him.' If he had been such as they depict, how could Rome (or for that matter Geneva, or Constantinople) have known how to ' use ' him, and is it possible to ' waste ' what has already run to seed ?

Granting for the sake of the argument that ' Rome ' refused to use this reed shaken by the wind, merely because it had sprung up on the banks of the Isis and not by the Tiber, imagining for a moment that the Church did not ' use ' Cardinal Newman, let us recall for a moment how Canterbury dealt with her ' best sons ' among his fellow Tractarians, and with their successors in the generation which he lived to see suffer similar persecution in the House of their friends.

Canon Ollard, one of Canterbury's best-known sons at the present day, draws the parallel many of his colleagues love to draw, but with a truer inference. This is what he says of the treatment dealt out to the leaders of the Oxford Movement, men of exceptional learning, piety, and zeal, by the Church in whose service they spent their lives :

' Dr. Newman was, after a time, recognised and honoured in the Roman Catholic Communion with all but the highest honour that Communion could give ; Dr. Pusey, like Mr. Keble and many another of that band, received no mark of trust here . . . no mark of honour from the Church he served so well.'[1]

No man, he tells us, was more cruelly attacked, no man more bitterly abused. He was suspended from preaching for two years, in May 1843, by the Vice-Chancellor ; on the ground that in a sermon on the Real Presence preached in S. Mary's before the University of Oxford he had taught doctrine contrary to the Church of England. When the foundation-stone of

[1] *Persons and Principles of the Anglo-Catholic Revival,* by Canon Ollard.

Margaret Chapel (later to be rebuilt as All Saints, Margaret Street) was laid, Dr. Pusey's presence had to be concealed lest it should cause a riot; and his little girls were sent away from the school in Clifton where he had placed them, as the parents of some of the other children could not tolerate the presence of Dr. Pusey's daughters under the roof which sheltered theirs. His last public act was to publish two moving appeals in *The Times* on behalf of one of the new generation of Tractarians (now called Ritualists), the Rector of S. John's, Miles Platting, imprisoned in Lancaster Gaol under the Public Worship Regulation Act of 1874.

Active and violent persecution by the mob, as well as his Bishop's inhibition from officiating in the diocese of Chichester, befell John Mason Neale—' poet, hymn-writer and translator, founder of a religious order, Church historian, preacher; the first man who unlocked the door of that wonderful treasure-house of the ancient hymns of the Church.' [1]

The inhibition took place in 1848 and was not removed till 1861, five years before he died at forty-eight, worn out by ' the neglect, opposition, and persecution ' which, like a sort of prophet's mantle, seems to have fallen on him as it had done some years earlier on Dr. Pusey. The cause of the trouble was the erection of a screen with a large Cross on it in the Chapel of Sackville College, the placing of a cross on the Altar; the use of two lights at celebrations; and the innovation of flowers in vases on the Altar and a set of altar frontals. The mob showed their approval of the Bishop's action by trying to burn down the College; and made another attempt to do so in 1851, undeterred by the presence in the house of his wife and small children, ' some of whom were very ill,' and were

[1] *Ibid.*

soothed in their terror by their dauntless parents ; who bore all that came to them, as one of their children wrote many years later, ' in a quiet matter of fact way.' This second outbreak took place because Neale instituted the use of a bier and pall at funerals. In 1857 the police had to intervene to protect him and the Sisters of S. Margaret of Scotland, the Anglican Sisterhood he had founded three years earlier, from the fury of the mob. The Sister whose funeral was the scene of the riot had died of scarlet fever, caught from a case which Neale had sent her to nurse in a poor quarter of the town. Protestant agitators incited a mob to attack him at the graveside by saying he had hoped for this to happen so that his new Sisterhood might benefit from the money she was supposed to have left ; and the police found it no easy task to rescue him and the Sisters who were with him from the angry crowd. Just before his death in 1866 he was again mobbed, this time in the streets of Liverpool after a sermon he preached there.

John Keble escaped both mob violence and episcopal censure, though the latter was incurred by his curate, who remained a deacon for twenty years as the penalty of holding the same view as Keble on the Real Presence. The penalty affected Keble also, as it meant that till the Bishop consented to ordain Mr. Young to the Anglican priesthood he could not celebrate Holy Communion or give absolution. So for twenty years Keble had a curate whom he could not leave in complete charge of the parish for one single day.

But though active personal enmity was never shown him, the man whom Newman had declared in 1823 to be ' the first man in Oxford,' the brilliant scholar who had obtained a Double First in Classics and Mathematics when only just over eighteen, the poet whose

'Christian Year' is a classic of Anglican devotional poetry which has helped to deepen the spiritual life of countless devout souls, lived and died as Vicar of a small country parish in Hampshire. John Keble's gifts were used in God's service *in spite of* Canterbury; he met with no aid nor appreciation from the Mother who seems unable to recognise so many of her best sons.

Lowder and Mackonochie, Stanton and Dolling, with other less-known but equally devoted missioners and parish clergy, were subjected to constant persecutions by the Church Association, inhibitions by their Bishops, and, in the case of Lowder, to mob violence instigated by the Church Association, for practices now in common use, and legally allowed to be part of Anglican doctrine and ceremonial. Others were sent to prison for similar practices; the last survivor of such imprisonment, Mr. Tooth, died only two years ago. Bishop King was prosecuted in 1892 by the Church Association for the same offence as that which Dr. Pusey committed in 1843, though this time the Archbishop of Canterbury upheld that doctrine of the Real Presence which his predecessor denied. It is heartrending to think how differently 'Rome' would have dealt with those splendid men, and how she would have 'used' their learning, their piety, their devotion, and their zeal. And the end is not yet, as the recent history of the diocese of Birmingham can testify.

'O my Mother, whence is this unto thee, that thou hast good things poured upon thee and could not keep them, and bearest children, yet darest not own them, why hast thou not the skill to use their services nor the heart to rejoice in their love . . . ? Thou makest them stand all the day idle as the very condition of thy bearing with them, and thou biddest them begone where they will be more welcome.' True when they were spoken, proved true over and over again since then, those words are part of the last sermon Newman ever preached in an Anglican pulpit. 'After preaching it he tood off his B.D. hood and threw it on the altar rail, to mark that he had ceased to be a teacher in the Church of England'; which had borne him yet dared not own him, and had not the skill to use his services or rejoice in his love. So he did her bidding, and went where he was more welcome; to the Church which set him among her princes as a reward for his services, and still rejoices in his love. 'Give Her the living child and in no wise slay it: *She* is the Mother thereof.'

An article entitled 'Musings upon Newman' which appeared in the *Church Times* during February 1930, sounded the note upon which the creators of the legendary Newman have harped ever since.

It may be mere coincidence that articles of the kind have become increasingly plentiful as the Centenary celebrations draw nearer; but it is difficult to imagine any other reason for such an otherwise inexplicable belittling of one of the greatest Englishmen of the nineteenth century than a desire to minimise an influence whose power they still fear. As Pius IX said of him in 1849 'he has a European name.' His influence still lives on in the books he wrote as a member of the Church which is said to have 'wasted' him; the marks and scars of the battle he fought before he could win his way into her Fold inspire others also to endure hardness in order to gain the same reward; and his powerful advocacy of her teaching draws men to her who have never known her, and helps those who have lapsed from that knowledge to return to her, at home and abroad alike.

Pius IX saw that the Oxford Movement was preparing the way for Catholicism by setting before English

Churchmen 'the principle of Authority, which is the first thing in religion.' To souls naturally Catholic the rest follows, and Newman's books are still there to expound that principle ; and to tell Anglicans to-day as he told them in 1850 that 'a movement is a thing that moves.' His pen is as powerful now as his voice was then to point out that a bridge, even a bridge Church, is not a dwelling-place ; and that the Via Media leads to a maze of cross roads, dangerous and perplexing ; like Carfax in that 'city of lost causes and impossible loyalties' from which the Oxford Movement took its name.

It is small wonder that his books live on in his own country, for their spell goes out into all lands. Some years ago Paul Claudel, whom critics have declared to be the greatest of living Christian poets, was asked by a young friend seeking to regain his faith : 'Help me to understand the Mass—give me a commentary on the meaning of each phrase.' He answered : 'How speak worthily of this adorable mystery ? I have tried several times, and always found it beyond my power.' But a few days later he sent him another letter—with no end to it nor beginning, but just a heading, 'On the Mass ;' and then in perfect English came what his friend desired. The French Catholic had not gone to the many great spiritual writers in his own language, whose books he must know well. The long extract was taken from *Loss and Gain*, and the person he found most able to speak worthily of that adorable Mystery was John Henry Newman.

So it is perhaps not surprising that papers like 'Musings upon Newman' are written at this juncture ; whether in the hope of lessening Newman's power to attract those who may have heard little of him before the Centenary propaganda, or in order to console those in charge of the celebrations for the great blank his absence leaves among the names of the leaders they are about to honour.

The 'Musings' are apparently provoked by a book published last spring, *A Newman Synthesis*, compiled by Father Erich Przywara, S.J., who is said to occupy the first rank among German interpreters of Newman. That such a book, produced by a foreign Jesuit, should be welcomed by Catholics all over Europe forty years after Newman's death is in itself a refutation of the legend that the great Cardinal was not appreciated by his fellow-Catholics.

The author of the 'Musings'—a frequent and usually well-informed contributor to the *Church Times*—says :

'Newman, like many others, demanded Truth, but demanded it from the lips of the living Church. . . . He began the Tracts with the idea that the Church of England had only to be shown the Truth in order to acquire a corporate conviction no less vigorous than his own, of the justice of Truth's claims. . . . But the Church of England betrayed little readiness to be convinced, and its official leaders manifested considerable reluctance to be instructed ; and though Newman was entirely in the right, he was at once badly shaken. Instead of relying on the concrete fact of episcopacy, he relied on the support of the Bishops ; when the poor startled Bishops proved themselves a superficies of duckweed, Newman fell into the pond. While Pusey, ensconced upon the cumbrous but substantial platform of antiquity sat safely, Newman found his confidence in the solidity of living vegetation had been utterly misplaced.'

The writer seems to be unaware of, or wilfully ignores, the fact that it was when Newman began to examine that substantial platform on which, the article tells us, Dr. Pusey so safely sat, that he first saw why 'the poor startled Bishops' had so little power to represent 'the concrete fact of episcopacy'; on which, *pace* the writer of that article, I think Newman did rely. It was not his fault if the Anglican bishops personally turned out to be duckweed on a pond instead of stones in that great Building of which Jesus Christ himself is the Chief Corner Stone.

'The shock cost him his faith in a Church whose spokesmen appeared to repudiate the Truth, and he was forced to seek elsewhere for a Church which should look more complacently upon his deepest convictions. Newman was genuinely consumed with wholehearted anxiety for the Church to teach him; but he exercised a scrupulous discrimination in the choice of doctrine he was prepared to suffer it to impart.' (These last words, entirely unsubstantiated, are most unfair and untrue.) 'As an Anglican,' the writer says, 'faith meant to Newman rational uncertainty; from his later Roman standpoint, the same unnatural divorce between faith and reason remains, but the word "faith" has now come to mean irrational certitude.'

And he ends his article with these words, put into the mouth of 'my Uncle Thomas,' a sort of literary ventriloquist's dummy, whom this author uses at times, as Mrs. Gamp did her friend Mrs. Harris; possibly for the same reasons.

After saying 'Newman submitted his reason to the claims of a supernatural authority that overrides the Church with an infallible afflatus' he lets his dummy speak thus. '"He did nothing of the sort," exclaimed my Uncle Thomas, looking over my shoulder; "he had all the rhetorician's passion for romantic efficiency and poetic order, and yielded himself to the spells of the sorceress. He struck his rational colours and hoisted the same emblems as those fellows flew at the fore in the Dutch wars ! " " Dutch wars ? " I murmured feebly : " we are not discussing the Holy Inquisition." " Van Tromp, man," he rejoined : " doesn't ' tromper ' always mean ' deceive ' ? The Broom of Christian Fanaticism which sweeps aside objection and enquiry with the plea of faith in its own infallibility, and the Whip of Christian Imperialism, which scourges man into submission on the plea of visible unity under its own necessary authority. The spectacle of Newman casts a dismal reflection of the efficaciousness of praying for light." '

So much for Cardinal Newman. ' Uncle Thomas ' has spoken, and his nephew evidently feels that with this last amazing sentence the matter is finished indeed. All that he can add by way of epilogue is this ambiguous statement. ' Indeed, that is an opinion widely held.'

No one who has carefully read the *Apologia pro Vita Sua*, and the two volumes of lectures in which Newman met and answered in his own masterly way ' Certain Difficulties felt by Anglicans in Catholic Teaching ' in 1850 can possibly hold such an opinion ; and those who have not done so have no right to hold, far less to express, any opinion of Newman at all.

But as Newman foresaw while he was still an Anglican, his conversion has delivered him up, unprotected by any scruples on their part, into the hands of critics who draw upon their imagination to supply the knowledge of him and of his motives which they lack.

In 1844 he predicted in a letter to his sister that if he changed his religion, the view among those he left would be ' that there must be something wrong at bottom ; that I must be disappointed or restless, or set on a theory, or carried on by a party, or coaxed into it by admirers, or influenced by any of the ten thousand persuasions which are as foreign from my mind as from my heart, but which it is easy for others to assign as an hypothesis.'

The truth of that prediction was immediately fulfilled, and the second and third generation of them that misjudged him seem inclined to imitate their forefathers.

But, luckily, in 1874 Newman decided that steps should be taken in good time 'to meet . . . vague and random accounts derived from the ephemeral literature and controversy of the last forty years'; and five years before his death he not only chose for himself some one well qualified to do so, but gave her ample material for her future task. His view was that if a memoir of him should be published, 'a Protestant Editor must take the Protestant part,' in justice to those who had worked with him in the great Movement from which he had once expected so much, and to the Church to which he had belonged in the best years of his manhood.

In 1885 he found his Protestant Editor in the person of Miss Anne Mozley, whose two brothers, both Anglican clergymen, had been close friends of Newman, and had married two of his sisters.

No better choice could have been made. Miss Mozley claimed to possess this qualification for her task; 'an absolute trust, under all changes of thought and circumstances, in the truth, sincerity, and disinterestedness of the one subject of the work.' Under the special circumstances of the case there could be no better qualification. That absolute trust in him, avowed by a loyal Anglican to whom the 'change in thought and circumstances' which culminated in 1845 must have been particularly painful, is the most complete answer to those who, by 'the vague and random accounts of him ' which he long ago foresaw, so frequently misrepresent a man they never knew, and cannot or will not understand.

It is a great temptation to quote page after page of Miss Mozley's work. Her loyalty both to her own Communion and to the great leader who had left it makes the impartiality with which she writes as valuable as it is rare. Her Anglican beliefs leave her testimony as unbiassed as her intimate friendship with Newman makes it informed ; and every word she writes shows how consistent his character was, and how unlike the petty, querulous, disappointed nature which some who never knew him now try to depict as his.

Her opportunities to study that character extended over forty years at least. She wrote to his sister in 1849, after a visit to Littlemore, and says of him : ' I was hardly prepared for the strong hold Mr. Newman seems to have gained over their affections ' (his old parishioners, the cottagers at Littlemore), ' that is, I imagined his power lay in a different class, though of course all must value his care and kindness ; ' and in 1890, after his death, her respect and affection shines undiminished in the words which explain her purpose in publishing, as he had wished her to do, his *Letters and Correspondence.*

' That purpose is,' she says, ' to place John Henry Newman before the reader as he was to his family, to his friends, to his correspondents ; as he was in early youth and in manhood ; in public and in private ; and in his actions in, and for, the English Church while he remained in her communion. With his secession the Editor's task as being a member of that communion is ended. Under the total change of circumstances the work, if pursued, must be carried on by another hand. Yet because only half a life furnishes the material and matter of these volumes, the reader need not imagine that the letters of a later date may or must contain intimations of a changed character. Perhaps no man, passing through a course of change, ever remained more substantially the same through the lapse of years and revolution of circumstances and opinions.' In the following extracts from her work, forty years after its publication, I hope to carry on the torch, for its light seems still to be needed.

As my purpose is only to show the steps by which Newman was led to the Catholic Church, from the indisputable evidence provided by his correspondence during the six years' struggle which preceded his reception, I am limiting these extracts to letters only; and to no other letters than those written between 1839, when the first gleam of the truth dawned on him, and October 8, 1845, when he sent that note to his sister from the Parsonage at Littlemore which told her: 'This night Father Dominic, the Passionist, sleeps here.'

My reason for this limitation is best expressed in Newman's own words.

'It has been a hobby of mine,' he writes to his sister in 1863, twenty-two years before Miss Mozley began her task, 'though perhaps it is a truism, not a hobby, that the true life of a man is in his letters. . . . Not only for the interest of a biography, but for arriving at the inside of things, the publication of letters is the true method. Biographies varnish, they assign motives, they conjecture feelings, they interpret Lord Burleigh's nods: but *contemporary letters are facts.*'

Some may say that the *Apologia* was a brilliant piece of special pleading; written so long after the critical years it recounts that the convictions set forth may owe more to emotion and less to reason than the author's memory allows; or they may discount the personal touches in the Lectures of 1850 as being tinged with a proselytising zeal which unintentionally colours the actual facts so as to fit his purpose. But they cannot possibly bring either charge against the letters written to Newman's most intimate friends, and received from them in reply, during the long-drawn-out crisis which caused so much pain on both sides.

Till 1839, as his letters show, Newman never for one moment doubted that the Church of England was inherently Catholic, and that the errors and losses of the Reformation could be made good if the changes, doctrinal and ceremonial, then made could be revised, explained, or reversed. In 1833, with this object in view, he wrote the first three Tracts for *The Times;* and published them just two months after Keble's famous Assize Sermon had been heard in the University Church of S. Mary the Virgin. Keble, Froude, and, a little later, Dr. Pusey, the Regius Professor of Hebrew and one of the first men in Oxford, joined him in this work; and the Movement advanced from strength to strength, gaining adherents amongst the best brains in Oxford and meeting for some years with little or no opposition.

A letter to Hurrell Froude, dated November 17, 1835, shows how little Newman then dreamed that in ten years' time he would have come to agree with the criticism he so indignantly quotes. 'Bunsen,' he says, 'has pronounced on our views with singular vehemence. He says that if we succeed we shall be introducing Popery without authority, Protestantism without liberty, Catholicism without universality, and Evangelism without spirituality.'

Baron de Bunsen, who was Prussian Minister at the court of S. James for many years, was not only a diplomatist, but 'a scholar of world-wide repute, a historian, a philosopher, and a theologian.' His Protestant mind saw their peril; but the Tractarians, drifting in mid-Channel between the true Catholic Faith of their forefathers and the 'Reformed religion' which had robbed them of it, were unconscious of the helplessness of their little boat, with no rudder, on uncharted seas.

No one who reads the religious press representing the three parties in the Church of England to-day can fail to see how right Bunsen was, and that in spite of the great progress made in restoring Catholic practices, and to a lesser extent, Catholic doctrine, since he wrote those words, 'Popery without authority' is as impossible now as it was when Henry VIII first attempted Catholicism without the Pope. The conditions which Bunsen prophesied must be inevitably fulfilled so long as the first part of his forecast remains a true description of a part, or even of the whole, of the Church of England.

The first glimpse of the truth of Bunsen's estimate of the Tractarian position seems to have come to Newman in September 1839. In a letter to Mr. Rogers, dated September 22, he says: 'Since I wrote to you, I have had the first real hit from Romanism which has happened to me. R. W.,[1] who has been passing through, directed my attention to Dr. Wiseman's article in the new *Dublin*. . . . It certainly does come upon one that we are not at the bottom of things. . . . I seriously think this is a most uncomfortable article on every account, though of course it is *ex parte*. . . . I think I shall get Keble to answer it. As to Pusey, I am curious to see how it works with him. . . . It is no laughing matter. I will not blink the question, so be it, but you don't suppose I am a madcap to take up

[1] Robert Wilberforce—who became a Catholic in 1856.

notions suddenly—only there is an uncomfortable vista opened which was closed before. I am writing upon my first feelings.' Those feelings, as we know, were destined to deepen and strengthen, and 'the hit from Romanism' to prove, as far as Anglicanism went, a knock-out blow.

Cardinal Newman, who supplied Miss Mozley with much of her material himself, gave her the following extract from an article by Henry Wilberforce in the *Dublin Review* of 1869 for insertion as an amplification of the above letter.

'It was the beginning of October, 1839, that he made the astounding confidence, mentioning the two subjects which had inspired the doubt—the position of S. Leo in the Monophysite controversy, and the principle "securus judicat orbis terrarum" in that of the Donatists.[1] He added that he felt confident that when he returned to his rooms, and was able fully and calmly to consider the whole matter, he should see his way completely out of the difficulty. But he said, "I cannot conceal from myself that, for the first time since I began the study of theology, a vista has been opened before me, to the end of which I do not see." He was walking in the New Forest and he borrowed the expression from the surrounding scenery. His companion' (H. W. W. the writer of these words), 'upon whom such a fear came like a thunderstroke, expressed his hope that Mr. Newman might die rather than take such a step. He replied with deep earnestness that he had thought that if ever the time should come when he was in serious danger [of losing faith in the Church of England] of asking his friends to pray that if it was not indeed the will of God, he might be taken away before he did it.'

[1] See Note 2, Appendix.

It is difficult to think charitably of 'Uncle Thomas's' dismal reflection on 'the efficaciousness of praying for light' with that reply, made 'with deep earnestness,' to his horror-struck friend, in one's mind.

On November 17, 1839, he writes to his sister, Mrs. J. Mozley: 'I should not wonder if my situation got unpleasant at S. Mary's. Had I my will I should like to give up preaching. . . . The question of the Fathers is getting more and more anxious. For certain persons will not find in them just what they expected. People seem to have thought that they contained nothing but the doctrines of Baptismal Regeneration, Apostolical Succession, Canonicity of Scripture and the like. Hence many have embraced the principle of appeal to them with this view. Now they are beginning to be undeceived. . . . Our Church is not at one with itself, there is no denying it.'

Miss Mozley says:

'Such notes of warning as are sounded in the above letter were doubtless very trying to the receiver; but Mrs. Mozley was assisted to bear them with sincerity; both by her high esteem for her brother's character, and by her own unworldliness. The loss of position [to him] and the world's estimate would tell little with her. The question would be one of right and wrong. And trusting her brother as she did, and full of faith in her own Church, she hoped, and held her peace.' How hard that question was for him to settle, and how truly she estimated the pains he would take to solve it rightly, the following letters show.

That full faith in the Church of England which he had shared with her, and had helped to deepen in her and in many others, died hard in him. And the inborn distrust of the Roman Church, which keeps so many outside her communion from even attempting to find out how far that distrust is justified, was as grave a hindrance to Newman then as it is to so many devout non-Catholics still. Miss Mozley says that 'his mind returned to its allegiance' after the misgivings caused by Dr. Wiseman's article; but those who have experienced the natural re-assertion of former beliefs and prejudices which takes place in the mind as it reacts from the first shock of Truth will realise that there was no real returning.

In a letter dated January 8, 1840, to Mr. Rogers, he shows that strange distrust and dread of 'the priest' which still exists in many non-Catholic minds, in his impression of 'Mr. Spencer, the R.C. Priest.' He refused to dine with him, he says, because 'if R.C.'s and A.C.'s met together, it should be in sackcloth rather than at a pleasant party,' but consented willingly to receive a visit from him. He found him 'a gentleman-like, mild, pleasing man, but sadly smooth,' and wonders whether it is their [R.C.'s] habit of internal discipline, the necessity of confession, etc., which makes them so. 'He did not come to controvert—his sole point was to get English people to pray for the R.C.'s . . . we should be soon agreed if we really loved one another . . . such prayers would change the face of things.'

Two days later he writes to Mr. Bowden: 'Things are progressing steadily; but breakers ahead! The danger of a lapse into Romanism, I think, gets greater daily. I expect to hear of victims. Again, I fear I see more clearly that we are working up to a schism *in* our Church; that is, a split between Peculiars and Apostolicals; the only hope is that the Peculiars may be converted or broken up.'

That hope has acted as a will-o'-the-wisp to each generation of Anglo-Catholics. But 'the Peculiars' are safely entrenched behind Parliament; and 1928 showed English Churchmen, to the despair of many of them, what heavy fetters an Established Church must wear. One of her own sons said during the Prayer-book crisis: 'The Church of England must make up her mind whether she is the Bride of Christ or the hesitating friend of Parliament.' It is impossible to be both.

Soon after he tries to counter Dr. Wiseman's 'palpable hit' in an article in the *British Critic*, January 1840, entitled 'Catholicity of the English Church.' His anxieties and prejudices are again shown in the following:

'I am extremely pleased at your liking my Article. It is one that has given me much anxiety. I have no fear of the Movement [not] progressing at this moment, but great apprehension of lapses to Romanism. It is written in answer to the Article of Dr. Wiseman, which (I acknowledge) is striking.'

A month later he writes: 'I have got into a desponding way about the state of things, and I don't know why quite. Right principles are progressing doubtless, but it seems as if they were working up to a collision with Puritanism which may split the Church. . . . Pusey is at present very eager about setting up Sisters of Mercy. I feel sure that such institutions are the only means of saving some of our best members from turning Roman Catholics. . . . I am told that Mr. Spencer expressed himself quite puzzled why I would not dine with him. So I wrote him a letter about a fortnight since which he has not answered, perhaps from fear of getting into controversy. I merely said it was useless for them to attempt amiable intercourse between themselves and us while *acts* were contrary—while they allied themselves to Dissenters and Infidels and were plotting our ruin. The voice was Jacob's voice, but the hands were the hands of Esau ; that he did not come as an individual Roman Catholic, but as a priest on a religious purpose.'

Such a letter must have been so difficult to answer politely that it is not, perhaps, surprising that Mr. Spencer refrained from attempting to do so.

The next letter shows how the leaven is working—and that the true cure for schism is to end, not try to mend it.

'Everything is miserable. I expect a great attack upon the Bible—indeed, I have long expected it. . . . His' (Carlyle's) 'view is that Christianity has good in it, or is good as far as it goes, which, when applied to Scripture is, of course, a picking and choosing of its contents. Then again you have Arnold's school . . . giving up the inspiration of the Old Testament, or of all Scripture (I do not say that Arnold himself does). Then you have Milman clenching his *History of the Jews* by a *History of Christianity* which they say is worse, and just in the same line. Then you have all your political economists who cannot accept (it is impossible) the Scripture rules about almsgiving, renunciation of wealth, self-denial, etc. . . . All these and many more spirits seem uniting, and forming into something shocking.

'But this is not all. I begin to have serious apprehensions lest any religious body is strong enough to withstand the league of evil but the Roman Church—at the end of the first millenary it withstood the fury of Satan, and now the end of the second is drawing on.'

This quotation from a letter to Mr. Bowden, November 6, 1840, is interesting, as it shows that 'Continental Churches' repelled some and drew others nearly a hundred years ago just as is the case to-day.

'I do not think anything great of the Continental

Churches as you seem to think, or of the Roman Catholics at home. Were there "sanctity" among the Roman Catholics they would indeed be formidable.'

A letter to Mr. Rogers, November 25, 1840, gives further light on his reasons for leaving S. Mary's and why he did not act on them for another three years.

'I wrote to Keble some time since telling him at full my difficulties about S. Mary's, and resolving to go by his judgement. I had three heads: (1) my inability to get on with my parish; (2) my exercising an influence on Undergraduates to which I was not called; (3) the tendency of my opinions to create Roman sympathies. The third was the only ground he thought much of, and he gave me full leave to resign, if I could do it without creating scandal. At the same time he said he wished me to remain, and did not think it a reason necessitating resignation. Upon this I felt I ought to remain. . . . These considerations have gone far to reconcile me to it since his decision: (1) That we don't know yet what the English Church will bear of infused Catholic truth. We are, as it were, proving cannon. I know that there is a danger of bursting; but still, one has no right to assume that our Church will not stand the test. (2) If I fear the tendency of what I teach towards Rome, it is no more than I see in Hooker or Taylor. . . . We all create a sympathy towards Rome so far as our system does not realise what is realised in Rome. (3) For what we know, Liberalism, Rationalism is the foe at our doors. S. Mary's pulpit may be given me against an enemy who may appear to-morrow. I am more certain that Protestantism leads to Infidelity than that my own views lead to Rome.'

In the same letter he speaks of a dilemma which has recurred since then. 'W. Palmer of Magdalen seems to have difficulty to convince the Russians that we are much of a Church ; their definition of us was a Church which had cast off its Patriarch, was somehow Calvinistic, and had no discipline.' And in a later letter : 'Palmer of Magdalen is returning ἄπρακτος [without success]. The Russians will not believe him against the evidence of all the English they ever saw before. They think him a theorist or worse.'

The change now beginning to dawn in him is shown in this passage : 'Last evening Bowden's volumes came. Either one has drifted, or he is most intensely Anglican in his theory, but he is quite consistent' ; and again in this passage, where in contrast to his former opinion of Continental Churches and English Catholics he says : 'I think you are apt to be unfair to those unhappy Romanists. As to the ceremonies, I confess I liked what I saw as little as you ; but there is such a thing as uncharitableness. We are much cautioned by Scripture not to go by appearance. How often has a person a pompous, etc., manner in England whom we think well of. Demureness is the Roman manner, as pompousness is the Church of England's. Marriott says upon it, "The impression of hollowness in ceremonies is almost necessarily exaggerated, unless one enters into them with complete enthusiasm." You may be right in being so suspicious of Rome, but still such prejudice and suspicion, I do think, disqualify you as a witness of fact against her. You *seem* to *like* to catch at something bad.'

Now come the letters relating to Tract 90,[1] which was condemned by the Bishop of Oxford in March 1841 ; an event which was, Newman said five years later, 'a far greater crisis than March 1836.' The reference is to the events detailed in a paper entitled 'Chronological Notes,' and attached to a packet of

[1] See Note 3, Appendix.

letters which he gave to Miss Mozley as material for her book, in the preparation of which he took much pains to help her.

In these notes he says : 'March 1836 is a cardinal point of time. It gathers about it, more or less closely, the following events :

1. Froude's death.
2. My Mother's death and my Sister's marriage.
3. My knowing and using the Breviary.
4. First connection with the *British Critic*.
5. The tracts becoming treatises.
6. Start of the "Library of the Fathers."
7. Theological Society.
8. My writing against the Church of Rome.
9. Littlemore Chapel.'

He brackets these nine landmarks in his life under the heading 'a new scene gradually opened' ; and, in the entry he added in 1841, states that the affair of No. 90, March 1841, was 'a far greater crisis than March 1836, and opened an entirely different scene.'

The 'new scene' of 1836 must have been the vision of the Church of England purified from the errors of the Reformation, teaching the doctrine of the Fathers, using the ancient prayers of the Catholic Church, and clear from the later corruptions of Rome. What he saw 'far different' in 1842 one can only guess ; but it was probably his first clear view of the City that hath foundations, whose Builder and Maker is God. The mirage of 1836 truly marked 'a cardinal point of time,' but the far greater magnitude of this new crisis is easy to appreciate.

The story of the famous Tract and its results has been told so often, and can be found in such perfect form in the *Apologia*, that I will only quote parts of the letters which show how calmly he took the storm.

On March 5, 1841, he writes :

'Do you know I am getting into a scrape about Tract 90 ? Yet it must be ; I cannot repent it a bit ; unless indeed it should get Pusey involved in it. . . . People are so angry, they will attempt to do anything. . . . I repeat, I cannot repent it.'

He writes to Dr. Jelf, at the same date : 'The only peculiarity of the view I advocate, if I must so call it, is this—that whereas it is usual at this day to make the particular belief of their writers their true interpretation, I would make the belief of the Catholic Church such.'

To his sister, Mrs. T. Mozley, on March 9, 1841, he says : 'I have got into what may prove a serious mess here. I have just published a Tract [90] which I did not feel likely to attract attention. . . . But people are taking it up very warmly.' And on March 12 he tells her : 'I fear I am clean dished. The Heads of Houses are at this very moment concocting a manifesto against me. Do not think I fear for my cause.'

He writes to Mr. Bowden, March 13, 1841 : 'I expect the very worst—that is, that condemnation will be passed in Convocation upon the Tracts as a whole, by the non-resident Establishment men, Liberals, and Peculiars. . . . I am making up my mind to it, and so is Keble. . . . That it will turn to good I doubt not ; but we have been too prosperous. I am only sorry my friends should suffer through me.' And on March 15 : 'The Heads, I believe, have just done a violent Act ; they have said that my interpretation of the Articles is an *evasion*. Do not think that this will pain me. You see no doctrine is censured, and my shoulders shall manage to bear the charge—if you knew all, or when you know, you will see that I have asserted a great principle, and I ought to suffer for it ; [i.e.] that the Articles are to be interpreted, not according to the meaning of the writers, but (as far as the wording will admit) according to the sense of the Catholic Church.'

His hopes for the Church of England and his distrust of Rome still persist; and find expression in letters such as these, which are so exactly like those written to dissuade converts or to deplore recent conversions at the present day that it is hard to believe they are dated so far back as 1841.

In April of that year he writes to a lady: 'I am not surprised at anyone being drawn to the Roman Church under your feelings, wrong as I think it. And I lament as much as anyone can our present state in the English [Church] in which high aspirations have so little means of exercise. If you will allow me to add it, I think you were *hasty* in your resolve. So great a matter as a change of religion ought not to be thought of without years (I may say) of prayer and preparation. Nor do I think it God's way, generally speaking, for *individuals* to leave one religion for another—it is so much like an exercise of private judgment. Three thousand at once were converted on the day of Pentecost. Where miracles are brought before an individual, the case is different. However, it is of course most satisfactory news to me that your purpose was arrested, and a cause of much thankfulness that any work of mine was a means of it.'

(That stock argument 'the exercise of private judgment,' employed against so many on the threshold of the Church, would surely make the conversion of a Unitarian, for instance, or of a Quaker, to the Church of England, or of a Moslem or Buddhist to Christianity of any kind, quite as misguided as that of an Anglican to the Roman Church.)

On the same subject he writes to Keble, July 23, 1841: 'I fear that poor —— is going to Rome, but one is apt to anticipate the worst. I have just stopped a man (not one you know) i.e. for the time, and other friends have stopped another. This in great confidence.'

In the same year he writes to discourage a lady from the same step as 'poor —— ' seemed likely to take: 'Your letter has given me the most heartfelt pain; though I do not feel at the moment quite as much myself as I should like to be in answering so very serious an appeal, yet I do not like to delay. . . . I will never say such a thing as that the Church of Rome is apostate; but still I am sure you have seen but the fair side of that church as yet. Join it, and you will see our Saviour's prophecy fulfilled there as with us, that she is a net cast into the sea and gathering of every kind.'

Keble's letter telling him of his (Keble's) Bishop's refusal to confer priest's orders on his curate (who remained a deacon for twenty years in consequence) on account of his belief in the Real Presence, elicits these attempts at encouragement, which again have a modern ring about them.

'I cannot help hoping that things are better with you than you anticipate. . . . On the whole, as things have before now been at the worst as regards the Clergy, so they are now as regards the Bishops, and they will improve, I think. Recollect the Clergy left off their wigs before the Bishops did. All in good time.'

An important divergence between his view and Dr. Pusey's is given in this short passage: 'I think he is beginning, however, to understand that we differ historically and not doctrinally; but though it is a relief to him, yet I do fear that his historical view of the Reformation is his great bulwark against Rome, which is not a comfortable thought.'

That difference goes far to explain why Pusey stayed when Newman went. Earlier in this letter Newman says : 'But then he never reads anything' ; by which of course he must have meant anything modern. Dr. Pusey's great reputation for learning (based on what 'Musings upon Newman' calls 'the cumbrous but substantial platform of antiquity') was acknowledged by all his contemporaries—friends and foes alike. But there have been important men since Agamemnon as well as brave men before him ; and the type of mind which believes that 'Art stopped short in the cultivated Court of the Empress Josephine' has its counterpart, which will learn nothing from History unless its lessons come down through many centuries, from a past which is indeed far away and long ago.

The Jerusalem Bishopric negotiations[1] greatly added to Newman's distrust of the English Bishops. On October 5, 1841, he writes to Keble : 'It really does seem as if the Bishops were doing their best to uncatholicise us, and whether they will succeed before a rescue comes who can say ? The Bishop of Jerusalem is to be consecrated forthwith, perhaps in a few days. M. Bunsen is at the bottom of the whole business, who, I think I am right in saying, considers the Nicene Council the first step in the corruption of the Church.'

On the 12th he writes to his sister : 'Have you heard of this atrocious Jerusalem Bishop affair ? He was consecrated last Sunday. The Archbishop is doing all he can to unchurch us' ; and to Mr. Bowden, the same week, he says : 'Have you heard of this fearful business of the Bishop of Jerusalem ? I will send you some papers about it soon. It seems we are in the way to fraternise with Protestants of all sorts, Monophysites, half-converted Jews, and even Druses. If any such event should take place, I shall not be able to keep a

[1] See page 37.

single man from Rome. They will all be trooping off sooner or later.'

In another letter on the same subject to Mr. Bowden, on October 12, he says :

' I did not speak of Oxford friends in what I said nor of anything immediate ; but the case is this : Many persons are doubtful whether we have the Notes of the true Church upon us ; every act of the Church, such as this of coalescing with heretics, *weakens* the proof. And in some cases it may be the last straw that breaks the horse's back. . . . The Archbishop is really doing most grave work, of which we cannot see the end.'

To Keble he writes on October 24 : ' For myself, I am too anxious for others, nay for myself, to say anything light about going to Rome. Our Church seems fast Protestantising itself, and this I think it right to say everywhere (not using the word " Protestant ") but not lightly.'

To Mr. Hope (later a convert) he writes these important words on October 17, 1841 : ' I think then we must be very much on our guard against what Cowper calls " desperate steps." Do you recollect the sheep in " The Needless Alarm " ?

> Beware of desperate steps. The darkest day,
> Live till to-morrow, will have passed away.

. . . I cannot deny that a great and anxious experiment is going on, whether our Church be or be not Catholic ; the issue may not be in our day. But I must be plain in saying that if it does issue in Protestantism, I shall think it my duty, if alive, to leave it. . . . I fear I must say that I am beginning to think that the only way to keep in the English Church is steadily to contemplate and act on the possibility of leaving it. Surely the Bishops ought to be brought to realise what they are doing.

But still, on the whole, I hope better things. At all events, I am sure that to leave the English Church, unless anything very flagrant happens, must be the work of years.'

To Keble, on October 31, he writes on the same subject: . . . 'I have no hope at all at present that certain persons will remain in our Church twenty years, unless some accommodation takes place with Rome; but I see no sign at all of any *immediate* move. I think that men are far too dutiful; and in twenty years things must either get much better, or the poor Church must have got much worse or have broken to pieces.'

A fortnight later he writes again to him: 'It seems there are certainly plans on foot in some quarters (but I don't wish it mentioned) for effecting a great extended union of Protestants, the Church of England being at its head. I distrust Bunsen' (who, Prussian by birth and Lutheran in religion, would naturally use all his Court influence to forward such a scheme) 'without limit.'

On the same day he writes to Mr. Bowden to tell him that 'it is quite plain our rulers can unchurch us'; and that there is imminent danger of 'a great scheme afloat to unite us in a Protestant League—the limits of which no one can see.' He encloses a draft of the Protest which 'after much anxious thought' he has sent to the Bishop of Oxford. With great respect, but very plainly he tells him:

'I do this very serious act in obedience to my sense of duty. If the English Church is to enter on a new course and assume a new aspect, it will be more pleasant to me hereafter to think that I did not suffer so grievous an event to happen without bearing witness against it.

May I be allowed to say that I augur nothing but

evil if we in any respect prejudice our title to be a branch of the Apostolic Church ? That article of the Creed, I need hardly observe to your Lordship, is of such constraining power, that if we will not claim it and use it for ourselves, *others* will use it in our own behalf against us. Men who learn, whether by means of documents or measures, whether from the statements or acts of persons in authority, that our Communion is not a branch of the One Church, I foresee with much grief, will be tempted to look out for that Church elsewhere.'

The main theme of Newman's Protest is too long to transcribe here ; and the Jerusalem Bishopric, in its short duration, made so many converts to the Church that all students of the Oxford Movement are fully conversant with its conditions ; viz. that the Lutheran Church and the Church of England were to provide alternately for the consecration of a succession of Bishops to shepherd Anglicans, Lutherans, and Calvinists in the east of Europe.

The fine preamble to his Protest, so full of painful interest to those forced to tolerate the Modernist school of theologians as their clergy and fellow-laity, has already been given, but its conclusion is repeated below as a link with what follows :

'On these grounds, I, in my place, being a Priest of the English Church, and Vicar of St. Mary's, Oxford, by way of relieving my conscience, do hereby solemnly protest against the measure aforesaid, and disown it, as removing our Church from her present ground, and tending to her disorganisation.

John Henry Newman.

November 11, 1841.'

His last sentence shows that he does not yet "despair

of the Republic," though after the letters to Keble and Bowden, it seems odd to read the certainty of 'our Church's future' expressed in the following, written to his sister, Mrs. J. Mozley, on November 16. He is probably actuated by that fear of giving pain to others, as well as of one's own suffering, which is a powerful factor in the struggle most converts unconsciously make to shut their eyes to the truth, when he says: 'Do not believe any absurd reports. They talk in the papers of secessions among us to Rome. Do not believe it. No one will go. At the same time I cannot answer for years hence, if the same state of things is persevered in . . . but I assure you, my dearest Jemima, unless some strange change comes over me, there is *no fear* at present.'

At the same date he writes to Keble in the same strain:

'Of course no one can read your sermon without being struck by it, but my feeling is you had better not preach it. I think it will add to our excitement, without effecting any object.

It will increase, upon a separate authority, the impression which is not well founded, that there are men in Oxford who are on the point of turning to Rome, with a sort of confession to the world at large, and as a triumph of the foe over you and us.

I know of none such—there is no doubt great danger in prospect; but the persons in danger are far too serious men to act suddenly, or without waiting for what they consider God's direction, and I should think very few indeed realise to themselves yet the prospect of a change, nay, would change, provided [that] their brethren kept from saying or believing of them that they would change. In that case, dangerous seed might lie dormant like a disease, for *many years*. It is a very bad policy to accustom them to the thought that the world *thinks* they will change. . . . I must tell you on the other hand that Cornish, whom I thought I might give a sight of your sermon, wishes it preached. But he has seen very little of men[1] this term, and believes, what I think a mistake, that there are men[1] here hanging on from day to day.'

On December 1 he shows his misgivings in this letter to Mr. Rickards—and again strikes a note which must be only too familiar to many a perplexed and conscientious Anglican to-day.

'. . . For two years and more I have been in a state of great uneasiness as to my position here, owing to the consciousness I felt that my opinion went far beyond what had been customary in the English Church. Not that I felt it any personal trouble, for I thought and think that such opinions were allowed in our Church fully; but that looking on my position here, I seemed to be a sort of schismatic or demagogue, supporting a party against the religious authorities of the place. In what I have done in my parish, whether in the ordinary routine of duty or any improvements or additions which I have attempted, I have uniformly kept my parishioners before my mind and wished to act for *them*. But in almost every case my endeavours have fallen dead upon them as a whole, but have been eagerly apprehended and welcomed by University men, and of these many Undergraduates. In proportion, then, as I had reason to believe that the Heads of Houses were dissatisfied with me, did I seem to myself in the position of one who was interfering with those committed to the charge of others, against their will, and that for the propagation of feelings and opinions which I felt were not so truly those of the English Church as their own. . . . In consequence for two years past my view of my duty and my prospective

[1] *i.e.* University men.

plans here have been very unsettled. I have had many schemes floating in my mind how to get out of a position which of all others is to me most odious—that of a teacher setting up for himself against authority. . . . The most persistent feeling in my mind is to give up St. Mary's. . . . As to this Jerusalem Bishopric, I seriously think that, if the measure is fairly carried out, it will do more to unchurch us than any event for the last three hundred years. With these feelings it is not wonderful that I should see my position here in a very different light. O my dear Rickards, pray excuse all this sad talk about myself, which disgusts me as I make it, and I fear I am writing you a most pompous sort of letter, but I think you would like to hear about me, and it is a comfort to me to write it out, and I have no time to pick and choose my words. But to return. It really seems to me that the Heads of Houses are now not defending the English Church, but virtually and practically, though they may not mean it, joining with this heretical spirit and supporting *it*; so that the contest is no longer one of what would be represented as a quasi-Romanism against Anglicanism, but of Catholicism against heresy.'

He ends the letter with these key-words: 'And thus, to my mind, at present, a much broader question follows up the particular one.'

In the answer each man found to that great question lies the true reason why Newman went, and Keble and Pusey stayed; why Father Maturin left the Society of S. John the Evangelist and became a Catholic, while the saintly Father Congreve, who remained his life-long friend, died in the Anglican Communion; why year after year, amongst men equally devout, intellectual and sincere, the one is taken back to the Church of his forefathers, the Holy Catholic and Apostolic Church, and the other is left, hampered at every turn by the anti-Catholic legislation which rules the Church of England 'as by law established.'

The clergy who disobey their bishops in the matter of Devotions, or of Reservation, are the true heirs of Keble and Pusey, and of the other Tractarian clergy who continued to teach, and, when not inhibited, to preach the Catholic doctrines the bishops whom they have sworn 'reverently to obey' had forbidden them to inculcate. They say now, more boldly perhaps than their predecessors, that wherever the individual Bishop departs from Catholic doctrine or tradition, they must follow the teaching of the Church, not of the Bishop. In insisting on some particular doctrine, whatever it may be, against the authority of their Bishop, they forget that they thereby cut across 'a much broader question,' the Catholic doctrine of Authority, which makes it as impossible for a Catholic priest to decide that he is right and his Bishop wrong on a point of faith or morals as for a Catholic Bishop to advance his opinion against an Article of Faith.

'The spectacle of Newman'[1] enabled at this crucial time to see a cardinal point of truth which was hidden all their lives from men as good and sincere as himself 'casts a reflection on the efficaciousness of praying for light' which can only seem 'dismal' to those who shrink from the crags and torrents a man must battle against before he reaches the heights to which that light leads him on.

He was still some way from realising the full implications of that much broader question, and the confidence his sister expresses in the following letter shows how she hopes 'this trial' will end. On December 3, 1841, she writes: 'I do feel very anxious about prospects in general, especially since your last alarming letter. My

[1] See page 17.

great trust is that you will be supported through this trial; that you may act as firmly as you have hitherto done. You must not think that I am at all afraid of you or doubtful of you. . . . I only feel more and more thankful that you have more judgment and clear-sightedness than the rest of the world, so as to steer through a most difficult course.'

In the middle of December came another blow. This time it was Keble's turn to send a Protest 'in his place, being a Priest of the Church of England' to the Archbishop of Canterbury, against the Bishop of Winchester's refusal to ordain his curate, the Rev. Peter Young, on account of his belief in the Real Presence. Newman offers him his sympathy regarding this in a letter dated December 16, 1841, but his main preoccupation seems still to be the same; what will its effect be on 'secession' which he is still endeavouring to prevent? The letter ends: 'I wish you would impress on all bystanders, patrons, friends and the like what a miserable effect is impressed on the minds of young and sensitive persons when they are accused or remonstrated with as suspected Romanists. This is now going on largely. It is bad enough to be rudely told by enemies that they have no business in the English Church but are dishonest in remaining in it (and this is going on without scruple or limit) but when *quasi* friends take up the tone of alarm . . . then a man says to himself, "I certainly fear there is something in *me* which I am not aware of" just as if every-one were to stare at him as he walked in the streets. Then the familiarity it creates with the idea of Romanism is miserable, and the dreadful unsympathetic chilling atmosphere created around him by it is a distinct evil. All this [is] added to his inward scarcely recognised tendencies towards Rome.' A fragment of unconscious autobiography which shows how fierce the struggle in him was now growing.

To Mr. Bowden, on December 21, 1841, he writes courageously: 'On the whole I am in good spirits about the Jerusalem matter. If the Prussian plan is carried out it will cut my ground clean from under me. For eight years I have been writing, either to prove, or on the ground, that we *are* a branch of the Catholic Church, that we were committed to nothing inconsistent with it, therefore I have a sort of right to make a protest, and a pretty strong one. Certain people will believe nothing but acts, and assuredly I will waste no more *words*. I am sanguine that acts will tell; and this protest is an act.'

On Christmas Eve he writes a letter to the Rev. R. W. Church—who later became Dean of S. Paul's and a historian of the Movement—which was evidently intended to lessen 'M.'s' (probably Mozley's) fear of secessions; but it reads as if he were also striving to reassure himself as to the possibility of remaining Anglican.

'I suppose it would be no relief to M. to insist upon the circumstance that there is no immediate danger. Individuals never can be answered for, of course, but I should think lightly of that man who for some act of the Bishops should leave the Church. Now considering how the Clergy really are improving, considering that this row is even making them read the tracts, is it not possible we may all be in a better state of mind some years hence to consider these matters? And may we not leave them meanwhile to the will of Providence? I *cannot* believe this work has been of man; God has a right to His own work to do what He will with it. May we not try to leave it in His hands, and be content?'

The postscript to this letter is an ironic comment on his argument.

'P.S. The Bishop of London has rejected a man for holding (1) any sacrifice in the Eucharist; (2) the Real Presence; (3) that there is a grace in Ordination.'

Next day he sends another letter to Mr. Church, which gives further reason to suppose that what he said to Keble about the dangers of imputed Romanism was based on personal experience.

'Christmas Day, 1841. I have been dreaming of M. all night, and so write again. . . . Should not M. and the like see that it is unwise, unfair, and impatient to ask others "what will you do under circumstances which have not, which may never come?" Why bring fear, suspicion, and dissension into the camp about things which are merely *in posse*? . . . I speak most sincerely when I say that there are things which I neither contemplate nor wish to contemplate, but when I am asked about them ten times, at length I begin to contemplate them. . . .

And again, M. surely does not mean to say that *nothing* could separate a man from the English Church, e.g. its avowing Socinianism, its holding the Holy Eucharist in the Socinian sense. Yet he would say it was not right to contemplate such things. . . . But let this be considered as the alternative. *What* communion could we join? Could the Scotch or American [Communion] sanction the presence of its Bishops and congregations in England without incurring the imputation of schism, unless indeed—and is that likely—they denounced the English as heretical? . . .

Has not all our misery as a Church arisen from people being afraid to look difficulties in the face? They have palliated acts when they should have denounced them . . . and what is the consequence? That our

Church has through centuries ever been sinking lower and lower, till a good part of its pretensions and professions is a mere sham, though it be a duty to make the best of what we have received. . . . The truest friends of our Church are they who boldly say when her rulers are going wrong and the consequences ; . . . if the clergy of —— denounced the heresy of their diocesan they would be doing their duty and relieving themselves of the share they will otherwise have in any possible defections of their brethren.'

Next day, December 26, 1841, he writes to Keble : 'It is not love of Rome that unsettles people, but heresy at home. And your Protest is very important as a bold looking of facts in the face. The Church of England has been ruined by people shutting their eyes and making the best of things.'

Miss Mozley here points out that now (January 1842) Newman's sisters were beginning to realise the trend of events, and that he always tried to give them the hopeful side, whenever such presented itself, of his hopes and general expectations. In February he begins to stress the possibility of his leaving S. Mary's, which had been present in his mind for some time. On the 15th he writes to Mrs. J. Mozley from Littlemore, where he had gone to live 'for good' a few days before :

'I am in Oxford only on Saturday evening and Sunday morning. . . . For some years, as is natural, I have felt that I am out of place at Oxford, as customs are. Everyone almost is my junior. And then, added to this, is the hostility of the Heads, who are now taking measures to keep the men from St. Mary's. But I think I have made up my mind, unless something very much out of the way happens, to anticipate them by giving up St. Mary's. . . . A year and a half since (as Harriett knows) I wanted to retire from St. Mary's, keeping Littlemore. If I could do so at the cost of losing my Fellowship I think I would.'

On February 21 he writes to her again :

'I have several things that puzzle me about St. Mary's pulpit. One special thing is this, which I have felt for years : is it right to be preaching to those who are not, in any sense, my charge, and whose legitimate guardians, the Heads of Houses, wish them not to be preached to ? This seems to be a view, to which others might be added, cogent also. But as you say, there are great difficulties on the other side. Of course I shall not pledge myself to anything for the future.'

He is most careful not to unsettle any of those who come to him for advice while he himself has any doubt as to the truth of his own misgivings. A letter dated February 27, 1842, to a lady who became a Catholic almost at the same time as he did, shows how scrupulously he avoided precipitancy in himself and guarded against it in others.

'Will you let me turn your thoughts, if I have not done so already, to the duty and, in one sense, task of cultivating *interior religion*, and in doing so, of leaving all matters of opinion for your Almighty Protector to determine for you in His good time ? So far is certain, whatever misgivings you may have had about the catholicity of the English Church, that men may *in it* be far, far holier—may live far nearer to God than most of us do. Let us beg Him to enable us to aim at those inward perfections, which He certainly does vouchsafe in our Communion. We cannot be wrong here, we must be pleasing Him in this proceeding ; we are in the safest way putting ourselves under the shadow of His wings. Depend upon it, at this day and in our present state, we are unequal to the great work of judging Churches, and had better leave it alone.'

A letter on May 24, 1842, is interesting evidence that Newman's departure was not in any way due to a belief that he had been singled out for individual censure by the Bishop or to a sense of injustice at his hands.

He writes to Keble : 'You will be glad to hear that the Bishop's Charge delivered yesterday was very favourable to us, or rather to our cause, for some of us suffered. He began by a description of the Movement, and of the bitterness with which it had been assailed ; spoke against newspaper writers and meeting-spouters, and praised us in contrast. This took up some time. Then he went to the Tracts. . . . I understood him to say that he thought No. 90's interpretation not the obvious, that he wished to take the obvious, that he was against all interpretations which made the Articles anything or nothing, and yet he did not see why Calvinists and Puritans should be allowed to consider that the Articles admitted them, but men who agreed with Bull, Beveridge, Andrews, etc., might not have the same liberty the other way.

Then he went to the disciples of the Movement, and here his regular censure began : (1) Palmer's Anathema (Magdalen Palmer) ;[1] (2) Vestments ; (3) Oakeley's Translation of St. Buonaventura ; (4) the speaking against the Reformers ; (5) leaning to Rome, and an unreal unity. He concluded by saying that he expected hardly any clergymen to go to Rome, but only very young persons ; and that if people attempted to dam up the Movement there would be a great inundation

[1] There were two Tractarians of that name, one a Fellow of Magdalen, the other of Worcester ; the former became a Catholic later on.

and a fearful schism. And he also said some strong things against the Church of Rome.'

This letter clearly shows that the Bishop saw some justice in Newman's contention, and that his particular censure was directed against Palmer and Oakeley, the other three points being held by all the Tractarians equally.

On July 16, 1842, he writes to the Archdeacon of Maidstone, the Ven. W. R. Lyall, at some length. It shows that the difficulty in answering the Archdeacon's question was too great for even an intellect like his to accomplish.

'Your question is just the difficult one of English theology, and as time goes on it will be more and more felt. It is as deeply feeling it that some persons have been called ultras, and thought to sympathise with Rome. While the Catholic Church is broken up into fragments it will always be a most perplexing question, "What and where is the Church?" . . . I consider that, according to the great Anglican theory (by which I mean the theory of Laud, Bull, Butler, etc., upon which alone the English Church *can* stand, as being neither Roman nor Puritan) the present state of the Church is that of an Empire breaking or broken up. At least I know no better illustration. Where is the Turkish Empire at this day? In a measure it has been, and is no more. Various parts are wrested from it, others are in rebellion. There is no one authority which speaks; individuals in particular localities know not whom to obey or how they shall be best fulfilling the duty of loyalty to the descendants of Ottoman. Sometimes the truest allegiance is to oppose what seems to come with authority. In many cases there is only a choice of difficulties. For the most part, a Turk speaking of precepts, prerogatives, powers, speaks but of former times. He appeals to history ; he means the earlier empire when he speaks of Ottoman principles and doctrines. In whatever degree this is true of the Turkish power, at least it is true of the Church. Our Lord founded a kingdom ; it spread over the earth and then broke up. Our difficulties in faith and obedience are just those which a subject in a decaying kingdom has in matters of allegiance. We sometimes do not know what is of authority and what is not : who has credentials and who has not : when local authorities are exceeding their power and when they are not : how far old precedents must be modified in existing circumstances, how far not. This view might be illustrated in detail to any extent from the controversies and difficulties of the day. . . . Under these circumstances when we are asked " Where is the Church ? " I can but answer, " Where it *was* "—the Church only *is* while it is one, for it is individually as He Who animates and informs it. . . . In such strange circumstances as those in which we find ourselves we can but do what we think will best please the Lord and Master of the Church—what is most pious ; we rule ourselves by what the Church said and did before this visitation fell upon her ; we obey those that are set over us, first, because they are set over us ; next, because at least the Apostolical Succession is preserved (which is like *de facto* rulers being of the Blood Royal) ; further because they are the nearest representatives we can find of the whole Church and are to a very great extent her instruments. We consider the local Church the type and deputy of the whole.'

The marvel is that he could stay nearly four years longer in ' a local Church ' after his definite statement that ' the Church only *is* while it is One ' ; seeing too so clearly, as this letter shows, the chaos caused by the 'unhappy divisions' lamented in the Prayer Book compiled by those who caused them.

On August 28 he writes to Mr. Bowden: 'I fear these Americans have done a most serious thing, about which a row must be made. I have seen nothing in print, but am told that their presiding Bishop, Griswold, has formally admitted a Nestorian, as a Nestorian, to Communion, expressing at the same time the concurrence of his people, or a good part of them. Acts like these will drive men out of their Church.'

In March 1843 he writes to Mr. Rickards about the break with S. Mary's, which he has not yet brought himself to make, Keble, his spiritual adviser, being against it. He says: 'I assure you, nothing has haunted me more continually for years than the idea that undergraduates are trusting me more than they should, and I have done many things by way of preventing it. I should not wonder if the feeling ended by separating me from St. Mary's, about which I have thought many times.'

He writes another letter advising patient self-discipline where she was, and no thought of change, to the lady to whom he gave similar advice a year before.

He tells her: 'Religious truth is reached, not by reasoning, but by an inward perception. Anyone can reason; only disciplined, educated, formed minds can perceive. . . . Consider that you have this great work to do, to change yourself; and you cannot doubt that, whatever be the imperfections of the English Church and whatever the advantages of the Roman, there are gifts and aids in the former abundantly enough to carry you through this necessary work.'

In June another severe trial befell his loyalty. On the 4th he writes to a lady: 'I dare say by this time you have heard the rights of Dr. Pusey's matter. This day three weeks he preached a Catholic, not over strong, sermon in the Cathedral, and for it he has been suspended from preaching for two years. . . . It is difficult to predict the ultimate effects. If his cause it taken up extensively it will damage the Heads. If not, it will tend to alienate still more from the Church persons of whose attachment to it there is already cause to be suspicious.'

On July 25 he mentions in a letter to Mr. Bowden that ' the papers tell us that Lord Ashley [later Lord Shaftesbury] has had a meeting in London in some public place ' to decide whether to petition the Duke of Wellington to put down Puseyism in Oxford.

On the 27th his sister, Mrs. J. Mozley, writes to condole with him on being ' out of spirits ' and makes a gallant, if not very logical or convincing, effort to cheer him.

'I really think while there is one Bishop like your Bishop, there is every reason for hope. Indeed, if there were not, yet how soon everything might be changed! The principles you fight for must react on the higher clergy in time.' In fact, if only the tail is undaunted in its energy it *must* some day wag the dog.

After this very feminine attempt to imbue her brother with her own certainty that nothing he undertakes can ever come to grief, for no better reason than her own faith in him, she encourages him with the 'great difference between our time and that of the Non-jurors. Then Catholic doctrines were on the decline, and Liberal doctrines rising into fashion. . . . Now surely the Catholic movement will prevail if we are not utterly unworthy. . . . Indeed, dear John, I cannot but believe many in our day will live to see things very different.' How many hundreds of times since 1843 has consolation been offered on exactly the same grounds to those despairing of Anglo-Catholicism as a practical possibility ?

But yet another blow falls a month later, which he breaks to her in a letter dated August 25.

'Perhaps you know already from your proximity to Loughborough that Lockhart, who has been living here with me for a year past has, at Dr. Gentili's at that place conformed to the Church of Rome. . . . This occurrence will very likely fix the time of my resigning St. Mary's for he has been teaching in our school till he went away. . . . These are reasons enough to make me give up St. Mary's, but were there no other, this feeling would be sufficient, that I am not so zealous a defender of the established and existing system of religion as I ought to be for such a post.'

She replies by return of post : 'Your letter has, as you may imagine, concerned me greatly. I do hope you may not have quite settled on the step of giving up St. Mary's just at this critical time. I know you have long had your thoughts turned to this point, and I have by degrees learnt to reconcile myself to the prospect, but I cannot think you are aware of the effect of everything you do upon people in general, to decide upon this step just at this moment. Of course I allude to Mr. Lockhart's change just now, with which your step would naturally be associated by friends and enemies in a manner you would not wish. There are so many anxious minds waiting and watching your every motion, who would misunderstand your proceeding, and consider it a beginning of a formal disengaging of yourself from your own Church, whose perplexities would be sadly increased. I trust you will think not only of yourself, but of others, before you decide on it.'

His answer has not been kept ; but what he said can

be to a certain extent guessed from her reply two days later.

September 1, 1843. 'I am very sorry indeed if my letter increased the pain you must feel. I know well that must be very great. In return, I must say your to-day's letter has greatly lessened mine. You have such a clear view on the subject that I cannot for a moment wish you to do otherwise than you have decided. It must be right for you to act when you feel so strongly.'

In this letter she encloses one from a lady who wrote to her on hearing the rumours, now widespread, that Newman was about to leave not only S. Mary's, but the Anglican Communion. The writer says: 'I have been thinking that among all the opinions and feelings your brother is called upon to sympathise with, perhaps he hears least and knows least of those who are, perhaps, the most numerous class of all, people living at a distance from him, and scattered over the country with no means of communicating with him . . . who all have been used to look upon him as a guide. These people have a claim upon him: he has witnessed to the world and they have striven to be obedient pupils. He has formed their minds, not accidentally: he has sought to do so, and he has succeeded. He has undertaken the charge and cannot now shake them off. His words have been spoken in vain to many, but not to them. He has been the means under Providence of making them what they are. Each might have gone his separate way but for him. To them his voluntary resignation of ministerial duties will be a severe blow. If he was silenced, the blame would rest with others; but giving them up of his own free will, they will have a sense of abandonment and desertion. There is something sad enough and discouraging enough in being shunned and eyed with distrust by neighbours, friends, and clergy, but while we have had someone to confide in, to receive instructions from, this has been borne easily. A sound from Littlemore and St. Mary's seems to react on us even here, and has given comfort on many a dreary day ; but when that voice ceases, even the words it has already spoken will lose some of their power ; we shall have sad thoughts as we read them. Such was our guide, but he has left us to seek his own path ; our champion has deserted us—our watchman, whose cry used to cheer us, is heard no more.

In spite of the sorrow and fear that such a step may excite, I know it may be right to do it—and if your brother does so, I shall try to think it is ; but it seems right that he should know all the consequences. We shall not leave the Church as others may. We have no longings for Rome, but it is a strong step to make our home feel cheerless, and this will tend to do it—at least for a time.'

This letter must have been terribly hard for Newman to read. But it may help others to whom the same stern duty has fallen, or on whom in future it may fall, to see how clearly it was put before him that he was leaving many sheep in the wilderness without a shepherd, and how courageously he faced that knowledge with his ' Ought it to be done ? '

He writes the day he receives the letter to Mrs. Mozley : ' I am sorry to put you to such pain. Your letter and ——'s to you would have brought me to many tears unless I had so hard a heart. You must take what I do in faith at least ; if not, I fear I cannot find a better way of consoling you.

I wonder my late letters have not prepared you for this. Have you realised that three years since I wished to do it . . . and that then only a friend prevented me? It has been determined on since Lent. All through Lent I and another kept it in mind; and then for safety's sake I said I would not act till October, though we both came to one view. October is coming!

My dearest Jemima, my circumstances are not of my making. One's duty is to act *under* circumstances. Is it a light thing to give up Littlemore? Am I not providing dreariness for myself? If others, whom I am pierced to think about, because I cannot help them, suffer, shall I not suffer in my own way?

Everything one does honestly, sincerely, with prayer, with advice, must turn to good. In what am I not likely to be as good a judge as another? In the consequences? True, but is not this what I have been ever protesting against? the going by expedience, not by principle? My sweetest Jemima, of whom I am quite unworthy, rather pray that I may be directed aright, rather pray that something may occur to hinder me if I am wrong, than take the matter into your own hands.'

On the same day he writes to Keble, by whose advice he had acted all along in the matter of S. Mary's, as follows. What he says to him shows how scrupulously he carried out the condition '*with advice*'; which he had just told his sister played so important a part in finding out God's will for each individual soul. If any ever guarded himself so far as he could against self-deception, surely Newman was he.

'I have just got your note. I am ready still to keep St. Mary's if you think best. Will you turn it in your mind however? (1) That a noise will be made at my resigning whenever I resign. . . . Will not resignation become more difficult every quarter of a year? (2) That Lockhart's affair gives a reason for my resigning, as being a very great scandal. So great is it that, though

I do not feel myself responsible, I do not know how I can hold up my head again while I have St. Mary's.' And then, which is difficult to understand in the light of what he says in the confidential letter to his brother-in-law, written the same day, he adds: (3) 'If it did for a moment alarm people, as if something were to come of my resigning which they did not know, yet a very little time would undeceive them.' At the end of the letter, he tells Keble that Lockhart's reception at that moment had taken place in spite of a promise he had exacted from him 'that he would put aside all thought of change for three years.'

The fact that Newman had thought it wise to exact such a promise may help to explain why he himself waited two years more before joining the Church to which, as his letters from now onwards show, he was most definitely drawn. He seems to have considered it not only possible, but in fact most necessary, to wait for 'conviction to become certainty' with a cautious patience difficult to understand.

His sister Jemima's husband, the Rev. J. B. Mozley, must have written to him about the same time as she did, and to the same effect. He writes to him on September 1, the day after his moving answer to Mrs. Mozley's dissuading letter, and tells him the true reason of his leaving S. Mary's.

'. . . Really it is no personal feeling of annoyance under which I do it. I hope I am right in speaking openly to you, which I have not done but to a very few, but now I will tell you the real cause—which others besides those to whom I have said it may guess—but which (as far as I recollect) I have only told to Rogers, H. Wilberforce, R. Wilberforce, Keble . . . Tom may suspect it and Copeland, so may Church and Marriott. Indeed, I cannot name the limit of surmisers.

The truth then is, I am not a good son enough of the Church of England to feel I can in conscience hold preferment under her. I love the Church of Rome too well.'

Three weeks later he writes to Mrs. J. Mozley, who seems to have written far more often to him at this juncture than his other sister, Mrs. T. Mozley :

'You cannot estimate what so many (alas !) feel at present, the strange effect produced on the mind when the conviction flashes, or rather pours, in upon it that Rome is the true Church. Of course it is a most revolutionary, and therefore a most exciting, tumultuous conviction. For this reason persons should not act under it, for it is impossible in such a state of emotion that they can tell whether their conviction is well founded or not. They cannot judge calmly. . . . It pains me very deeply to pain you, but you see how I am forced to it.'

To Mrs. Thomas Mozley he writes a week later (September 29, 1843) :

'I do so despair of the Church of England, and am so evidently cast off by her, and on the other hand, I am so drawn to the Church of Rome, that I think it *safer*, as a matter of honesty, not to keep my living.

This is a very different thing from having any intention of joining the Church of Rome. However, to avow generally as much as I have said would be wrong for ten thousand reasons. People cannot understand a man being in a state of *doubt*, of *misgiving*, of being unequal to responsibilities, etc. ; but they will conclude that he has clear views either one way or the other. All I know is, that I could not without hypocrisy profess myself any longer a *teacher* and a *champion* for our Church.'

Mrs. J. Mozley writes to him on October 8 a letter

which shows how one of those who knew him best believed in his sincerity.

'Knowing all I do of you and your present opinions, I do not call in question anything you have done or your manner of doing it. I may deeply lament, but I cannot find fault: I cannot accuse you of being impatient, precipitate, or insincere. Far from me ever be the thought of this last. I cannot say you have not acted wisely under the circumstances, and I am sure you have acted kindly and considerately. But for many years I have anxiously watched the course, and endeavoured to ascertain particulars concerning converts to Romanism, and I must say I have never heard of anyone like yourself. All other conversions I have known anything of, men and women, seem more the fruit of excitement and restlessness than of straightforward, honest conviction.'

On October 25, 1843, Newman wrote to a friend 'who has every claim upon his frankness': 'I must tell you then frankly (but I combat arguments which to me, alas, are shadows), that it is not from disappointment, irritation, or impatience, that I have, whether rightly or wrongly, resigned St. Mary's; but because I think the Church of Rome the Catholic Church, and ours not part of the Catholic Church, because not in communion with Rome; and because I feel that I could not honestly be a teacher in it any longer. This thought came to me last summer four years . . . I mentioned it to two friends in the autumn. . . . It arose in the first instance from the Monophysite and Donatist controversies, the former of which I was engaged with in the course of theological study to which I had given myself. This was at a time when no Bishop, I believe, had declared against us, and when all was progress and hope. I do not think I have ever felt disappointment or impatience, certainly not then ; for I never looked forward to the future ; nor do I realise it now.

My first effort was to write that article on the Catholicity of the English Church ; for two years it quieted me. Since the summer of 1839 I have written little or nothing on modern controversy. . . . You know how unwillingly I wrote my letter to the Bishop in which I committed myself again, as the safest course under circumstances. The article I speak of quieted me till the end of 1841, over the affair of No. 90, when that wretched Jerusalem Bishopric (no personal matter) revived all my alarms. They have increased up to this moment. At that time I told my secret to another person in addition. . . .'

He had already told the same friend in an earlier letter that he intended to resign S. Mary's. Knowing that his friends feared that this step was the forerunner of one they dreaded he would eventually take, he took pains to give his reasons for it as clearly as he could.

'The nearest approach,' he writes, '. . . to a general account of them is to say that it has been caused by the general repudiation of the view, contained in No. 90, on the part of the Church. I could not stand against such an unanimous expression of opinion from the Bishops, supported, as it has been, by the concurrence, or at least silence, of all classes in the Church, lay and clerical. I fear that I must confess, that, in proportion as I think the English Church is showing herself intrinsically and radically alien from Catholic principles, so do I feel the difficulties of defending her claims to be a branch of the Catholic Church. It seems a dream to call a communion Catholic, when one can neither appeal to any clear statement of Catholic doctrine in its formularies, nor interpret ambiguous formularies[1] by the received and living Catholic sense, whether past or present. Men of Catholic views are too truly but a party in our Church. I cannot deny that many other independent circumstances, which it is not worth while entering into, have led me to the same conclusion.'

This letter is a complete refutation of the contention that the 'great blow' which Newman felt when Tract 90 was condemned was due to his personal discomfiture. It is unmistakably clear from what he now writes that what so shocked him was the anti-Catholic position taken up by the bishops, which had caused its condemnation.

His correspondence at this juncture with the Mozleys must have been very distressing reading for all concerned. He writes to the Rev. J. B. Mozley, on November 24, 1843: 'Your note made my heart ache —it is the simple truth, so I may say it. I don't know whether it will comfort you, yet I hope it may (as *omne ignotum pro magnifico*), to tell you that my present feelings are not new, nor have they come upon me gradually, nor from disgust and despair, nor have they been indulged.

Last summer four years [i.e. 1839] it came strongly upon me from reading first the Monophysite controversy and then turning to the Donatist, that we were external to the Catholic Church. I have never got over this. I did not however yield to it at all, but wrote an article in the *British Critic* on the Catholicity of the English Church, which had the effect of quieting me for two years. Since this time two years the feeling has revived and gradually strengthened. I have all along gone against it and I think I ought to do so still. I am now publishing sermons, which speak more confidently

[1] The Thirty-nine Articles.

about our position than I inwardly feel, but I think it right and do not care for seeming inconsistent.

I trust you may quite rely on my not admitting despair or disgust, or giving way to feelings *which I wish otherwise*, though from the experience of the last four years, I do not think they are likely to be otherwise.'

On May 24, 1844, he writes to Mrs. J. Mozley: 'I am very sorry to make you anxious, but do not know what to do. I don't like you to be ignorant of my state of mind, yet don't like to tease you by my rigmarole statements. Unless anything happened which I considered a divine call, and beyond all calculations, I never should take anyone by surprise, and therefore you need not alarm yourself as if anything were happening. But if I judge of the future by the past, and when I recollect the long time, now nearly five years, that certain views and feelings have been more or less familiar to me and sometimes press on me, it would seem as if anything might happen, and I must confess they are very much dearer to me and stronger than they were a year ago. I can no more calculate how soon they may affect my will, and become practical, than a person who has long had a bodily ailment on him (though I hope and trust it is not an ailment) can tell whether or when it may assume critical shape, though it may do so any day.'

On June 3 he tells her: 'You must not suppose I put on a cheerfulness because people do not find out I have cares; the truth is (thank God!) I *am* cheerful. And though it so entirely depends on Him that I might be cast down for good and all any day, and know not, of course, what is before me, yet having sound sleep at night and quiet days, and trying to serve Him without aims of this world, however imperfectly, how can I but be cheerful, as I am? And I trust He will overrule all painful things which myself or others have to bear, to our good. Of course the pain of my friends is what cuts me, and I do not know how I shall bear it; but He gives us strength according to our day.'

On June 12 Keble writes him a most kind letter, in the hope, of course, of settling him once more as an Anglican, but ending with this assurance of continued friendship whatever happens.

'The other thing I wanted to say to you, or rather to make you feel, was [the conviction] of one of your friends at least, and he believes a great many would be of the same mind, that nothing which may happen will make any kind of separation or hinder confidence. It is so utterly different from a change in the other direction, but of course one fears how it may be on your part—I mean, what duty may suggest to you.'

On November 20, Mrs. Mozley writes to reassure him as to her response to his need of sympathetic interest, as he seems to have complained in a letter to her husband of feeling a lack of this in both of them at this time. She tells him that any appearance of intentional silence about his state of mind on her part is 'not because I did not enter into your feelings, but because I did so too much. . . . I know reserve, and all feelings and habits connected with it are a great fault in me.'

In his reply, November 24, 1844, he tells her that in his opinion, she *had* given him cause to think that she found the whole situation too painful to mention, and was therefore purposely refraining from alluding to the confidences he had made to her as to his feelings; and then goes on to say: 'Besides the pain of unsettling people of course I feel the loss I am undergoing in the good opinion of my friends and well-wishers, though I can't tell how much I feel this. It is the shock, surprise, terror, forlornness, disgust, scepticism to which I am giving rise ; the differences of opinion, division of families, all this it is that makes my heart ache.

. . . I cannot make out that I have any motive but a sense of indefinite risk to my soul in remaining where I am. A clear conviction of the substantial identity of Christianity and the Roman system has now been on my mind for a full three years. It is more than five years since the conviction first came to me, though I struggled against it and overcame it. I believe all my feelings and wishes are against change. I have nothing to draw me elsewhere, I hardly ever was at a Catholic service ; even abroad I knew no Roman Catholics. I have no sympathy with them as a party. I am giving up everything. I am not conscious of any resentment, disgust, or the like, to repel me from my present position ; and I have no dreams whatever—far from it indeed, I seem to be throwing myself away. Unless something occurs which I cannot anticipate I have no intention of an early step even now. But I cannot but think . . . that some day it will be, and at a definite distance of time.

What keeps me here is the desire of giving every chance for finding out if I am under the power of a delusion. Various persons have sent me kind letters, and I really trust that many are bearing me in mind in their prayers.'

His loyal-hearted sister in a long letter dated November 29, 1844, says : 'This is my especial trouble that I cannot defend you as I would desire through everything ; and I have to throw a damp of reserve and discouragement on unsuspicious and generous spirits who are ready to answer for your steadfastness. I am afraid of adding to your trouble, but I really do wish you would take the matter into account, and consider it, not merely as counting the cost, but as Mr. Oakeley[1] puts it, whether such impediments as the troubling of the minds of the better sort of people and long-chosen friends, etc., may not be providential warnings of the course in which we should walk.'

Then after telling him as gently as she can how impossible the step he is plainly about to take would be to her, she says: 'I should not have said this; but that I thought it fair that you should know how I stand, or rather where, in these shifting days. But you must also believe that I can in spite of all this, appreciate the pain and struggle which causes you suffering, and indeed sympathise entirely with it, looking upon it, in your case, as truly a matter of conscience. . . .

Many thanks for your kind promise, as I take it that we shall not be taken by surprise by anything you do. This gave me hope before. I hope you will forgive anything wrong I have said in this letter, and believe that my first wish is that you should see the truth as it is. I hope and trust I desire this for you above all things.

Worldly fame is a vulgar thing enough. With your talents you are sure to have plenty of that . . . but I have valued for you the deepest respect and admiration of good people, but this I would give up if I could feel sure you were in the right course. I trust you will have the blessing of that conviction.'

Next day, November 30, he replies, after answering some anxious enquiries after his health with which her letter ends:

'I am not unwilling to be in trouble now, and for others to be—for it is what must be—and the more of it

[1] Later a convert.

the sooner over. It is like drinking a cup out. I am far from unmindful of what you say about the unsettlement of others being a providential intimation; but there must be a limit to its force, else Jews could never have become Christians in early times; or Nestorians or Monophysites Catholics in more recent. How St. Paul must have unsettled quiet Jews who were serving God, and heard nothing but ill of Our Lord as a Samaritan and "deceiver"! And this suggests what has ever been said against the Church at all times—namely that it was corrupt, anti-Christian, etc. This has ever been a Note of the Church. . . . It is no new thing that the Church has been under odium and disgrace. I think the unsettlement of quiet people quite a reason for not moving without a clear and settled conviction that to move is a duty. I throw the *onus probandi* on the side of moving, were it not so before. And this is what has kept me quiet hitherto. Still there is a point beyond which this impediment will not act.'

On December 22, he writes to her again: 'I do not wonder at anyone's first impression being when he hears the change of religion of another, that he is influenced by some wrong motive. It is the necessary consequence of him thinking himself right; and I fully allow that the *onus probandi* that he is not so, lies with the person who is influenced. While then, I think you are rather hard on the various persons who have joined the Church of Rome, I think you are justified in being so, for they have to prove that they do not deserve a hard opinion. I say the same of myself. A person's feeling is that there is something wrong at the bottom; that I must be disappointed, or restless, or set on a theory, or carried on by a party, or coaxed into it by admirers, or influenced by any of the ten thousand persuasions which are as foreign from my mind as from my heart, but which it is easy for others to assign as an hypothesis. I do not quarrel with people so thinking.

But still I think that as time goes on, and persons have the opportunity of knowing me better, they will see that all these suppositions do not hold; and they will be led to see that *my motive simply is that I believe the Roman Church to be true.*'

These words, quoted earlier in this article, show his true motive so clearly that it seems strange that any others should ever have been assigned to him; except, as he acutely remarks, as 'the necessary consequence of his thinking himself right which so often blinds a man to any point of view except his own.'

On March 13, 1845, Mrs. J. Mozley writes a distracted letter in answer to one in which her brother tells her of his intention to resign his Fellowship in October, with a view to a subsequent step.

'You may imagine rightly in thinking the communication at the end of your letter would give me a great deal of pain. I can think of nothing else since, and yet seem to be without the power of writing to you. Yet I can hardly say why it is so, for I am far from taken by surprise, indeed I have been dreading to hear something of this sort for some time past. You have sufficiently warned me of it. Yet I have so much sanguineness in my composition that I always hope the worst misfortunes may be averted till they are irremediable, and what can be worse than this? It is like hearing that some dear friend must die. I cannot shut my eyes to this overpowering event that threatens us any longer. What the consequences may be, I know not. Oh, dear John, can you have thought long enough before deciding on a step which, with its probable effects, must plunge so many into confusion and dismay ? I know what you will answer—that nothing but the risk of personal salvation would lead you to it ; and I quite believe it. I know you have all along the greatest regard for others, and acted upon it for some time past. But think what must be our feelings who cannot entertain your view, but can only deplore it as a grievous mistake ! And I feel bitterly how many good sort of people would not do you justice, but judge you very hardly indeed. It is a real pain and grief to think of you as severed from us, as it were, by your own sentence. I am very much afraid, dear John, you may be taken by surprise by what I say, and expect I shall receive this event more easily. Indeed I cannot ; it is to me the great proof of the badness of this world, and the unfortunate times we live in, that such a one as you should take the line you have taken.'

He answers by return of post : ' I have just received your very painful letter, and wish I saw any way of making things easier to you or to myself. . . . If I am right to move at all surely it is high time not to delay about it any longer. Let me give my strength to the work, not my weakness—years in which I can profit the cause which calls me, not the dregs of life. . . .

As to my convictions, I can but say what I have told you already, that I cannot at all make out *why* I should determine on moving, except as thinking I should offend God by not doing so. I cannot make out what I am at except on this supposition. At my time of life men love ease '—he was now forty-four—' I love ease myself. I am giving up a maintenance involving no duties, and adequate to all my wants. What in the world am I doing this for (I ask myself this) except that I think I am called to do so ? I am making a large income by my sermons. I am, to say the very least, risking this ; the chance is that my sermons will have no further sale at all. I have a good name with many, I am deliberately sacrificing it. I have a bad name with more ; I am fulfilling all their worst wishes, and giving them their most coveted triumph. I am distressing all I love, unsettling all I have instructed or aided. I am going to those whom I do not know, and of whom I expect very little. I am making myself an outcast, and that at my age. Oh, what can it be but a stern necessity which causes this ?

Pity me, my dear Jemima, what have I done thus to be deserted, thus to be left to take a wrong course, if it is wrong ? I began by defending my own Church with all my might when others would not defend her. I went through obloquy in defending her. I in a fair measure succeed. At the very time of this success, before any reverse, in the course of reading, it breaks upon me that I am in a schismatical Church. I oppose myself to the notion ; I write against it—year after year I write against it—I do my utmost to keep others in the Church. . . . May not one hope and believe, though one does not see it, that God's Hand is in the deed, if a deed there is to be ; that He has a purpose, and will bring it to good, and will show us that it is good, in His own time ? Let us not doubt, may we never have cause to doubt, that He is with us. Continually do I pray that He would discover to me if I am under a delusion ; what can I do more ? What hope have I but in Him ? To whom should I go ? Who can do me any good ? . . . May He tell me, may I listen to Him, if His Will is other than I think it to be.

(Palm Sunday.) If you can suggest any warnings to me which I am not considering, well, and thank you ;

else do take comfort, and think that perhaps you have a right to have faith in me, perhaps you have a right to believe that He Who has led me hitherto will not suffer me to go wrong. . . . Have I not a right to ask you not to say, as you have said in your letter, that I shall do wrong? What right have you to judge me? Has the multitude who will judge me any right to judge me? Who of my equals has a right? Who has a right to judge me but my Judge? Who has taken such pains to know my duty, poor as they have been, as myself? Who is more likely than I to know what I ought to do? I may be wrong, but He that judgeth me is the Lord, and "judge nothing before the time."

His ways are not our ways, nor His thoughts our thoughts. He may have purposes as merciful as they are beyond us. Let us do our best and leave the event to Him; He will give us strength to bear. Surely, I have to bear most; and if I do not shrink from bearing it others must not shrink.'

On Good Friday she writes a long letter in answer thanking him for writing to her 'so promptly and at such a length.' She feels, she tells him: 'almost vexed with myself for having said anything that should have, as it were, compelled you to write so much. For I feel it is a great effort to you to write, and I fear I cannot altogether receive all you say as you wish. . . . Indeed I must say that thinking as you do, with such a strong view of what is right, I cannot ask or wish you to act otherwise than you contemplate. I know on a point of conscience we must not be drawn aside by persuasions or arguments, which tell with others, but which are only mere excuses if we act by them when they do not touch ourselves. Indeed I do pity you, for I know you are just the person to feel the force of the sacrifices you are making more than most, without the excitement which carries most persons through such changes; and it needs no assurance from you for me to be sure that you do it simply because you think it right, when interest or love of ease would naturally draw you another way. This is my hope and my consolation. . . . O may you be rewarded now and hereafter in the way God thinks best! I believe I do not wish to choose for you—so [long] as you are doing His Will and His Work, what more can one desire.'

A little later, April 2, he shows something of the strain he is undergoing in a letter to his brother-in-law, the Rev. J. B. Mozley.

'I say to myself, if I am under a delusion, what have I done, what great sin have I committed, to bring such a judgment on me? O that it may be revealed to me, and the delusion broken! But I go on month after month, year after year, without change of feeling except in one direction; not floating up and down, but driving one way. . . . I cannot promise myself to remain as I am after Christmas, perhaps not so long, though I suppose in the event I shall linger on some little while longer. By November I expect to have resigned my Fellowship, and perhaps may publish something. . . . What complicated distress! I suppose it will be less when the worst is over.'

On April 3, in a letter to the Rev. R. W. Church he reverts once more to his resignation of S. Mary's.

'Just now I have been overset by James Mozley's article in the C.R. Yet, really, my dear Church, I have never for an instant even had the temptation of repenting my leaving Oxford. The feeling of repentance has not come even into my mind. How could it? How could I remain at St. Mary's, a hypocrite? How could I be answerable for souls (and life so uncertain) with the conviction, or at least persuasion which I had upon me ? It is indeed, a dreadful responsibility to act as I am doing; and I feel His hand heavy on me without intermission Who is all wisdom and love, so that my mind and heart are tired out, just as the limbs might be from a load on one's back ; that sort of dull aching pain is mine. But my responsibility really is nothing to what it would be, to be answerable for souls, for loving confiding souls, in the English Church, with my convictions.'

After this letter, except for one, dated April 10, in which he asks Mrs. Mozley to show the long letter he sent her on Palm Sunday to James Mozley, there is a blank in his correspondence till October 1845, just before the final step was taken. Mrs. J. Mozley seems to have stayed with her brother at Littlemore in July, and writes to her sister-in-law, Miss Mozley, on the 17th, saying : 'He (J. H. N.) looks just the same as when I visited him last, and seems tolerably well. He has been with us an hour this morning and will dine here. We are going to Church in ten minutes, the times here are 11 and 3. After Church I am to pay calls in the village with J. H. N.' Miss Mozley added this comment many years later : 'Everything shows that Mr. Newman attended service at Littlemore till the final step was taken.' She thinks that the village people had no suspicion of his reason for leaving the parish—'It seemed clear to me,' she says, 'that he had never spoken a word to them that might set them thinking.'

On October 6, Mrs. Mozley again writes to her sister-in-law : 'I have had a letter which I have been suspecting and half-dreading to receive, this week from J. H. N. to say he has written to the Provost to resign his Fellowship. He adds that now anything may be expected any day.'

Two days later this letter reached her.

'Littlemore,
Oct. 8, 1845.

I must tell you what will pain you greatly, but I will make it as short as you would wish me to do.

This night Father Dominic, the Passionist, sleeps here. He does not know of my intention, but I shall ask him to receive me into what I believe to be the One Fold of the Redeemer.

This will not go till all is over.'

For some time, as we have seen, it had been 'noised abroad that Mr. Valiant for Truth was taken with a Summons.' Now at last, after months of heart-searching, he 'had this for a token that the Summons was true, that his Pitcher was broken at the Fountain.' Broken through the sins of his forefathers nearly three hundred years before his birth, his efforts to piece it together again had failed.

'Then said he, "I am going to my Fathers, and though with great difficulty I am got hither, yet do I not repent me of all the Trouble I have been at to arrive where I am. My Sword I give to him that shall succeed me in my Pilgrimage, and my Courage and Skill to him that can get it. My Marks and Scars I carry with me to be a witness for me that I have fought his Battles who now will be my Rewarder."'

The Passage Perilous had brought him within sight of the Port Pleasant at last.

Forty-four years of his life had gone, forty-five remained. Were those long years in the Catholic Church 'wasted' and unused? No one, as he said himself, can judge his life-work but his God.

Yet of the measurable success which those years brought him, his writings—to take a single instance of his achievement—give abundant witness. 'The

Second Spring,' said to be the greatest sermon in the English language, sells in its thousands up to the present day. His magnificent *Apologia* (unequalled by the many which have followed it), the *Essay in Development*, the *Grammar of Assent*—all the works which made Froude class him with Carlyle as one of the 'two writers who have affected powerfully the present generation of Englishmen'—were written after he became a Catholic; and they still affect powerfully, not only Englishmen, but French and German thought in particular at the present day.

As to the impression given by those who speak of him as a disheartened and hopeless man ending 'his chequered life in the Roman Communion,' and infer that he never found fresh heart or hope within it, let this passage, written forty years after he became a Catholic, remove it once for all.

'For myself, now, at the end of a long life, I say from a full heart, that God has never failed me, never disappointed me, has ever turned evil into good for me. When I was young I used to say (and I trust it was not presumptuous to say it) that our Lord ever answered my prayers. And what He has been to me, who have deserved His love so little, such will He be, I believe and know, to every one who does not repel Him and turn from His pleading.'

CHAPTER II

THOMAS W. ALLIES

An article entitled 'A Great Lost Leader' has lately appeared in an Anglo-Catholic magazine in preparation for the Tractarian Centenary celebrations next year. The writer, speaking of the time when Newman's influence at Oxford as a Tractarian was at its height, says:

'As is often the case, the "disciples" too often went beyond their great leader, mixing up essentials with non-essentials. Several then, or later, joined the Church of Rome from various reasons, one probably from ambition, others attracted by Roman Catholic services, or by seeing Church work on the Continent, some by the possession of a sheep-like nature.'

But none of these reasons would have enabled them to enter the Church. Neither a liking for Catholic services nor an admiration of 'Church work' abroad, far less a desire to realise ambitions doomed to disappointment in other spheres of religion, would be considered a proper qualification for taking such a step. And the possession of a sheep-like nature does not in itself confer the right to enter the One True Fold.

Readers of *A Spiritual Æneid* will remember how Father Ronald Knox, when still an Anglican, went to Father Martindale, S.J., who happened to be a guest in the same house, and told him of the misgivings that had troubled him since he had had 'a glimpse of the possibility that the Church of England might be wrong.' He did not come to him for actual direction he says, 'but for advice as to whether, in his view, such a state of mind made it right for me, or a duty to me, to shut my eyes and take a plunge. His answer was the last thing I expected: "Of course, you couldn't be received like that."' Probably the majority of non-Catholics think, as Father Knox says he did then, that nothing more than a 'decent doubt about Anglicanism' (or whatever may be their present form of faith) is required of a convert to the Church. But those who seek to enter her Communion soon learn that she demands, again to quote Father Knox, 'positive faith;' not mere dissatisfaction with another creed.

In the article just quoted, a foot-note, 'see Allies's *Diary in France*,' not only shows which convert the writer had in mind as having been 'attracted by seeing Church work on the Continent,' but makes it an easy matter to refute this statement as to his motives. For Thomas Allies left on record, in a contemporary diary and in an account written soon after his conversion, his true reason for 'joining the Church of Rome.' Like Newman (who received him into her Communion) he did so because he believed the Roman Church to be true.

As the difficulties of the Anglican position which first roused his misgivings still exist to a great extent in the Church he left, it is possible that some who read this account of them may be standing at the same crossroads in 1932 as he did over eighty years ago. And perhaps his experience may serve as a sign-post to direct them along the road he took.

His conversion from Rationalism to the Tractarian position, and from that position to the full Catholic

Faith, was so largely due to Newman as to make his account of its progress interesting, if only as a mirror of the workings of that great mind on one of the many who under his influence went from strength to strength.

It has been said that Newman seemed 'destined to sound to its depths every reason for staying where he was[1] so that no one who came after him might be able to say that he had discovered a reason for remaining which was not at some time or other present to his [Newman's] mind.' And certainly Allies's letters and journal give the impression that for him, as well as for others in whom Newman's sermons had, in his Anglican days, awakened 'a want which they could not supply,' the path to Rome had been to some extent cleared and its rough places smoothed by the experience he bought so dearly.

The part he played in Allies's conversion was of great importance, both direct and indirect.

For the first step Thomas Allies trod on the road to Rome was taken on December 20, 1838, when he dined with Ward; and, though 'shocked at what he told him of the Newmanites,' decided to read some of Newman's lectures on Church doctrine. He 'thought them Jesuitical now and then,' but on re-reading them four lays later they seemed to him 'just the truth.' It was not long before he followed Ward's example, and 'from being greatly opposed' to the Newmanites, became one himself.

The second step followed in 1841; when the Bishops' condemnation of Tract 90 became, little though he then guessed it, a turning-point in his life. That episcopal condemnation was, as we saw in the preceding chapter, one of 'the three great blows' which still further loosened Newman's foothold in the

[1] In the Church of England.

Anglican Church, already shaken by Dr. Wiseman's article on Donatism published two years before. And the blow which was destined to dislodge Newman from S. Mary's and send him into retirement at Littlemore also laid Allies's ambitions in ruin around him.

For Bishop Blomfield was naturally much displeased when his young chaplain, as Allies had become a few months earlier, expressed his disapproval of the Bishops' action in no measured terms. As a mark of the episcopal displeasure Allies was very shortly given a small country living; whereby his ambition 'to have a large and influential congregation such as Dodsworth's' and to become a force among London preachers was completely shelved. The result was that, 'quite shut out from society' in what he felt to be a deliberate exile, Allies turned into other channels the mental energy which the Launton villagers, in his opinion, could not fully absorb. Almost his first step was to buy 'at a single stroke, a hundred pounds' worth of the Fathers,' and the reading and study he now undertook led eventually to a complete reversal of all his views—Newmanite and pre-Newmanite alike—as regards the position of the Church of England.

The account he gives of what may be called his pre-Newmanite spiritual growth is very interesting.

'Born and bred a Protestant,' as his father, the Rev. Thomas Allies, was 'as strongly Evangelical and as far removed from Church doctrines as clergymen of his generation,' his early religious training seems to have done little to help him when he first went out into the world. And though he tells us that his mother's early piety and her firm trust in God left a deep impression on his memory, what he learnt from her does not seem to have played any positive part in the early struggles of his soul.

After his 'education was "completed," as it is called,' he was sent abroad for 'three years' travel in Catholic countries,' but returned from them 'no Catholic; but rather with strong rationalistic tendencies.' But in 1837, when he was twenty-four, his life 'encountered a great change.' He fell, he says, into a great sorrow, in consequence of which he hovered between life and death so keen was the stroke; till 'from the furnace seven times heated into which God had cast him' he 'came out a fresh creature. Feebly and most imperfectly at first' he began to make Him his object, whereas the world had occupied him before.

He made up his mind to take Anglican Orders, and was ordained deacon the following year, 1838, the year also of his father's death. As from that time forward he never mentions either parent in his book, it is probable that his mother had died some time before.

That year was, he tells us, 'a struggle after fixed principles and a settled mind,' in which his training for ordination seems to have played very little part. But his old Eton tutor, the Rev. Edward Coleridge, by a chance remark, led him 'to the frequenting of Mr. Dodsworth's church.' This church was Margaret Chapel, the first church in London to provide Tractarian doctrine and ceremonial for its congregation. Here Allies heard, he says, 'what was destined to lead me on in what were called Church principles. One after another I took in the higher views of Anglicanism as to the Church, the Episcopate, the Sacraments.' These 'higher views' gave him an ideal which made it impossible for him to rest contented as Bishop Blomfield's chaplain, or as the Vicar of Launton later on.

How he became imbued with 'Newmanism' is told in two entries in his diary which have already been mentioned, and are now given in full.

'December 20, 1838. Dined with Ward; shocked at what he told me of the Newmanites. He is become one himself from being greatly opposed. Read some of Newman's lectures on Church doctrines: thought them Jesuitical now and then.'

'December 24. Saw Coleridge; talked a good deal, chiefly about Oxford School. C. says every reasonable man agrees with them. Curious the great force of opinion from one liked. I have since been reading Newman's lectures again, and they seem to me just the truth. Is this an accession of light, or is it mere weakness of judgment? How wonderfully one's own state of mind influences one's intellectual judgment!'

These entries are valuable, not only as a forecast of Allies's future, but in the light they throw on Newman's power, even by means of 'cold print,' to change men's hearts and minds.

Mr. Coleridge's influence also caused him to get a volume of Newman's sermons, which afterwards had, he tells us, a very marked part in his spiritual growth, and 'increased a sense of want they did not supply.' But, as he goes on to say, at this critical time when his whole spiritual being cried out for guidance, 'in nothing was I more unfortunate than in that I had no living guide to direct me in studies, or mental or spiritual growth.'

But 'a certain substratum, gathered at Eton and Oxford, which had strong affinities' with Tractarian doctrine, remained intact; and during 1838 and 1839 he seems to have been 'unlearning his foreign radicalism,' and to have gained that conception of 'the Church as one visible society, and of the sacraments as channels of grace' which, as he truly explains, involves all the rest. Newman's mind, he tells us, was the instrument through which he did this, 'so that the idea which I gradually formed of the Anglican Church was neither more nor less than Newmanism: something which, as a whole, and with that relative proportion of parts, that *mixture*, really had no existence before him; which, however, in the spring of 1840 I should have stoutly maintained to be the true, historic, and only Church of England.'

In that spring two important changes in his life took place. The first was his marriage, and the second his appointment as chaplain to the Bishop of London, which he tells us 'affected no alteration' in his opinions, though he felt himself 'stronger and more advanced in Church views' than his Bishop. He explains: 'There was besides in him a truckling to expediency, and an attempting to act between two stools, which freed me from all danger of being Lambethised. Perhaps I erred in the other direction. Instead of keeping my counsel and holding my tongue, when Dr. Blomfield produced, at his own table or elsewhere, some sentiment extremely un-Catholic . . . I not seldom ventured to oppose it.' He seems, however, to have produced an extremely un-Catholic sentiment of his own: 'We must educate our Bishops.'

His zeal was not yet according to knowledge, as he was then, he tells us, utterly ignorant of Catholic theology. 'Yet,' he says, 'I preached two sermons then on the Unity of the Church, which are quite Catholic in doctrine, and which entirely contemplate the Church as one visible perennial society. I dwelt on the *sacramentum* of unity as all-important, whilst, curiously enough, it did not strike my mind that such principles alone carried with them an utter condemnation of the Anglican position. Looking back, it seems hard to discern how it was possible, *bona fide*, to believe and to speak in such a manner and not to see the necessity of becoming a Catholic. Now, my belief in such a doctrine of unity, as again in the doctrine of the Real Presence, of baptismal regeneration, and the apostolical succession (however wrongly conceived), was stronger even at that time than my belief in the Anglican Church. And this singular contradiction went on. Doctrine after doctrine I reached by the process of my own mind, feeding like a bird on the pastures which it most fancied, but without any design. And each succeeding doctrine I held with stronger faith than I held the communion itself in which I was doing this. Consequently the *ground* of my belief was diametrically opposed to that of the Catholic. It was private judgment; whether biased by supposed historical inquiry, or formed by logical synthesis, or drawn by moral coherence, and developed by inward affinities; it was not trust in a teaching body which alone, by a divine commission, has the truth entrusted to it, and alone is guaranteed in the perpetual possession and transmission of it. Yet if I had been asked in 1842, before I left the Bishop, why I believed a certain doctrine, I should doubtless have answered, because the Catholic Church believed it—i.e. something which I had loosely fancied in my mind as the Catholic Church, just as I, the individual, imagined it, without any precise locality or time. Here, again, if asked, I should probably have said then, and certainly later, the Church of the fourth and fifth centuries; as if it were in my power, or the power of any individual, to know what that Church believed, by historical inquiry, which was my supposed informant.'

Very naturally, the Bishop soon became restive under the rebukes of his young chaplain; and 'two days after a warm discussion in which the Bishop had censured some of the Oxford party . . . and I had defended them,' a discussion in which 'the Bishop got very heated,' he gave Allies the living of Launton. Allies comments: 'When I think of this appointment and all its circumstances I am reminded of Lord Rochester's remark to a cur biting his heels in the Park, "I'll get you a living in the country."'

Soon after his induction (in June 1842) he attended a visitation at Oxford, 'and was delighted at the dinner to sit next Mr. Newman,' whom so far he had never met. The influence which had already brought him so far was evidently deepened by this first personal encounter; and soon after he wrote to Newman asking for guidance in the study of the Fathers. Newman's reply, dated September 30, 1842, marks another stage in his progress. For that letter began the personal direction which with no real break, as even after Newman's conversion he used to seek his advice from time to time, led him step by step towards Rome. The final stage was not reached, however, till the September of 1850. Almost exactly eight years after that first letter of advice, on September 11, 1850, he 'was received by conditional baptism into the Catholic Church by Father Newman.'

In the account Allies wrote in 1853 of his conversion (three years after it took place) he describes its final stages in a chapter entitled 'My tent pitched upon an iceberg.' But when we read his account of Newman's influence in his life during those critical years, it seems more apt to think of him as scaling an ice-wall; advancing step by step, by means of the notches cut in the steep and slippery ascent by the ice-axe of his guide; till after a long pause half-way he reached the ridge, and the clear invigorating air which blows off the ice-field gave him strength to gain the summit.

Having found his guide, he was now led to a suitable

base from which to start his climb. As the Bishop's chaplain, he probably would have remained a rather cocksure young curate till he blossomed out into a sort of Reverend Charles Honeyman ; and, as he acknowledged later, 'Dr. Blomfield's mode of punishing me for having entrapped him into the discredit of having a pronounced Puseyite as his examining chaplain was one of the turns of Divine providence.' But at the time the Bishop's action in removing him 'out of the way of distinction ; from friends and connections ; and from the power of influencing others, especially the young,' seemed to him not only a disgrace unjustly incurred for following his principles, but the destruction of his prospects.

He was 'burning to have a large and influential congregation, such as Dodsworth's'—which, he thinks, had always been before his eyes as a sort of model—and 'longed to carry out my Puseyism on a large field. Without, I think, any bent to the pastoral office, I had considerable love of preaching, and a very great feeling and love of theology as an organic structure of Divine doctrines. I was yearning after the Catholic system in its fullness, without the least suspicion where it was to be found.'

Nor does he seem to have suspected that the Catholic system values the souls of country villagers as highly as large and influential congregations in fashionable London churches, and that the power to influence others, old or young, for good does not need density of population to make itself felt. But Thomas Allies had never heard of the Curé of Ars.

The self-confidence, combined with a lack of humour, which is noticeable in him at times makes it hard to say how far the self-revelation which follows is intentional. It shows him to have been quite unfitted for 'the weekly office of teaching and worship, sick and dying calls' which as 'a beneficed clergyman' it was his duty to fulfil. Writing ten years after he had ceased to be Vicar of Launton, he tells us that his former position as examining chaplain had been as agreeable to him as his parish duties were distasteful. He 'did not want *general* pastoral work at all' and liked his 'small portion of government at the centre of a great system' better than his 'relegation to serve at one of its extremities.' As he 'knew all along' that 'this extremity was devoid of any vital heat' and made up his mind beforehand that it would 'refuse his efforts at calefaction,' it is small wonder that 'it never disappointed him' by responding to his exhortations.

When he was inducted at Launton on February 12, 1842, his twenty-ninth birthday, he felt that his banishment there was a great loss to the Movement. 'I was keenly interested,' he says, 'in the success of the Puseyite cause, and I thought my removal from a very responsible place of influence at Dr. Blomfield's side a considerable blow to it; an opportunity lost; an omen of success gone. . . . In short, what God was doing I knew not then, but I know now.' There was no false modesty in the Vicar of Launton's estimate of his own powers.

Then came the turning-point. He had, as has been said, 'become possessed at a single stroke of a hundred pounds' worth of the Fathers': S. Augustine, S. Chrysostom, S. Basil, S. Athanasius, and some others. 'Up to this time I had never fallen in their way,' he tells us, 'and knew nothing of them, save a quotation here and there. This was done before I left London; and this itself, of course, was an effect of Newman's teaching. Even when I was ordained deacon, I knew as little of the Fathers as the man in the moon, and answered a question of Archdeacon Clerke [with the statement] that St. Justin was a Latin Father. It was Newman's continual setting the Fathers forth as the witnesses and sure guarantee of orthodoxy which wrought this change.' Another result of his change of occupation was that being 'quite shut out from society,' and 'having his mornings entirely free,' he 'began to compose parochial sermons; and in doing so used constantly to see what St. Augustine said on the subject first.'

Then came his first personal contact with Newman, which has been already mentioned. The meeting at the Oxford dinner was followed by that first request for guidance which was to have so far-reaching an effect. The letter on the study of the Fathers which it elicited gives most interesting details of the effect which that study had had on Newman, and of his views as regards undertaking it from the Protestant angle. In his own case it had meant that he had 'managed to spend a good deal of time on them and got nothing from them.' Unfortunately it is too long to quote fully.

Writing three years after his reception into the Church Allies admits that so far he has 'never done anything more with the Fathers than dip into them.' However he 'learnt even in this way to look up to an objective ground of faith; and became aware that whatever early Christianity and the Church system of the fourth and fifth centuries were, they were at least most unlike Protestantism.' He felt they were 'unbiased witnesses between Rome and England' in a sense post-Reformation writers could not become. 'As I saw their mighty folios ranged round my room, I felt,' he says, 'that I was not alone, that I had a ground for what I believed, that I stood on a higher footing than the system in which I lived, and was acquainted with those who enabled me to *judge* that system. Thus my mind acquired a strength and resolution it had not possessed before I came to Launton. I was struggling with the Reformation theology, often losing my way among its miserable débris, but at length overmastering it and casting it away as a *caput mortuum.*'

His description of his work at Launton is worth quoting in full. The state of affairs in that country parish in 1842 will seem only too familiar a picture to many of the English country clergy to-day.

'Of course, as a beneficed clergyman I had practical work to do, a weekly office of teaching and worship, sick and dying calls. The whole practical working of the Anglican system was thus brought before me. And I found daily and weekly that it *would not go. Cela ne marchait pas.* Theoretical difficulties had a new edge given to them by practical daily disappointments. My people obstinately refused to discern the difference between the Church and the meeting-house, unless, indeed, by the unacceptable way of preferring the latter. I preached to them over and over again what schism and heresy were, and they never would understand that there was any sin in them, or cease from the unlimited practice of them. I strove to make them frequent the sacrament, in vain. Low, disunited, immoral, conceited, brutally ignorant and brutally obstinate, they were and they would be. Reverence for my office they had none; consideration for me as gentleman and landlord, and occupant of a large glebe, they had. I tried to make myself their friend in every conceivable manner, and with profuse expenditure; but with little success. And then, whenever I tried to rest on the Church's regulations and means of grace, they seemed to produce no effect. The experience of death-beds was appalling to me, but not to the patient. From a life of wickedness, unbelief, and ignoring or blaspheming God, they seemed to drop into eternity with utter indifference, and a passive profession of God's unbounded mercy. They seemed not to have the need of my warnings or consolations, and valued neither. I looked around, and saw parishes all about me more or less in the same condition. Thus my reading and my life-theory and practice—thought and works, seemed to fit into each other, and together produce dissatisfaction with the Anglican Church.' . . .

He had now begun his sojourn in No Man's Land; dissatisfied with the Church of England and prejudiced against the Catholic Church. In 1843 he spent fifteen days in France; and saw for the first time, though still dimly, the beauty of the Catholic Faith. The three years he had spent on the Continent before the crisis which he experienced in 1837 had, as we have seen, merely fostered Rationalism in his mind. But since then, as he puts it, 'from irreligious he had become serious; from idle and purposeless, a minister with a strong feeling of responsibility, and the most anxious desire to do good.'

And he had his reward. Looking back ten years later on an account of his tour written on his return home, he points out that 'the observations in it on the state of religion prove incontestably that then, for the first time, my mind was grappling with the great fact of Catholicism. . . . I saw "men like trees walking." For the first time it seems to have been brought home to me that Our Blessed Lady had a share in the Incarnation.'

His Journal is, as he says, 'the most curious mixture of ignorance and candour.' He gives a long and quite interesting description of the Cathedrals he visited, and notices at Chartres 'a stone screen containing a delineation of our Saviour's life,' the scenes ending with 'the crowning of the Virgin by God the Father and God the Son, which I almost shudder to put down.' A pillar supporting 'an image of the Virgin' was kissed by 'respectable women,' which obviously surprises him.

The great difference which at once strikes him between religion in England and on the Continent, consists, he says, in this. 'Abroad, the church, however lamentably it has been assailed by revolutionary impiety, or decorated in false or meretricious taste, is still recognised by all who have any sense of religion as the house of prayer, intended primarily for worship, not for instruction, still less for the display of the priest's oratory.' This undoubtedly 'favourable point' seems to him possibly to 'make up for all the disadvantages of the Roman worship.' He disapproves of 'non-communicating attendance,' and expresses his disapproval in words which, in my turn, I 'shudder to put down.'

He has other objections; but decides that the corruptions he deplores are atoned for by the practice of daily communion among the priests; and by the fact that 'the poorest parishioner of the poorest parish' has 'the opportunity of communicating *daily*, which is a wonderful privilege, and contrasts strangely with our quarterly or monthly celebrations.' He also notes with approval that 'the service of the Mass is still the central service of the Church,' and that 'the discipline imposed upon the Roman clergy is far stricter than that with which our own Church contents itself.' As regards 'the otherwise prevailing Mariolatry' he considers that 'how far the prominence given to the service of the Mass keeps it in check may be a question.'

But even now the truth of the Catholic doctrine

concerning Our Lady is clearly beginning to emerge from the mists with which his Protestant upbringing had naturally clouded it. He says: 'I do not think the Romanist is in danger of confounding the reverence due to the Mother of God with the worship due to her Son—it rather seems as if, in his mind, she were the connecting-link between us and Him, so that the Virgin is inextricably mixed up in his feelings with the Incarnation; whereas, if I mistake not, the Protestant tone of thought seldom rests upon the Virgin at all, or considers the part she had in the mystery of the Incarnation.'

Another Protestant prejudice in him is about to be dispelled; and he touches the fringe of truth when he writes:

'It is beyond a question that the Romanists (people and priest) attribute to the Saints and Angels, and above all, to the Blessed Virgin, offices which we are wont to restrict to the Redeemer; but it is not at all clear to me that the immeasurable distance between the Redeemer and the Saints is thereby lessened to their minds. To them His intercession differs in kind from that of the Saint. There must be some far deeper principle in the universal reverence paid to the Virgin than we are accustomed to allow; at the same time it certainly seems to me the black spot of the Roman Church.'

The other comparisons he makes have lost much of their force, thanks to the revival in the Church of England due to the Oxford Movement. 'Churches open all day and people praying in them' may be found in all English towns and in many villages; and 'the use of vestments, holy water and the Crucifix' is becoming more and more common in churches all over England, in spite of Mr. Kensit's apparent conviction that the whole country is his parish, and that he has a right to act 'the aggrieved parishioner' wherever he pleases.

Allies's remark that 'bowing to the altar has lately been approved of by a bishop' is interesting, as it shows what a complete dead letter the canons drawn up for the Church of England in the seventeenth century had become. *All* English bishops are bound by them not only to approve but to enjoin this canonical practice of their Church.

Many and startling as 'the series of damaging contrasts' he noted were, he seems to have drawn no logical inference from them. Much as he deplored them, he had no idea where the regret they caused him would eventually lead him.

Ten years later, looking back on that eventful fortnight, he says: 'I am sure that this time the thought had never even crossed my mind of the possibility of my becoming a Catholic. I wrote these things in the exuberance of my strength as an Anglican. I made large admissions, noted strong contrasts, endeavoured "to creep into the skin of others" (to use de Bammeville's expression), with a conviction that I was quite safe where I was—that there was simply a Church with Divine powers to be restored, and that a great party had risen with strength to restore it, if the Bishops would only let them.'

'Plus ça change, plus c'est la même chose.' How often those same large admissions are made, those same strong contrasts noted, that same conviction that the Bishops are the only bar to Catholic progress in the Church of England expressed by Anglicans to-day.

But though in 1843 he had no idea where his impressions would lead him, others had immediate misgivings. His old tutor, Mr. Coleridge, to whom he sent his little journal, showed it to a friend who had not at that time met Allies. When the Journal came back, between its pages was a note 'cautioning the writer of the Journal as to whither he was being carried.' This caution Allies then thought 'very unnecessary.'

He little knew his own mind. The leaven soon began to work. In 'the dull, flat and moral desert of Launton' his memories of Chartres, Amiens and S. Ouen were not only 'a keen delight,' but spurred him to further thought.

'The state of my parish,' he says, 'drove me daily to reflect on the advantages which I had observed in full and peaceful possession by the French clergy. How often, when unable to get at the conscience of some hardened old sinner, when sighing over the closed breasts, to me, of my school children, did that hurried visit, while the horses were changing, to the Church of Poix, on the eve of the Assumption, and the people waiting at the confessional, recur to my thoughts! What is the reason of this difference? I said mentally. Why does the priest do there what I can never arrive at here? Why has the Church in France, overthrown and impoverished fifty years ago, risen in her strength, and set about doing a work for the people, while the Church here, possessing for three hundred years the high places of the land, is despised and powerless just in the points where she ought to be strong—the trust of her people?'

A third force, as he now began to realise, was acting on him. To the theology of the Fathers and the practical state of his own parish had been added a fresh incentive; that is, 'the actual sight of the Church abroad watched with a religious and yearning eye.' The questions which that sight had awakened would give him no peace till he had at least made every effort to find an answer to them.

He tried to leave Launton, but the Bishop of London 'never condescended' to answer his application, so he made up his mind to remain there; and consoled himself by writing a volume of sermons. This work he dedicated to Newman; who at first demurred at the compliment. In a letter dated January 8, 1844, he gives the reason; which the date makes particularly significant: 'I have a very great dread of committing others to any association, however faint or vague, with myself. I will say to you what the occasion makes me say, but which I should not like repeated as from me, that I am not to be trusted.'

Allies sent a copy of his book to Mr. Gladstone, whose letter of thanks, written in June of that year, has a reference to Newman which shows that others distrusted him besides himself. He considers that Allies has 'acted courageously in his acknowledgments to Mr. Newman,' and 'has used a caution' which Newman's own work on the subject of Justification apparently seemed to lack. As an offset to this seeming disparagement he adds that the Editor of the *Quarterly*, Lockhart, told him lately that he thought Newman the finest writer of the day.

As regards the general public the book fell rather flat, and Allies decided not to publish one on the nature of the Church 'which he had much at heart.' But Keble 'gave him some praise'; and he also had a long letter from 'the late gifted Mrs. Henry Coleridge,' who tells him that surrounded as she is, 'like most of my neighbours in these printing days with new works, and engaged with my boy and girl,' she has only had time to tackle one of the eight Sermons. It seems to have been the one on Justification; and (unlike Mr. Gladstone) she does not approve his handling of the question, though otherwise she thinks the sermon 'remarkably clear and happy in expression,' and 'well reasoned.' As regards Justification, she evidently fears that he is in danger of being led astray, and warns him that though 'Aquinas set his wits, and they were right keen ones, to work on the subject with right good will,' she doubts whether either he or John Henry Newman can prove the opinion they hold in common regarding it so explains learnedly and at great length—('driving at the point a great deal'; as it seems to her 'a cardinal one') why their joint belief is 'a contradiction in terms.' She would like to hear what Allies thinks of Mr. Newman's last volume ; as Mr. Percival and, she believes, others of the Oxford school are full of grief and displeasure at a part of its contents, though she 'can see nothing in it of an un-Anglican tendency which is not already plainly indicated in the "Church of the Fathers."' The boldness of its views does not surprise her ('the author's position considered') as much as does the 'strangeness of the reasoning.'

This letter, dated April 1844, must have come as rather cold comfort to Allies ; who just at that time was experiencing a deepening of his anxieties 'on the whole position of Anglicanism.' So far these anxieties had not affected him personally ; but he had just asked Newman to hear his first confession, and had learned that 'he rather wished to excuse himself, as having doubts on certain points.' These doubts were not hard to guess, and soon Allies also became a prey to them.

'Hitherto the discouragement in my parish, and the plain inability of Anglicanism to grapple with a disaffected or heathenised people, to nurture the young or receive back the wandering, together with the glimpse into the early Church which my dippings into the Fathers have given me and the sight of the actual living Church, had done no more than this: they had produced a mind sensitively alive to practical evils, and searching for their causes. . . . I was perpetually asking myself why we were not better; why our bishops cared so little for the Articles of the Creed; why our clergy had such varieties of belief, and so unsacerdotal a bearing; why our people loved the meeting-house and their own way; why they felt no confidence in the clergyman, and had no sense of needing his services?' To these questions he now must add another—Why had the clergyman he most trusted no confidence in his power to render those services?

'The great effort of conscience made in confessing' was rewarded, he believes, by an accession of light as to where confession and absolution were really to be found. 'In July 1844,' he says, 'my spirits sank'; for his trust in the Church of England was shaken; and even when he looked at 'the material fabric' these questions haunted him: 'Is the Divine Presence here? Am I right in being here? How long shall I be here?' Those three fateful questions which every convert knows.

Ward's *Ideal of a Christian Church* gave him a key to his questionings, and supplied him with reasons for his difficulties. But 'as long as Mr. Newman remained, his mind was curiously suspended.' His attitude was that enjoined on the child in the Smuggler's Song:

'Steps and voices round the house; whistles after dark,
There's no call for running out till the house-dogs bark,
Trusty's here, and Pincher's here, and see how dumb they lie.'

But very soon (in little more than a year in fact) one after another the house-dogs began to bark, and that tide of conversions which swept so many men from the

Movement began to flow. 'From April 1844,' Allies says, 'I saw Mr. Newman from time to time, and my chief comfort and support were derived from what he said to me ; but still more, I think, from *seeing him where he was*.' At length this support was to be taken away.

Eight months before that happened, on February 12, 1845 (his thirty-second birthday), Allies writes in his diary : 'Since my last birthday one very important change of view has developed itself—a secret and yet undefined dread that we are in a state of schism. All that I see around me seems so little like the Church, as either revealed in the Bible, or realised in early ages.' The entry ends, 'In all things may I know God's will, and at all times be ready to fulfil it' ; and the inverted commas show that he had read (though probably had not actually heard) that most moving farewell sermon preached in the church at Littlemore, which ended with Newman's appeal to his hearers to pray for him in those words.

'On May 19th,' Allies tells us, 'I went to Littlemore in company with Mr. Dodsworth. We had an interesting conversation with him [Newman], of which I have the notes, and he disclosed to us that he had made up his mind to leave Anglicanism. My record of this interview is as follows. He said : "I cannot conceive how we can be said in any true sense to be parts of one kingdom with the Church abroad. I see everywhere in the Prophecies the Church set forth as a kingdom. Now we Englishmen would say at once, in temporal matters, that where there are separate legislatives or sovereign powers there cannot be one kingdom. For instance, we hear everyone saying that if the Union with Ireland were repealed, there would be a dismemberment of the Empire. We are in no sense one kingdom with America. This is readily admitted in temporal sovereignties; how then can we in any true sense be members of one kingdom with the Church abroad?" '

He quoted Guizot in support of his contention that Englishmen, though admirable as practical statesmen, never carried out a principle, which he obviously felt was the reason why the argument he had just stated did not automatically convince all thinking men as soon as they heard it. When he was told that it would cut off the Russian and Greek Churches, as well as the Anglican, from the right to be considered part of the Catholic Church, he replied 'Certainly it would. You must see how far your principle would carry you.'

He explained the painful similarity between 'our actual position' and that of 'the ancient heretics,' and when asked if he meant the Donatists replied 'Yes, and the Monophysites also.'

But the rest of the conversation led them to hope that he did not intend to make any movement himself, but seemed 'to gather up throughout the difficulties attending a change, rather than to encourage it in any way.'

The melancholy interview was brought to an end by the approach of church-time. Newman said he would show the church to them, but the bell was ringing, and they had only a moment to look at it. 'As he attended us out to the churchyard gate, and was taking leave, he said to D.: "Was there any other question you would have liked to ask me?" D. replied: "You must not answer what I am going to say if it is in any way impertinent. But it is said in London that you desire it to be known generally that you are going over to Rome. I should like to be able to contradict it." "That is too strong," he said. "There were persons to whom I have wished it to be known—friends, but not generally." He shook hands and went into church; but I saw an immediate change pass over his countenance, which became very pale and firm; he seemed to have said what cost him a great effort, and to have recovered his calmness. We both remarked how contrary was this conclusion to what had seemed to us the bearing of his conversation. He took us entirely by surprise. He had the mein of a man who saw all manner of difficulties in the course he was taking, who wished his example to be followed by no one [merely] because it was *his*; but who yet was decided by some immovable and overpowering conviction which he had not communicated.'

Both men wrote down and exchanged accounts of this interview; and Dodsworth adds a few points to Allies's statement, from which the foregoing is taken, and amplifies others. As they are fully discussed in the *Apologia* and in 'Certain Difficulties' I will only give a brief summary of them.

Newman had said that it would be unsafe to argue from the supposed corruptions of a community *as they appear to an individual*, and that over and above the difficulties which beset the whole question of the Tractarian position would be that of '*knowing* whither one is going.' Dodsworth says that this last remark of Newman's, italicised by Allies in his account of the interview, was in reply to a criticism of 'the tawdry waxen images of the Blessed Virgin,' on the part of either Allies or Dodsworth himself. Newman had also spoken of 'the loss sustained by the Roman Catholics by the absence of the Saxon element.' He thought that the State connection with the Church of England had been of benefit in some ways; under Hoadley, for instance, or in the generation just passed. But he assented to the remark that the State connection had helped to produce those moribund conditions in the Establishment which the Tractarians had set themselves to cure, and also such bishops as Hoadley.

Dodsworth's account ends with some admissions made by Newman in answer to his friends' arguments, which show how very hard put to it they had been to defend the Anglican position. They got him to agree that the Church of England flourished most in poverty; that there was an absence of the ascetic element in the Church among the Roman Catholics as well as among ourselves; and that as the Church of England had produced such men as 'Hammond, Nicholas Ferrar, etc.' (he would not allow living examples to be cited—'We do not know what Pusey will be') 'in this respect it might be unlike the Donatists.'

Dodsworth winds up with: 'This is all I have in addition to yours. I agree with you that the less said the better of him and his probable movements. I cannot bring myself to think that his secession from us is certain—though but too likely.

Ever yours,

W. Dodsworth.'

Allies had very little doubt of what those movements would be after the visit just recorded. He writes at the time: 'As soon as I could escape observation I wept bitterly over it': and a footnote (added four years later) alluding to 'the wars and rumours of wars which followed immediately on Ward's book,' shows how much that visit had upset him. He says:

'From time to time I consulted J. H. N., who always quieted me. My visit to him with Dodsworth, May 19th, 1845, when we learnt his determination to leave us was a terrible blow. I think I have never felt the same person since. . . . His mind had been for many years educating mine : his books were the instruments by which I was drawn out of my foreign radicalism and loose, incoherent Protestantism. His influence was my real *point d'appui* in the Anglican Church.'

From this time onwards, 'by the prospect of Newman's leaving us, as well as from its own internal progress,' his mind, as those who have experienced a similar shock will readily believe, 'was put wholly into a controversial state.' He was drawing nearer and nearer, as he says, to the great contest and trial of his life, approaching the problem which day after day agitated and tormented him. 'Was there standing ground in the Church of England at all ? Or was I, like Abraham, to go out, knowing not whither I went ? ' Newman's movement struck away the τὸ κάτεχον which had hitherto held me back from simply facing that question.'

From that time forth 'till the crowning act, September 11th, 1850,' he passed through a time, as he says, 'of the severest spiritual trial which a man can go through : a very intricate and complicated question of religion involving all the dearest interests of life ; on the one hand the dread of acting or concluding from any but conscientious motives ; on the other hand the perpetual destruction of one's worldly position depending on a particular conclusion.'

In June 1845 he again went to France, 'on a tour which was destined to open my eyes to much of the power and sanctity of the Catholic Church, and to bring the whole question of the Anglican position, touched already by Newman's expected movement and my own growth, in the liveliest manner before me.' Marriott, the friend with whom he travelled, introduced him at Yvetot to a Catholic priest he had met in Oxford ; which not only began 'a most valuable friendship,' but led to the month abroad being spent 'in searching out Catholic sights, and getting as far as we could at the interior life of the Catholic Church.'

On his return to Launton, he writes in his diary (August 10): 'Since my return home I have been more troubled in mind than for near eight years past I can remember to have been. I think this has arisen from a general but very vivid sense of the deficiencies of the English Church, and of her very dubious position, which has been impressed on me by what I have heard and seen in France. I have been unable to apply to anything. The prospects of the Church have appeared to me in the darkest view—all the arguments for our separate existence have been obscured: all those against it, vividly present. May God brace me to the vigorous discharge of daily duties, that light may spring out of this darkness.'

Under the dates August 11 and 17 are accounts of two visits to Newman, when he seems, as he says, to 'have been, as before, quieted' by him. The entries are so full of interest as regards Newman's direction of those he feared to unsettle, as well as showing some of the thoughts in his own mind, that I quote them in full.

'August 11. I went to Littlemore, the last time that I consulted him as a confessor and director. He said he could not use the form of absolution, so I only asked advice. He recommended use of 27th and 119th Psalms, and others, *with intention*, for illumination; and that being done, to put aside the direct consideration of doubts and troubles. If they are from God, they will force themselves again upon the mind.' And again, under date August 17: 'Blessed be God, since my visit to Oxford I have been more comfortable and composed in mind. I seem to feel that it is the will of God that I should remain quiet when I am in the discharge of everyday duties, and this is all I can desire. I have felt my interest in things around me restored. I have been quietly arranging for studies to come—have finished my diary, and hope soon to resume sermons, or a steady course of reading.'

When revising his diary three years later he adds: 'On this occasion—August 11—I also put to J. H. N. whether it was the abstract case of schism in Elizabeth's proceedings that made his difficulty. He said "I have never considered it in so technical a point of view. I am not sufficiently acquainted and care not to be, with the historical events, to judge. It is rather the existing state of separation, the heresy, etc." He quoted "Securus judicat orbis terrarum." I asked whether circumstances were not so changed since then as to make that inapplicable. He replied, "I tried for a long time to rest in that view, but I could not." Afterwards, "I have had, for four years in November, the strongest conviction that there is no choice between the Church of Rome and infidelity—not that I have ever been tempted to infidelity"—here he checked himself—"though one would not say that boastingly, lest a judgment should come upon one; but as a fact I have never been so tempted. I feared if I resisted this conviction, the other might come in judgment upon me." His state has been more comfortable since his present decision. He will probably resign his Fellowship in October, and after publishing he cannot say how soon the final step may follow. He took an affectionate leave of me, warmly grasping my hand, and saying, "God bless you!"'

In his search for further light Allies 'set about reading Petavius, and from him diverged to Newman's *Sermons on the Relation of Faith to Reason*.' He tells us of the disconsolate feeling with which he began to compare the ritual of the Catholic with that of the Anglican Church; and how 'as the thought came full before me that perhaps it would be my duty to become a Catholic, I said to myself, the divine command ought to be as clear as that given to Abraham, for the sacrifice would be as great. The thought of it,' he says, 'was most terrible to me.' He also read the Articles of the Council of Trent, the *Catechismus ad Parochos*, and the *Life of S. Dominic* and *Letter on the Holy See*, by Lacordaire, which last especially delighted him. He says: 'I don't think I had any difficulty as to the Council or its Catechism. And certainly the decision and clearness of their tone struck me much.'

Another entry from the diary tells how he heard that the blow had at last fallen:

'Friday, October 10, at breakfast with Marriott. I received from him the intelligence that J. H. N. had become Catholic, and I write: "I had been so long expecting the blow that it was almost a relief when it was come." On returning home I found a note from him telling me of the fact, and expressing the clearness of his intellectual conviction that he was doing right.'

The note, one of thirty similar ones written to Newman's closest friends on that eventful day, ran as follows:

'LITTLEMORE,
October 9, 1845.

MY DEAR ALLIES,

I am to be received into what I believe to be the one Church and the one Communion of Saints this evening, if it is so ordained. Father Dominic the Passionist is here, and I have begun my confession to him. I suppose two friends will be received with me.

May I have only one-tenth part as much faith as I have intellectual conviction where the truth lies! I do not suppose anyone can have had such combined reasons poured upon him that he is doing right. So far I am most blessed; but, alas! my heart is so hard, and I am taking things so much as a matter of course, that I have been quite frightened lest I should not have faith and contrition enough to gain the benefits of the Sacraments. Perhaps faith and reason are incompatible in one person, or nearly so.

Ever yours most sincerely,

JOHN H. NEWMAN.'

On November 5, nearly a month later, Allies paid his first visit to Newman after his conversion, and the entry in his journal again seems worth quoting in full.

'Went to see J. H. N. at Littlemore. I had resolved to give three full years to this dreadful Roman controversy, and *whatever* might be my convictions, to do nothing during that time. And I wished to ask him to set me upon a course of reading, and moral, and intellectual discipline for that time. When I asked him this, he said it would be better to wait and read his book, and then consult him on any particular point. It was such a *sea*. When I asked specifically whether there was anything wrong in taking a considerable time, whatever might be one's feelings, his answer struck me as very different in tone from what it used to be. (In truth, from April 1844 down to my last interview with him in August 1845, before his becoming a Catholic, he had uniformly quieted me by checking precipitation and advising delay.) He said he could not answer such a question without consulting those in authority—that, indeed, no general answer could be given—that it must depend on the subjective state of each individual. I alluded to his own case, and the many years taken since his convictions were what they now are. He said he had had such a distrust of argument. The great point seemed to be whether the conscience was touched; if it was, then great delay seemed not allowable. The Roman Catholics asked this, Is the conscience touched? It is not to be wondered at that N.'s tone is changed; but the change is very marked; before he was uniformly decisive about waiting, circumspection, etc. However, he admitted that a person in doubt was at worst in the position of a catechumen waiting for baptism. It was a great delight to see him again. One just feels that one would be content to do anything and to go anywhere with him.'

The 'book' was, of course, the Essay on Development, and Allies says: 'The whole of this interval since my return from France, I had in fact been waiting to see what account of his change Newman would give. Never had I waited so anxiously for any book; and doubtless this was the case with many others; for I find remarks' (in his diary) 'about persons still Protestants, which show in what state of suspense they then were.'

'Thursday, November 27. Went into Oxford to get J. H. N.'s book, so anxiously waited for, and with a combination of opposite feelings—love, fear, curiosity; returned in evening with my treasure.'

'Tuesday, December 2. Had a long talk with W. Palmer; he thinks J. H. N.'s book by far the most able defence of Roman Catholicism which has appeared. It promises to become ecumenical. It was portentous to think of such a book as Newman's being a new and most able defence of Catholicism, coming from without the Church.'

The book 'directed his studies for the next five

years'; and its preface determined him to single out the point of the Papal Supremacy and pursue it to its conclusion as being 'the key to the whole controversy, the centre of the whole position.' His resolution was made 'to go honestly to the Fathers, and to see if their witness was in favour of Rome or not.' His plan was to pursue every mention of such subjects as Primacy, S. Peter, etc., given in the index of each Father's works, and by this means he 'rapidly got a view. The Roman Primacy seemed confirmed on all sides.'

The 'view' was a very consoling one from the Anglican position, as it saw the Church 'governed by a Patriarchal system, at the head of which was the Bishop of Rome, whose power was limited by the canons and by usage.' He wrote an article on it for the *Christian Remembrancer*; which expanded into a book with the lengthy title of 'The Church of England cleared of the Charge of Schism upon testimonials of Councils and Fathers of the first six centuries.' This work not only helped to steady him after the shock of losing Newman, but earned him a very long and learned letter of praise from Mr. Gladstone, who rejoices in 'the weight of the consideration connected with the Eastern Church,' which has so little 'received its due from others' than Allies. Manning also writes to thank him for a copy sent him, tells him that he thinks the book is 'the most candid, and therefore the most satisfactory we have had on either side of late,' and gives a synopsis of letters he had written to a person shaken on the Supremacy question which show that he and Allies have come substantially to the same conclusion. Moberly thinks the author speaks with much more respect 'than appears to me deserved by Mr. Newman's "body of proof";' and quotes many pages of the book in which the instances of 'poor

J. H. N.' are utterly demolished. And Baron Alderson thinks he has made out his proposition, and done important service to the English Church.

The first edition, published in June 1846, was followed by another in February 1848, exhibiting the same view, but at treble the length! The reading on which he had based his book consisted, he says, chiefly of Gallican works, whose authors sought in certain points 'to limit the Papal prerogative.' His concentration on this blinded him at the time to the fact that 'every one of them held that communion with the Pope was essential to Church membership.' His eyes were opened to it later.

Between the publication of the two editions, an encounter with his Bishop, Dr. Wilberforce, took place; after a ruri-decanal meeting at which he had denounced as heretical, doctrines publicly affirmed by the vicar of a neighbouring parish. The Bishop refused to support him; so he sent him a letter 'tolerably strong, in which I drew the conclusion from his conduct that the Sacraments might be indifferently held or denied in his diocese.' This had no effect but to elicit a rebuke; and so 'the two ministers of adjoining parishes, Bicester and Launton, went on preaching contradictory doctrine such as they had done before, and just as is done all over England now.' Plus ça change!

It is hard to understand how he could, after this, publish a second edition of a book written, he tells us, 'in the utmost good faith, with daily prayers for enlightenment,' in 'ostensible defence of a communion which "he" thoroughly hated.' He seems to have sent a copy to Newman, who sharply rebuked his extraordinary attitude in the following letter:

'. . . Glad as I am to be of service to you, it pains

me more than you can understand to write to you. I cannot make out how you reconcile it with yourself to take up a position which so few people, if any, in the whole world ever did before you. You have, excuse me, no pretence to say you follow the Church of England. Do you follow her living authorities, or her Reformers, or Laud, or her Liturgy, or her Articles? I cannot understand a man like you going by private judgment, though I can understand his thinking he goes by authority, when he does not. I can understand a man identifying Laud with the Church of England, or Cranmer with the Church of England; but it amazes me to find him interpreting the Church of England by himself, and making himself the prophet and doctor of his Church. This, I suppose, you and a few others are now doing—calling *that* the Church of England which never was before so called since that Church was. I can't make out *how* you can be said to go by authority; and, if not, are not you, and all who do like you, only taking up a form of liberalism? It puzzles me that people won't call things by their right names—why not boldly discard what is no longer practically professed? Say that the Catholic Church *is not*—that it has broken up—this I understand. I don't understand saying that there is a Church, and one Church, and yet acting as if there were none or many. This is dreaming, surely.

Excuse this freedom. I don't wish, as you may well suppose, to get up a controversy, when we both have so much to do; but when I think of your position and that of others, I assure you it frightens me.

Ever yours most sincerely,

JOHN H. NEWMAN.'

The extracts which follow from the defence Allies

sent him, and his comment at the end of Newman's second letter give instances of that obtuseness which shows itself in him from time to time when his own actions are in question.

He answers Newman's warning a week later, in a letter which, as far as arguments go, might be taken from the *Church Times* to-day, so completely do they resemble those which frequently appear in its columns.

'LAUNTON, BICESTER,
Sept. 14*th*, 1848.

MY DEAR MR. NEWMAN,

I have been trying to make out what you mean in asserting "I have no pretence to say I follow the Church of England." Certainly I may deceive myself, and "think I am going by authority when I do not," but I *do* imagine that my book simply sets forth the *Idea* on which the Church of England has all along subsisted. I suppose that during three hundred years she has had men of holy lives and learned in Church matters and antiquity among her members, and those who would not have shrunk from a sacrifice had their conscience demanded it. Now I really do believe that Andrewes, Laud, Hammond, Ken, Wilson, and such like in time past, and Keble, Pusey, Manning, at present, and all whom they represent, subsisted or subsist on that *Idea* of the Church which my book gives. And what appears to me so greatly in their favour is, the strong historical evidence that this was the original *Idea* of the Church down to the very separation of the East and West, and much longer.

. . . I have at once the greatest admiration for the theory of Infallibility dwelling in the single Chair of S. Peter, and the conviction that the whole history of the Church for eight centuries runs counter to it. If I have mistaken history and councils, it would only be charitable to convince me of this—I am quite open to it. I thoroughly distrust my own judgment. I am most deeply pained and shocked at the state of the Church of England; but how can I take one class of difficulties instead of another? or how make so tremendous a plunge without the conviction that truth is entirely on the side for which I should sacrifice everything? The converts, you excepted, seem to me to have swallowed ultra-montanism whole, without inquiry. They have *assumed* its truth, and then argue from it. I can't do this. . . .

Perhaps you think that my book has already been refuted times out of number—if there be any treatise proving historically that ultra-montane view of the monarchy which we deny that you will point out to me, I will give it the best attention I can. I for one agree with Keble that "whenever R. Catholics will prove the supremacy of the Pope, with anything like the same mass of authority and argument as that by which S. Augustine proved the necessary imperfection of the visible Church, we will at once submit ourselves to him." (Preface, p. 61.)

Believe me, my dear Mr. Newman,

Ever gratefully yours,

T. W. ALLIES.'

Newman replies:

'MARYVALE, PERRY BAR,
September 16, 1848.

MY DEAR ALLIES,

I write you a line to acknowledge yours, lest you think it unkind in me not to do so—not as if I intended to take up your time, as I said in my former letter, with argument. Were it worth while doing so, and were time cheap, there would be much to say on various points you bring forward; but I intended my letter merely as a protest, lest you should think me other than I am, and assuring you I often think of you at sacred times, I am, my dear Allies, very sincerely yours,

JOHN H. NEWMAN.'

It is somewhat surprising to read the comment Allies added to this letter when including it in his book some years later: 'I may remark that I never understood why he sent this sort of answer to me; and could hardly avoid construing it as an admission of weakness. I fancy now that he thought I was not perfectly sincere!'

He now planned to write a defence of the Anglican Church on the charge of heresy, and consulted Dr. Pusey, who was now his director, on the difficulties which very naturally occurred to him. The account of the interview given in his Journal is worth transcribing, the momentous point raised by Pusey—'How far the allowance of heresy destroys a Church'—being apparently still in doubt amongst his successors.

'February 29, 1848. Called on Pusey last Tuesday, 22nd, and again yesterday, to set before him my difficulties. They consist in the inadequate expression, or omission altogether, of parts of the Catholic system, which our formularies, as settled at the Reformation, present. For instance:

1. The maiming and dislocation of the Liturgy.
2. The putting out of the doctrine of the Eucharistic Sacrifice.
3. The practical denial of the Priesthood.
4. The all but universal disuse of Confession.
5. The language about the five minor Sacraments.
6. The theory of Justification.
7. The not holding the Real Presence,

We conversed about an hour and a half on these. The *first* he allowed. The *second*, maintained that we had all that was essential to the Sacrifice. The *third*, said the Prayer Book put forth the Priesthood as strongly as could be desired. The *fourth*, that Confession was authorised. The *fifth*, that however badly the 25th Article, in that part, was drawn up, the English Church was borne out in setting the two great Sacraments above the others *longo intervallo*. The *sixth*, that our theory of Justification was S. Augustine's. The *seventh*, that our language really contained and authorised the Real Presence, and the restrictive assertions were directed against a *carnal* Presence. He allowed, then, that we were deeply suffering from certain changes made at the Reformation; that our present weakness and want of unity were the result of indecisive and ambiguous language, then adopted; that this was much to be deplored but that it did not unchurch us; that what we had must be devotionally used, with a prayer for better times. He seemed to think that no detailed study of these and other points would lead to any very satisfactory conclusion, because the point really at issue was—*How far the allowance of heresy destroys a Church;* and at the end of the discussion one would have got no further than this. He maintains most stoutly that no heresy is set forth in the Articles, or elsewhere.

He had shown my letter to C. Marriott, who had observed that if I considered the matter as honestly as I had done in the case of the Supremacy, the result would be the same. "J. H. N.," he said, "had been carried off by the Supremacy."

This may be considered a perfect specimen of Dr. Pusey's answer to theological difficulties. Is it any wonder that as soon as one was out of his presence all the doubts came back?'

The ' Defence from Heresy ' was never written, but just before the interview with Dr. Pusey just quoted he received the first copies of his ' Journal in France,' written in 1845 and revised in 1849, in which he gives the impression made upon him by the Church in France during visits abroad in 1845 and 1848.

It occasioned ' a great storm,' as many of his Tractarian friends prophesied. Manning would not allow it to be dedicated to him, as he did not want to be obliged to answer ' I do,' if asked if he believed its contents.

The author was delighted at its publication ; for as an entry on February 19, 1849, tells us, it so exactly set forth his mind, and paid a debt which he seemed to owe to the Roman Church. On March 19 he writes : ' I have had many letters ; one, very kind, from J. H. N. ; valuable, from W. Palmer ; good, from Gladstone, Wynne, Pollen, Allen, H. Coleridge, Dodsworth, Lady Alderson, Richards, Bishop of Brechin ; very good, from E. H. Thompson ; good from E. Coleridge, H. Wilberforce, Stokes, Patterson, Lord Adare, etc. Furious article in *Old Mother Gamp*, indescribably beastly in *Church and State Gazette*, unpleasant in *Guardian*, angry in *Britannia*.'

Of the ' many letters ' he prints a few. Gladstone's letter shows a distinct anti-Roman bias ; based on his experience, ' such as it has been,' of the Catholic system on the Continent ; and on his ' very limited reading ' on the subject. Keble's is in reply to one which Allies sent him enclosed with the ' Journal.' It shows how much the ' Trusty's here and Pincher's here ' argument then weighed with him ; and also helps to explain why Newman's rebuke in the previous September fell on deaf ears.

Allies writes :

'LAUNTON,
Feb. 19*th*, 1849.

DEAR MR. KEBLE,

I hope you will receive by this post a copy of a little book, a Journal in France. I am not, I am aware, entitled to beg your acceptance of it by any length or intimacy of acquaintance ; but it touches on subjects of more than deep interest at present to English Churchmen, and on which your judgment possesses, in my eyes, the greatest weight. If, therefore, you should have time to cast your eye on it, it would be a satisfaction to me to know how it affects you. I approach the whole subject of Rome, not with feelings of an author, but with those of the most trembling responsibility. To speak candidly, the existence of you, Dr. Pusey, Archdeacon Manning, and some others in the Anglican Communion is the strongest proof I can see at present of its being part of the Catholic Church. To such a degree does it appear to me to have sacrificed, and to sacrifice at present, all objective truth. I mean not the pen and paper English Church, but that Church which preaches every Sunday in some twelve thousand parishes, and energises through Dr. Sumner and his colleagues. I have been so strongly impressed with what, on the other hand, I have seen in the Roman Church ; and the profound ignorance, the wonderful misconception concerning it, which prevail almost universally among us, have been so brought home to me that it seemed to me almost a sacred duty to set before others what I have seen. On the whole subject no thought but one gives me any satisfaction—would that I could see any prospect of it !—the reunion of the two communions.

I hope you will think that times of peril authorise

one almost a stranger to speak so frankly. And believe me, dear Mr. Keble, faithfully yours,

T. W. ALLIES.'

The following extracts from Keble's reply show how much sounder his views were on the argument from Sanctity than those Allies had so far managed to grasp; quite apart from the modesty which made him dislike to have his personality considered as a reason for remaining in the Church of England.

'HURSLEY,
April 17th, 1849.
Tuesday in Eastertide.

MY DEAR MR. ALLIES,

Will you forgive my great unthoughtfulness, I fear I should say unkindness, in not having sooner thanked you for your kind present and letter? . . . I have only just finished my thorough reading of the journal, though I have read a great deal of it more than once. Will you pardon me if I own that in some respects it has deeply pained me? Perhaps it would not have done so, nearly to the same extent, if I had not all along been haunted by that sentence in your letter, where you say that, were it not for certain individuals you should feel inclined to give up our Church. This caused me, perhaps, to put a more unfavourable construction upon parts of the "Journal," and especially upon the conclusion, than I should otherwise have done, and would certainly embarrass me much if I had to plead for the book in conversation. But I think you must have written in a hurry, and could hardly mean what you say. Seeing that if the being of a Church (I do not say its well-being) depends on the more or less *apparent* sanctity of individuals within it, or even of the general mass, it must vary from time to time and from place to place in the same body ; e.g. if your knowledge of the excellency of the French Church at present is a reason for accounting it, κατ' ἐξοχήν *the* Church, you ought, I suppose, during good part of the eighteenth century, to have reckoned it *no* Church ; or if you saw it even now in some unfavourable light—in parts of Ireland, perhaps, or of South America (I do not know, but only put the case), it would be no Church *there*.

. . . It would not be quite candid in me were I not to own that I could not have said all that you say of the Roman doctrine of the Real Presence and of the honour due to the B. Virgin Mother, without adding something by way of caution : i.e. I not only believe that in both respects there is a good deal of popular error among them which is winked at, as many errors are among ourselves, but I *could* not, even were I turned out of this Church, adopt from my heart that faith on these two points which I must adopt to be a R.C. at all. I could not get rid of the impression that in both of them I was upon no sufficient authority pledging myself to definite statements on points which Scripture and antiquity had left indefinite. So that if, as the least of several evils, I *did* feel compelled to ask for admission among them, I should feel that I could not do it strictly in faith, but in the hope of being spared, if wrong, in consideration of invincible ignorance. Indeed, this matter, of being definite without sufficient warrant, seems to meet one in almost every part of the Roman system, and would, in my mind, more than counterbalance the deep satisfaction with which I might assist at R.C. services, and use their books of devotion unchanged. I hope that I shall not have startled you too much in saying this ; and I hope also, that if thoroughly carried out, this kind of feeling would not prove adverse to the reunion we all so earnestly desire, but in the end would tend towards it ; provided always it were accompanied with hearty, uncompromising faith in the great points which the Universal Church *has* defined for us.

I return the correspondence with the Bishop of Oxford, which W. B. H. also put into my hands. I trust that your very striking quotations will have their effect, and that you will soon be relieved from the great discomfort (how great, I know better than I could wish) of being in *polemics* with your Diocesan. I am sorry to see that the Bishop considers the report about an Encyclical letter of last February, concerning the Blessed Virgin's Immaculate Conception, as genuine. I had hoped it was a mere newspaper invention ; for it seems to me as much against unity as any one thing could be. Pray believe me always, my dear Allies, affectionately and gratefully yours,

J. KEBLE.'

One letter from Mr. Justice Coleridge contains a criticism which a certain type of apologist for the Church might well take to heart :

'No one can doubt that you have communicated to Englishmen a great deal of new and important information, useful for us to know in itself, and still more useful if it should have the effect of infusing a more catholic and charitable spirit respecting Romanism. And you have done this in an authentic and interesting form. Nevertheless I must frankly say that I think you have made two serious mistakes—the first in the form of the book ; seeing [that] your object was to make us know more and feel better about the Roman Church, and that this [object] assumed ignorance and prejudice to be existing more or less amongst us, the journal form was peculiarly unfitted for your purpose. What you had to say should have been put forward in the most careful and guarded manner ; but the journal, especially when the writer feels so strongly as you do, is almost sure to convey the truth in the most careless and offensive way—every bit of cake is accompanied by a slap in the face. This seems to me *now* so obvious that I almost wonder it did not occur to me when you mentioned your intention to me in London ; but I really wonder it did not occur to Manning when he read the journal. I uncommonly regret this mistake, because I think if you fail in doing the good you intended, it will be in a great measure owing to it, and it is a failure very difficult to set right. . . . The second defect depends in some measure on the former. When one pauses and begins to consider the book, it is impossible not to be struck with its *one-sidedness*, and the narrowness of the premisses compared with the breadth of the conclusion. You visit about a twentieth of France, and you see in it certain selected specimens, exhibited by certain selected clergymen, whom you knew, and who knew you beforehand—and from this you draw general conclusions affecting both Churches . . . but the journal was meant to do what an argument would have done—you meant to change men's opinions—and therefore either the journal ought to have fulfilled the conditions of an argument, or was an unfit vehicle for your matter. . . .

Now the absence of this not only diminishes the authority of your book, but serves to increase the very prejudice you wish to put down—it lets in somewhat of personal anger against the writer.'

To win wars, a British general has said, one must not exaggerate. The axiom seems a sound one as regards all battlefields.

Manning's criticism also shows that the damaging element of unfairness to one side—in this case against the side to which the writer officially belonged—was decidedly marked. He mentions several points in which Allies understates the progress made in the Church of England in the last fifteen years, and says that though 'the amount of valuable, instructing, shaming, stirring matter is great,' he had hoped to see the facts of the matter stated 'without any reflections,' and fears that in consequence of their unfortunate inclusion 'sore heads will remember only the reflections and forget the facts.' He finds thirty-one passages in the Journal which 'tell for the Roman Church,' and twelve 'against it, i.e. for us.'

Newman's letter of thanks for a copy of the book explains 'at least in part,' Allies thinks, the drift of the preceding letters from him in September 1848, which had so surprisingly 'perplexed' him. The letter gives an interesting contemporary glimpse of Newman's reasons for leaving Anglicanism.

'ORATORY, ALCHESTER STREET,
BIRMINGHAM,
February 20, 1849.

Thank you very much, my dear Allies, for your most interesting, and, if I might use the word without offence, hopeful book. It cannot be but it must subserve the cause of Catholic unity, of which you must know I think there is but one way. You do me injustice if you think, as I half gathered from a sentence in it, that I speak contemptuously of those who now stand where I have stood myself. But persons like yourself should recollect that *the* reason *why* I left the Anglican Church was that I thought salvation was not to be found in it. This feeling could not stop there. If it led me to leave Anglicanism, it necessarily led me, and leads me, to wish others to leave it. The position of those who leave it in the only way in which I think it justifiable to leave it, is necessarily one of hostility to it. To leave it merely as a branch of the Catholic Church for another which I liked better, would have been to desert without reason the post where Providence put me. . . .

Moreover, he [the convert] will feel most anxiously about those whom he has left in it, lest they should be receiving grace which ought to bring them into the Catholic Church, yet are in the way to quench it, and to sink into a state in which there is no hope.

Especially will he be troubled at those who put themselves forward as teachers of a system which they cannot trace to any set of men, or any doctor, before themselves; who give up history, documents, theological authors, and maintain that it is *blasphemy against* the Holy Ghost to deny the signs of Catholicism and divine acceptance, as a *fact*, in the existing bearing and action of their communion.

But of such as you, my dear Allies, I will ever augur better things, and hope against hope, and believe the day will come when (excuse me) you will confess that you have been in a dream; and meanwhile I will not cease to say Mass for you, and all who stand where you stand, on the tenth day of every month, unless something very particular occur.

Again begging you to excuse this freedom. I am, my dear Allies, most sincerely yours,

JOHN H. NEWMAN.'

A Journal such as the above letters show it to have been could hardly avoid episcopal censure; and on March 19, 1849, the Bishop of Oxford, Samuel Wilberforce, handed Allies a letter calling his most serious attention to the variance which in the Bishop's judgement existed between the language of the book, and the dogmatic teaching of the Church of England. He encloses a paper of extracts 'as to each of which' he says 'I must require of you either such explanations as shall show I have mistaken your meaning, and that they are reconcilable with the language of the Thirty-nine Articles; or failing that, their unqualified retraction.

Failing one or the other of these, nothing will remain for me but to call upon you solemnly, in the name of God, to discontinue that ministry and renounce those emoluments which you exercise and enjoy on the condition of holding articles of religion which you publicly contradict.'

The extracts the Bishop gives could not possibly be made to square with the Articles, but do not seem to give a very coherent system of Catholic belief. It is easy to understand why Newman was so dissatisfied with such an attitude of mind.

Allies's reply did not satisfy the Bishop; so on March 24 he wrote another letter requiring from him 'explanation, justification or retraction,' to which Allies made another very long reply; quoting Bishops Taylor, Andrewes, Forbes, Latimer, Montague, Hall, Bull, etc., as well as Hooker and Thorndike, in support of 'the Adoration of the Holy Sacrament, the Invocation of Saints, and the use of Relics, etc.,' being compatible with Church of England doctrine. The Bishop's answer was as follows:

'CUDDESDON PALACE,
April 9, 1849.

REV. AND DEAR SIR,

It gives me much pain to be obliged again

to express to you my dissatisfaction with your last letter.

It would not, I think, be difficult to show that the passages you have quoted in justification of your own statements either do not apply to the matter before us, or taken in their full context do not fairly bear the meaning you put on them, or are from writers who are of no authority on this subject.

But I take a higher objection to the line of defence you have adopted. My charge against you is that your words directly contravene the plain letter of the Thirty-nine Articles. A catena from other writers is no answer to this charge. The letter and grammatical meaning of the Articles themselves is that to which your statements must be referred.

I therefore deem it useless to enter further with you on the subject in the way of argument. But you will, I think, see that I cannot with a clear conscience allow doctrine which I judge directly to contravene the Articles on important points to be publicly put forth by one of my presbyters without my taking notice of his conduct.

At the same time I am most anxious to avoid, if possible, the scandal and the pain of calling you into a court of law. Neither do I desire myself to dogmatise. I therefore make you the following offer.

Will you engage to submit yourself to my judgment in this matter, if, on referring your book, and the letters which have passed between us, either (1) to the Archbishop of the province; or (if you prefer the judgment of your brother presbyters) to (2) the Regius Professors of Divinity, Pastoral Theology, and Ecclesiastical History in the University of Oxford, with the request that they will give me in writing their judgment as to *the fact* whether your statements do or do not contradict the Thirty-nine Articles or any of them, I receive their written confirmation of my own judgment upon this point ?

I am, Rev. and dear Sir, yours very faithfully,

S. Oxon.'

Allies made no reply: and a fortnight later the Bishop again wrote as follows:

'London,
April 23, 1849.

Rev. and Dear Sir,

Feeling the importance of the decision to which you came [*sic*[1]] upon the proposition laid before you in my last letter, I have waited your own time for your reply. But as it is now a fortnight since I despatched that letter, I cannot feel that I am wrongly pressing you for a decision when I say that I think the time is arrived at which I ought to receive your answer.

I am, Rev. and dear Sir, very truly yours,

S. Oxon.'

Allies sent him a long reply which I quote in full, as it is interesting to compare his views with those now held by the majority of Anglican clergy as to the mental reservations they may lawfully make when subscribing to the Thirty-nine Articles on Ordination.

'7 Marine Parade,
Brighton,
St. Mark's Day, 1849.

My Lord,

I thank your Lordship for the offer contained in your letter of the 9th, as plainly evidencing your desire

[1] The [*sic*] is in Allies's copy of the letter. The Bishop probably meant to write 'must come.'

to avoid a public trial, which would be equally painful to us both.

I also quite admit that "the letter and grammatical meaning of the Articles themselves is that to which my statements must be referred."

I feel unable, however, to accept in either alternative the offer your Lordship makes me, for the following reason: To decide whether my statements are or are not agreeable to the letter and meaning of the Articles, would be, in fact, to decide what the sense of the Articles[1] is on certain disputed points. This is a matter which for three centuries has been left open by the Church of England; and I feel that it would not be right to accept a particular sense put upon those Articles, from any individuals (however fitted by station or qualification to give a judgment) nor from any authority short of the Church of England herself, either assembled in Synod or represented in her courts of law—especially as a decision either way must produce an extensive and lasting effect on the Church herself.

For instance, I conceive that no authority short of the Church of England herself can determine what is the precise sense of the 22nd and 31st Articles, which are those on which the question would mainly turn. The sense of those Articles which entirely approved itself to my conscience is one entirely compatible with all the statements of my book. Others might form a different judgment; but in refusing to be bound by their judgment, while I respected it as far as they themselves were concerned, I should, I conceive, only be using the liberty which the Church of England has given to her children.

It may here be proper, for your Lordship's satisfaction, to state the sense in which I do subscribe the

[1] See Note 4, Appendix

Articles. I subscribe them, then, in their literal and grammatical sense, interpreting them, in due subordination to this, according to the canon of the Council which imposed them, and which I consider as the rule or type of the English Church : "Let preachers take care that they never teach anything to be religiously held and believed by the people, save what is agreeable to the doctrine of the Old or New Testament, and what the Catholic Fathers and ancient bishops have deduced from that very doctrine."

I subscribe them *not* as articles of *faith* (save as to those matters contained in them which are likewise contained in the creeds), but as articles of *peace*, for the following reasons :

1. Because it is not lawful or competent for any particular province of the Church to enact fresh and peculiar articles of faith, as Bishop Hall, quoted by Bishop Bull in his "Catholic Propositions," denies in general "that any Church can lawfully propose any articles to her sons besides those contained in the common rule of faith to be believed under pain of damnation."

2. Because the form and structure of the Articles themselves, save of the first five, prove that they are not intended for articles of *faith*, but for practical canons suited to a particular Church under special circumstances.

3. Because the Church of England does not require any lay person to subscribe them, which, were they articles of *faith*, she must require.

4. Because bishops of the highest eminence have declared that they are not subscribed as articles of *faith*, but as articles of *peace*. Thus Bishop Bull quotes Archbishop Usher as "expressing the sense of the Church of England as to the subscription required to

the Thirty-nine Articles " in the following words : " We do not suffer any man to reject the Thirty-nine Articles of the Church of England at his pleasure, yet neither do we look upon them as essentials of saving faith, or legacies of Christ and His Apostles ; but, in a mean, as pious opinions, fitted for the preservation of peace and unity ; neither do we oblige any man to believe them, but only not to contradict them." Archbishop Bramhall quotes these same words in controversy, and makes them his own. And contrasting the *subscription* to the Thirty-nine Articles with the obligation to *believe* the creed of Pope Pius the Fourth, he observes : " We do not hold our Thirty-nine Articles to be such necessary truth *extra quam non est salus*, nor enjoin ecclesiastical persons to swear unto them, but only to subscribe them as theological truths for the preservation of unity among us, and the extirpation of some growing errors." And Bishop Patrick writes : " I always took the Articles to be only articles of communion ; and so Bishop Bramhall expressly maintains against the Bishop of Calcedon ; and I remember well that Bishop Sanderson, when the King was first restored, received the subscription of an acquaintance of mine, which he declared was not to them as articles of faith, but peace. I think you need make no scruple of the matter, because all that I know so understand the meaning of subscription, and upon other terms would not subscribe." (Letter to Dr. Mapletoft.)

This therefore reduces the question to a single point, whether I have in any statement contradicted the literal and grammatical meaning of any Article. Your Lordship considers that I have. I feel convinced that I have not ; but the Church of England alone, and no individual, can decide the point ; for such decision will fix a certain sense on particular Articles which at present is not fixed on them.

I have the honour to be, my Lord,

Your Lordship's dutiful servant in Christ,

THOS. W. ALLIES.'

The result of the correspondence was the threat of a prosecution, which was only averted by the efforts of Alderson, Manning, Pusey, Bishop Forbes, and others. In the end they brought Allies to write a letter to the Bishop in which he regretted that anything he had published should appear to *him* to be contrary to the Articles, declared his adherence to them in their plain literal and grammatical sense, and engaged not to publish a 2nd edition. Someone (he thinks Dr. Pusey) bought up all the remaining copies, and so the matter apparently ended.

Manning's letter on the matter to the Bishop, his brother-in-law, may be of interest here, in view of the date when it was written, May 16, 1849, and Manning's own state of mind at the time.

'MY DEAREST BISHOP,

Allies has sent me the enclosed letter to forward to you; and in doing so I wish to say a few words on this matter, in which you have so kindly allowed me to communicate with you.

In the letter I wrote to you from Lavington I said that there are in Allies's book things I wish out, and things I wish otherwise. I may add that it is not exempt from criticism, to which every book is liable. But upon the main question at issue I am thoroughly convinced:

1. That it contains no Roman doctrine properly so called.

2. That it contains no proposition or word contrary to the Catholic Faith.

3. That it contains no doctrinal statement at variance with the Thirty-nine Articles.

In language, sentiment, and opinion there may be parts which, in the present state of feeling, in the present disorder of our ecclesiastical courts, and the present confusion of our theological interpretations, might give occasion to an adverse judgment.

But I believe that such a judgment would put not so much Allies's book in opposition to the Thirty-nine Articles, as the Thirty-nine Articles, and the living Church of England, in opposition to the faith of the whole Church, both East and West, according to Bishop Ken's rule, and from the beginning.

It is not, therefore, Allies's book, nor Allies himself, that is alone at stake.

I have his repeated and express declaration, both by word and writing, that he does not hold any doctrine in which the Roman Church differs from the East and from ourselves, but that his agreements with Rome are in points of faith where Rome agrees with all alike.

His statements on the Roman Supremacy and on Transubstantiation are full evidence on these cardinal points.

Indeed, the whole book he has published in defence of the Church of England against the charge of schism is direct and continuous proof, throughout. And it is a work which, so far as I know, stands alone for completeness, honesty, and truth.

Any judgment against Allies upon the language of his journal, these facts standing, would be a manifest injustice.

The case would be this: He disavows Roman doctrine: he has (let it be said) used language which may be urged by special rigour up to an appearance of opposition to the Thirty-nine Articles in some matter not of faith; but the condemnation would have the effect of declaring him and his book to be Roman. It is from this wrong I have desired to protect him, so far as I have been able, both for his own sake, and because I believe it would be a wrong the effects of which would recoil on the Church of England, as a Catholic body, in the face of all the Church.

May I now add one word as to what my wishes would have been and still are in this matter?

I could have earnestly desired that no written document at all had passed; that you, as his bishop, should have expressed your judgment, and he, in his turn, have answered, "Then I will publish no further edition."'

After this controversy, Allies suffered from a natural sense of Episcopal unfairness. The Bishop had passed over 'such propositions on Baptism and the Holy Eucharist as those publicly put forward by Mr. Watt and his friends,' while he attempted to punish Allies 'for statements *moderate in comparison*' on *his* side. 'But then the Bishop was faithful in this,' as Allies realises in looking back on it all, 'to the living spirit of the Anglican Church.' Allies had assumed that 'because a thing was true, ancient, and Catholic, therefore it was held by the Anglican Church,' but 'the real point of issue,' then as now, was whether what he 'considered true, ancient, and Catholic was tenable by the Anglican formularies.'

He consoled himself by a journey to Rome, in company with Wynne (also 'in the last stage of Anglicanism,') feeling that he 'had not a shred to love in

Anglicanism, yet all the while the speculative difficulty on the side of the Roman Supremacy remained.' He wished to present his Journal, so 'reprobated by my own Bishop to the real Bishop of bishops and . . . to kneel at the tomb of the Prince of Apostles.'

He took with him the conclusion of the Journal, translated into Italian for the Pope, and also the book itself, in English. In the course of a long and interesting interview, which he was fortunate enough to obtain through Dr. Grant's good offices, he presented them to Pius IX, who accepted both 'very graciously,' though regretting that he knew no English.

The account of this interview is most interesting. After giving a description of the Pope's dress and of the place where he received them, Allies reports a few remarks made by the Pope on his book, and says: 'His Holiness said, "I am satisfied when I see men earnestly desirous after the truth. Truth is one; and if men seek it with a single mind, I am convinced that God will give them grace to attain to it." . . . He then passed to political matters, and observed that we enjoyed great tranquillity in England; in this respect he much admired us. "I talked," he said, "many times, with Lord Minto; but he does not seem to me one of your leading statesmen; he speaks French ill; for though I have been accustomed to hear it continually for many years, I often could not make out what he said." Then he remarked on the danger of communism in religion, to which republicanism in politics was likely to lead. Catholics generally knew their duty, but too many did not practise it. He asked if I knew Mr. Newman. I said, very well—he had been my confessor while he was with us. "I was much pleased with him," said the Pope; "with his gentleness and calmness; he gathered some five of his friends about him at Rome, under my direction, with the view of becoming Oratorians. Then, as to ability, he has a European name. I remember his friends, though I cannot catch their names, save one—St. John." Then he asked after Dr. Pusey. "He has done," said the Pope, "much good; he has opened the door; he has set before his countrymen the principle of authority, which is the first thing in religion; he has prepared the way for Catholicism."'

Allies then 'took courage to begin a fresh subject' himself, and said, 'I consider it a blessing to have the opportunity of expressing personally to your Holiness that some ecclesiastics at least among us—I may say, several—deeply feel how great a calamity it has been to England, and to the whole British realm, that she has been separated from the Holy See. They ardently desire her reunion with it;' at which the Pope expressed his joy. When asked if he would give Allies and Wynne his blessing, he replied: 'That I will, with all my heart, and I will pray for you, for your friends, and for all England.'

'The comfort,' Allies says, 'which this interview gave is indescribable, and I feel sure that from the time St. Peter's successor gave me his blessing and promised me his prayers, the heavy cloud of confusion and misapprehension which had rested so long upon me, in spite of prayers and the most resolute efforts after the truth, began to dissolve, and the day-star to rise. We passed a delightful fortnight at Naples, Sorrento, Capri, etc., and I then returned by sea to Marseilles, leaving Wynne at Genoa, and on Thursday, September 13th, was again in England, renovated in mind and body, and carrying about with me the Pope's present' (he had given Allies a cameo of our Lord wearing the Crown of Thorns, and Wynne an intaglio bearing on the obverse S. Peter and on the reverse S. Paul), 'as a safeguard against all evil.'

His comments on what he saw of the Church in Italy are interesting, and the following is worth quoting, as the 'Northern mind' is still unduly sensitive at times, and the arguments Allies used to combat his own prejudices may help to overcome them in others.

'On the *festa* at the Mariners' Church at Santa Lucia: we went in and found a small chapel set out very gaudily with hangings, and on the left a large figure of the Madonna, gaudily dressed in gauze, with a tinsel crown, and the Child the same. A benediction was preparing, and the priests were robed at the altar, and many lights burning. I thought how much there was here to offend a Northern mind, and yet the law of charity would surely consider for whose worship this small chapel and its decorations were intended. This tawdrily-dressed figure of the Madonna and Child is probably the gift of poor boatmen; the ornaments they have bestowed on her are probably the costliest and finest which they could imagine, or at least procure. The worship is *to them* that which best represents the majesty of God, and their feeling of love and veneration for her whom all generations call blessed. This people, I conceive, and especially the lower classes, are very sensuous; they must see with carnal eyes, or *not at all.* Is it not so with the uneducated even in the North? Where is the love and veneration which the poor among us show to the person of our Lord and to His Mother? Judging from their demeanour in all holy places, they have none; nothing that meets their eye is to them holy. A man may kiss St. Peter's foot, or wear [*sic*] his knees in ascending the *Scala Santa*, or bow his head before the likeness of her who was the instrument of the Incarnation, without being a saint.

Nevertheless, these external acts of faith are more consoling than the attitude of the peasant who passes the broken cross without salute, who cannot fall on his knees even before the altar of God, whose notion of religion seems to be to sit out a sermon ! But, however, the North and the South are so far apart in feeling that only the charity which died on the Cross can reunite them.'

Allies had now reached the very threshold of the Church. The last remaining barrier was the question of the Supremacy. Like many others whom that barrier still repels, he tried to console himself by proving that many Catholic truths were held in common by the Church he longed to enter and the communion he could not bring himself to leave. He decided to set forth 'the true Patristic doctrine of the Eucharistic Presence and Sacrifice, fortified with quotations, and framed so as to bring matters "to an issue," in our communion—a favourite notion then with us poor *rari nantes in gurgite vasto*, who did not see that we were tossed and whirled like helpless logs of wood in the maelstrom of Protestantism, and who dreamt of the solid foundations of the City of God in that abyss of diabolic confusion, the seething turmoil of the outer darkness. On setting this purpose before Dr. Pusey, he encouraged it much ; he knew it would last some time, and keep me quiet, he might hope, in the interval.'

On September 24, 1849, his diary gives a vivid picture of his state of mind :

'Launton, Monday, September 24, 1849. Returned home, Saturday, September 15 : began the next week with finishing journals of tour : gradually fell into a state of deep despondency about our position. I try to make out the cause of this. I think it is the vision of the English Church thoroughly possessed by heresy, full of a schismatical spirit, and miserably impotent in discipline, which fills my mind and reduces it to a deplorable state of unhappiness. I have taken up any light book which came to hand to get a momentary relief. Saturday seemed a little better, and had made up my mind to prosecute the design which before I went abroad suggested itself to me repeatedly—to collect, that is, the most striking passages of the Fathers concerning the Holy Eucharist. That seems to me the ground on which to offer battle to the enemy.' Under date, Monday, October 1, he writes: 'Went to Oxford—to Pollen, and had a long talk with him. He has been to S. Saviour's most of the vacation, amid the cholera in fearful force, testing to the utmost our system. He seems in very low spirits about it: people quite in a state of heathenism. He got a sort of general confession, and absolved them without Holy Communion. Rest of week chiefly on Suarez' *De Eucharistica* with increasing assurance that the difference is not irreconcilable between us and Rome on *that* head.'

The entry on Saturday, October 6, says: 'Drew out with amplification the sketch of difficulties as to our position made last March for consultation with Pusey and Manning. P. writes urging at once increased pastoral work and a dogmatic treatise.' This advice recalls that which Father Ronald Knox, in *The Spiritual Æneid*, says that his brother gave him under similar circumstances in 1915. He adds: 'The same advice, it will be remembered, was given to Hugh Benson.'

The list of difficulties which Allies entitled 'Thoughts of an English Churchman on the Roman Controversy,' is put in full in his autobiography; the main points are included in this abridged version of it. It is dated October 6, 1849.

'As to the Roman claim and position there are :

For

(*a*) Communion with St. Peter's See.
(*b*) Unbroken descent.
(*c*) Continuity of dogma. (I do not mean that everything now held to be *de fide* in the Roman Church can be proved to have been held from the beginning, for this is not even asserted, but that the whole dogma is historically and logically coherent and homogeneous.)
(*d*) Unity and extent of communion.
(*e*) A defined religious dogma resolutely maintained.
(*f*) A Church living and in action, and exercising the most awful functions.
(*g*) The force and attraction of the Catholic system : under this may be ranged (i) Sacraments encompassing the whole spiritual life. (ii) Counsels of perfection. (iii) Religious orders providing for every development of Christian graces and every need of the Church. (iv) Celibacy in clergy.

Against

(1) The claim of Papal infallibility and with it absolute power, which seems necessary as a key-stone to the whole Roman system, both in doctrine and discipline, i.e. as to the question of heresy and as to the question of schism. The evidence not only fails for this but seems contradicted and over-powered.
(2) *Extent* of Saint worship and *Patronage* of the Blessed Virgin.
(3) Use made of Indulgences and their mediæval development.

(4) That the state of society, morals, religion, etc., in the world does not bear out the exclusive Roman claim to be the Catholic Church.

But these difficulties, which are very great to one placed externally to the Roman system, become very much diminished, if they do not disappear, to one *within* it, by recognising it as the Catholic Church.'

The progress of his thought is shown by two marginal notes added in the following year. The first, dated February 16, is: 'N.B. All the difficulties against Rome range themselves under excess and abuse of right principles. All those of Anglicanism are perversions or denials of the principles themselves—Feb. 16th, 1850.'

The second, written on the page opposite paragraph 1 of his statement, runs:

'With regard to No. 1 all my difficulties have been removed by a further enquiry, and the Papal Supremacy is now one of the strongest proofs on the side of Rome to my mind.'

Another serious flaw he discovers in the Anglican claim and position is that it reduces an article of the Creed, 'I believe in the Holy Catholic Church,' to a nullity. If, as the Anglican system maintains, the Catholic Church is made up of three branches, and these branches do not hold the same body of truth, but in certain points condemn each other, 'the Church has ceased not only to be one, but likewise to be "the pillar and ground of the truth."'

He points out that as the Anglican Church does not claim to be *the* Catholic Church, yet censures the other two for false doctrine, 'all she leaves to the believer in "one holy Catholic Church" is a ruin full of uncleanness, a fabric [which is] not *one*, for it is divided; and not holy, for each of the three parts, in the estimation of the other two, teaches false doctrine.'

'What avails it,' as he despairingly asks, 'to say that during six or any number of centuries, there *was* "one holy Catholic Church?" The question for men who are every day dying and called to judgment is, whether there is one in the year 1849, where she is, and what she teaches.'

He proceeds to show a further difficulty arising out of this separation from the Authority and Unity of the Church. When the Church of England differs in matters of faith and morals from 'the other branches of the Church,' she has 'no *authority* for *anything* she teaches save her *private judgment* of Scripture'; yet 'the private judgment of a province of the Church has no more the promise of being right than the private judgment of an individual.' As he says, 'This is so great and paramount a difficulty that it seems to destroy the habit of divine faith itself in members of the English Church. They can believe nothing simply because it is the belief of the Catholic Church, for that Church is a past historical thing to them, not a living power; and what that historical Church held is matter for a man's private judgment which the longest life and the greatest abilities will hardly enable him to solve.'

All this confusion dates, as he points out, from 'the changes of doctrine and the isolation of communion brought about at the Reformation.' Its three main results, he says, have been the spoliation of Church property by the governing classes, the subjection of the spiritual to the civil power in spiritual matters by the State, and the overthrow of the principle of authority in the minds of all. Thus a national system replaced Catholicism in England, and the Reformation developed itself 'among us in three main features,' which he proceeds to state as follows.

The first is Erastianism, which is responsible for 'the invasion of spiritual powers by the civil authority; the interference of mixed legislative lay bodies with dogma; the conferring of spiritual jurisdiction by the Crown (as in the late division of the Bishop of Australia's See);[1] the founding of bishoprics; dividing of parishes, etc.'

The second feature is the Church of England's 'disregard of unity; her practical Donatism'; and the third her 'disregard of dogma, truth made subjective and individual.'

In the distinctive system thus set up there is, as he says, no inward coherence and unity. The Prayer-book in the main reflects 'though faintly, the old Catholic system'; the Articles and Homilies represent 'the intruding Protestant virus.' Thus while the formularies themselves were 'shaded down to an imbecile neutrality,' the different parties whom the Reformers hoped to 'hold together in the joint use of ambiguous formularies by taking them each in their own sense,' remained fundamentally opposed. It is small wonder that the whole history of the Church of England in the three hundred years following the Reformation reveals 'an inmost disunion and struggle [between] Puritans and High Church Establishmentarians, Calvinists and Arminians, Latitudinarians and Non-Jurors, Evangelicals and Orthodox'; which, under different party names, continues to this moment. 'The very ethos of belief and conduct of these parties is,' as Allies says, 'antagonistic.'

One inevitable result of this opposition is, he says,

[1] This had its counterpart within recent years; when Parliament refused its assent to a Bill for the division of the unwieldy See of Hereford into two dioceses of workable dimensions.

'the absence of theology since the Reformation, since when no one writer, much less a catena, seems to have been possessed of a complete sense of doctrine.' Hence have come 'variations, defects and inconsistencies about the Holy Eucharist in our best writers, Hooker, Andrewes, Bramhall, Bull, etc.' He finds a sinister commentary on these discrepancies supplied by 'the state of the chancels and mode of administering the Holy Eucharist throughout England'; in the diametrically opposed teaching about Baptism, or Orders, or the Church; and 'in the allowance of every description of heresy on the Protestant side as respects the whole Church system and justification.'

He now specifies the 'corruptions of dogma which are chargeable on the English Church as a communion.' They are:

(*a*) Denial of the Eucharistic sacrifice.
(*b*) Denial of the Real Presence.
(*c*) Practical denial and universal disuse of the Priesthood.
(*d*) Practical denial of the power of the keys.
(*e*) Absence of a system of confession and guidance of the interior life.
(*f*) Prevalence of the Lutheran doctrine of justification, which is as much supported by the Articles as the Catholic doctrine by the Prayer-book.
(*g*) Putting aside the Communion of Saints.
(*h*) Language about the Seven Sacraments, and the abolition of extreme Unction, the alteration of the ceremonies in Baptism, the disuse of the chrism in confirmation, and the maiming and altering of the rites in conferring Orders.
(*i*) Rejection of the sacerdotal and episcopal robes.

He points out that though many of her members

have protested against some of these corruptions, the Anglican communion 'viewed as a whole, is guilty of them all, having introduced or suffered them by the changes wrought at the Reformation.' And he sums up his objections as regards dogma by deploring the ambiguous formularies, inconsistent precedents, and principles but partially developed, in the Anglican system.

The 'specific corruptions of discipline' which form the fifth division of his paper are overstated. 'Bigamy and trigamy, etc., in bishops and clergy,' is, thus expressed, a ludicrous and misleading charge ; and the section on 'General signs of [the Anglican] Ethos,' with which he ends, is almost entirely obsolete, owing to the influence of the Oxford Movement, not only amongst Anglo-Catholics but to a great extent also in the Anglican Communion as a whole.

He omitted to state 'the *for* on the Anglican side' ; an omission for which he accounts in 1853—when he first realised he had committed it—by the fact that he unconsciously 'took upon trust that the Communion in which I was born, educated and beneficed had a system which lay implicitly in my mind, and was the real basis of my conduct and opinions—so real that it lay after all, deeper than all my inquiries.'

Five days after drawing up this statement, on October 11, 1849, he records : 'Had a very pleasant evening with Archdeacon Manning and on Friday I set before him my paper of difficulties. He replied nothing. And when I recurred to them in the evening, I thought the tone of his Apologia indicated how much he felt them. He said the maintenance of *ideas* was more important to his mind than the maintenance of facts, in respect to extreme unction and chrism in confirmation. I suggested that in the Holy Eucharist the idea itself had not been maintained. He almost allowed this.

When I told him of my purpose to publish [a paper] on the whole doctrine of the Eucharist, and try the issue on that point, he concurred. On the *against* of the Roman side, he remarked that he felt a good deal the second, third, and fourth of my difficulties—the last (the state of society, morals, religion) he alluded to repeatedly. The purity of married life in England he considered a sort of set-off for the absence of virginal life. Nothing would ever drive Pusey and Keble out of the English Church. The subjective argument about the sanctity of individuals in the English Church worth nothing. All that Pusey was doing in maintaining the Real Presence, the Sacrifice, Confession, and Counsels of Perfection, was distinctively Roman and not English, said he had never had to give absolution when called in to a sick-bed; could never get them far enough advanced for that; had given it to poor persons in health. Expressed his firm belief in the validity of English Orders, Courayer's book many years ago had seemed to him conclusive. Altogether the state of his mind struck me as more than ever Roman. He thought, if there were a break-up of the English Church, the great mass would fall away.'

On Monday, October 15, he recounts the result of showing his 'paper of difficulties' to another Tractarian, W. Palmer, who 'first observed they did not settle the claim of the Greek Church.' He also objected that 'the rest were of much weight but did not *decide* the matter to his mind; that things could not be pushed to their *logical results* [!]; that he felt that there was something real in the English Church; that there was a genuine difference between our state and that of Presbyterians; and that the English Church taught what was enough "abstractedly" for salvation.' As Allies commented in 1853 in a note to his account of these two visits: 'Not much comfort for an uneasy Anglican to be got out of these two.'

After his visit to Lavington he 'sets to work on St. Thomas, Suarez and Vasquez on the Holy Eucharist' in preparation for the undertaking to which Manning had given his approbation during the visit just described. Three months, he says, passed happily in this way; for, as he wrote on October 28: 'I seem now to have a definite object. I always wished the battle to be fought on that point, *and I hope either to raise the doctrine of the English Church*, or to be cast out maintaining the Catholic Faith: either way a gain.'

Three years later, he comments on this entry. '*To raise the doctrine* of the communion to which one belonged. Herein lay the secret thought of Puseyism, herein the root of a certain pride and self-sufficiency which it was at least hard for those who thought themselves called to such a task not to fall into.'

Those three years had taught him that, as Father R. Knox puts it in the *Spiritual Æneid*: 'It is wrong to join the Church because the Church seems to you to lack support which you can give. You must come, not as a partisan or as a champion, but as a suppliant for the needs in your own life which only the Church can supply—the ordinary, daily needs.'

The three months' study brought him to the final stage of his journey. Almost all the steps up the ice wall had been taken. He had got rid, he says, of 'one of the most mischievous Puseyite assertions' (on the Real Presence), and had come to see clearly that Transubstantiation, far from being distinct from the doctrine of the Real Presence, was its 'most accurate and most spiritual exposition.' But he still feared to lose his foothold if he took the last step of all; as this entry of February 14, 1850, shows:

'As to my own mind, I find it in a curious state, which must surely be transitional. I am profoundly dissatisfied with the Anglican Church; its first principles, so far as it has any, seem to be founded on misconceptions of doctrine, and confusion as to the proper relation between the civil and spiritual power; and more than all, its moral atmosphere chokes me. Again, as to the Roman Church, I am at one with it on principle. I admire its spirit of asceticism, and its maintenance of independence. I think [that] the Papal Primacy [is] of divine institution, and that in doctrinal controversies between the two communions Rome is right, especially as to the whole sacramental and sacerdotal system, and justification. And yet I feel unable simply to accept Rome as *the Church;* unable to throw myself upon her with the calm conviction that I am doing right, and quitting a heresy and schism. Intellect points that way; but heart and will are divided, not through any fear of consequences as to temporal interests, but through incomplete conviction; and for such a step I feel that the whole trinity within one, body, soul and spirit, should be of accord. What can I do but wait and pray—"O send out Thy light and Thy truth"?'

Two days earlier he had written: 'I have been so long now, for nigh six years, in spite of myself, involved in doubts the most harassing on matters of the nearest concern. My life has been an unceasing cry in these years "O send forth Thy light and Thy truth that they may lead me and bring me to Thy holy hill and Thy dwelling," and that I may "go to the Altar of God." The "Altar of God" and the "Bread of Life," where are they? That one should have a doubt about this! that the doubt should not yield to prayer! that it should last for years!'

But that unceasing cry was now to have its answer; that doubt was at last to yield to prayer. All the controversial reading in which, as he says, he had been 'engaged with all his power' all these years, and all his efforts to find the truth had brought him 'no further than the above.' But now 'the elucidation was to come' (as it has come ever since the first and greatest convert saw the Light on the road to Damascus) 'by a sudden unblinding of the eyes,' which only God's grace can bring. It came about thus.

In February 1850, he finished the paper on 'The Identity of Transubstantiation with the Real Presence' which was to be 'the kernel' of his future work, and sent it to Archdeacon Manning to be criticised. Six days later, on February 27, he 'took up Cardwell and Gibson, and found overwhelming proof of the Sovereign being made by English law—accepted and acted on by the Church—the source of spiritual jurisdiction and the supreme judge of doctrine. This seems the foundation of Anglicanism.'

In these few pages a point he had missed in all those years of reading, 'the very simplest point' as he says, 'one which it would be thought a student of such a controversy ought to have secured at the very beginning of his work,' now became suddenly clear to him. He saw that: 'This making the Sovereign *Pope*, viewed not as an abuse of those in power, but as the real basis of Anglicanism, alters the whole face of things.' From that time forth his whole solicitude was to be sure that Cardwell and Gibson were right in their view of the matter. He immediately consulted Gibson, Maskell, 'and Suarez on the same point, in *De*

Erroribus Sectæ Anglicanæ,' and became convinced that their statements were true, and his deduction from them the only possible one.

If what they held concerning the Anglican subordination to the Crown in spiritual matters was the fact, then for him 'all doubt and controversy were at an end.'

'I applied at once,' he says, 'with all my might to St. Thomas and Suarez to get a clear view of Order and Jurisdiction'; and three weeks later he published a pamphlet on 'The Royal Supremacy in reference to the Two Spiritual Powers of Order and Jurisdiction' which he, as usual, 'sent to a number of friends'—amongst them Keble, Pusey, Manning, R. Wilberforce, Alderson, Coleridge, and, of course, Mr. Gladstone.

He evidently considered it unanswerable, but the criticism of his friends and the courteous amplification and corrections made by Cardinal Wiseman in a letter of thanks to the author, seem to show that it did not go into the subject with quite as much 'closeness and accuracy' as he prided himself was the case.

One passage from Cardinal Wiseman's letter is quoted here, as it seems an especially conclusive answer to the non-Catholic attack at a point where it is frequently made.

'A Catholic would view the contending claims thus. There are two powers that claim supremacy in this country—the Papal and the Royal. To raise a reasonable question, there should be at least parity of case between them—a sufficient quality of grounds to make it matter of discussion. If the trial has to rest on Scriptural grounds, the Catholic adduces the well-known words addressed to Peter, and then says, "If you admit a supremacy to be necessary, but deny that these charges are sufficient to establish it in St. Peter, quote me other passages stronger, in which it is bestowed on temporal princes." If it has to be a mere question of ecclesiastical reference, we must still require as strong declarations of the Fathers in favour of imperial as we can give [in favour] of Papal Supremacy. . . . The task is not to investigate what was the primitive doctrine of the Church, but to show that it must have been what now exists.'

A useful lesson is included in Judge Coleridge's criticism, when he speaks of the effect on his mind of some of the Oxford converts whom he, for want of a better term apparently, calls 'Seceders.' Whether he already fears Allies will join them, or feels that the similar tone which seems to underlie his writings will make him a hindrance to the Tractarian party of which at the time both were members, it is hard to say.

He says: 'I will freely confess to you that my mind has been much affected by what I have observed in the conduct of those whom, merely for convenience, I may denominate Seceders. I think I perceive an unfairness in the mode of their inquiry and reasoning. Even my little light lets me see that in the Roman history and practice are difficulties which produce marvellously little effect on the minds of men who are hyper-critical enough with things of the same sort in the English history. Further, I see with great regret a tone of personal unkindness and severity towards those who disagree with them, even where no provocation has been given, beyond that fact of disagreement, and which I should have said was foreign to the former nature of those who display it. . . . Further, I see a spirit of proselytism, and appealing to the public, which is strange to me in a matter I should have thought personally so painful; where a man's justification to himself is not, I should have thought, to be sought in polemic victory, and where the duty of converting others does not begin till all one's own struggles and scruples are over, and more than that, till some period of trial has ended in complete satisfaction at one's own change.

These, and such observations as these, I own, fill me with distrust.'

One result of the pamphlet, Allies says, was to elicit many letters to him from Archdeacon Manning (now greatly disturbed by the Gorham Judgement) showing how the Royal Supremacy affected him. In one of these dated April 5, 1850, he asks Allies, on whose intellectual judgement he seems to have relied, 'to take up his work again on the subject.' Owing to the Gorham case, it was of burning interest at this time; both to all who feared and to all who supported Erastianism in the Church of England. He ends the letter: 'The Gorham is the Dirige.'

Though another year was to elapse between the writing of these words and Manning's own conversion, for Allies they were almost immediately fulfilled.

On April 2, 1850, three days before the date of Manning's letter, the Diary has this entry: 'As for myself, since the Royal Supremacy, as the basis of Anglicanism, has broken upon me, I have had but one view—that it annihilates us as a Church: it seems, moreover, to supply the key that was wanting to our whole state. I no longer wonder at the dishonesty of our formularies, at the division of principle in the various parties comprising our community, at the slight hold which the Church system has on our people; in fact, at any or all the evils which afflict us. As to the judgement of the Privy Council in favour of Gorham, of course it involves us, if unreversed, in heresy; but important as it is, it seems to me quite subordinate to the question of the Supremacy itself.'

The effect of the Gorham Judgement on his mind was now evidently deepened by the determined action of his wife. 'She was,' he says, 'always very quick in leaping to conclusions, and generally right moreover'; and she had quietly noticed and listened to all that had been passing in his mind, without his having had any idea of what was in hers. 'And so, grace acting in and through these means,' she had 'seen the conclusion' before he did, 'having perhaps less obstinacy and more simplicity' than he. She had told him in February that 'she was satisfied of the falsity of Anglicanism'; on March 16, she took him 'somewhat aback by expressing her complete conviction that we were a sham, that she could not feel any reality in our ordinances, and that she wished to go over immediately.' He begged her 'to delay for a month,' as he wanted to see the result of 'a petition against the Gorham Judgement signed by thirteen persons.' It failed to obtain a reversal of the judgement; nor did the Church of England as a whole offer any support to this effort to uphold its 'office and authority to witness and teach as a member of the Universal Church.' That failure caused six of the thirteen sooner or later to attest their sincerity by submitting to the Catholic Church; amongst them H. E. Manning.

Having delayed, at her husband's wish, till the middle of May, Mrs. Allies very naturally then told him she would wait no longer; as her mind was quite made up and she wished to become a Catholic without further delay. At last he allowed her to follow where her heart and conscience led, and wrote to Newman about her; who answered that he would receive her into the Church, 'if all is well and it suits her, early on Thursday morning, Corpus Christi Day, if she wishes it.' He cannot come up to London before; but if she prefers not to wait till then, he recommends her to go to ' a quiet old priest called Wilds ' who would receive her. The letter is dated May 23, and on May 24, the day of its arrival, Allies took his wife ' to Mr. Wilds, when he received her with conditional baptism.'

The four months which elapsed between her reception and her husband's show a gradual drifting on his part. Though he ' had no thought of remaining an Anglican,' he felt that the time to make his submission had not yet come. Not till two months later did he lose his sense of reality in Anglican ordinances, and even then his ' old difficulties about the Primacy ' stood in his way.

But not only his wife, but a friend who had taken the same step as she had a few days later, ' made incessant demands to determine him '; and his friends Wynne and Pollen were received in June. Pollen, who came to see him soon after, saw the state of his mind and urged him to write a statement explaining his change of opinion on the subject of the Primacy. He took this advice, and the next six weeks were spent in collecting material for his treatise ; the next three occupied in writing it. On September 8, 1850, he preached his last sermon at Launton ; and ' to the great astonishment of every one ' told his parishioners that he was on the point of resigning his living, ' his faith in the Anglican Establishment having been utterly destroyed.' On September 11 he ' was received by Father Newman at St. Wilfrid's, in Birmingham.'

The contrast between Newman's preparation for the final step and that made by Allies is as great as that between the two men themselves. Even in the points of likeness the difference is great. Newman preached that most poignant farewell sermon, ' The Parting of Friends,' to his people two years before he became a Catholic ; then, giving up all active ministry among them, he spent his days at Littlemore in recollection and prayer ; till at last the Light shone clearly through the encircling gloom, and he knew God's Will and had strength to do it. Like Allies, he felt that a written explanation and retractation was necessary, but nothing could be less alike than their ways of carrying out the task. The picture of Newman standing at his desk in the study at Littlemore, often for fourteen hours a day, as he wrote and re-wrote, sometimes with tears streaming from his eyes, the Essay on Development of Christian Doctrine, is a very moving one. The manuscript lay unfinished on his desk on that October night when he knelt at Father Dominic's feet and asked admission into the One Fold of the Redeemer.

The account Allies gives us of his own reception shows a very different line of approach. It is hard to decide whether he wrote *The See of St. Peter* so as to clear up his own difficulties in response to Pollen's wise advice, or as he says some years later, 'in order that it might give to all who cared to enquire my reasons for taking the step.' But it is evident that he delayed his 'moving forward,' as he rather pompously says, 'with unfaltering step to the Catholic Church' till he could do so 'holding the retraction due to the truth in my hand.' With that strange obtuseness and lack of humour which dogged him, he dedicated this retractation to Mr. Gladstone, whose letter in reply to the surprising compliment is a model of dignified courtesy. It is hardly possible to imagine anyone to whom the dedication could have been more unwelcome, especially as there were no ties of friendship between them to explain it.

Mr. Gladstone's letter, written a month after Allies preached his last sermon, gives another instance of the overstatement and inaccuracy which seem to have neutralised, to a certain extent, Allies's power to convince his Tractarian friends. Here again his methods are a foil to Newman's outstanding genius in combating 'Difficulties felt by Anglicans' with a fairness and moderation which in no way added to them. I quote it in full.

'8 Carlton Gardens,
October 8, 1850.

My dear Sir,

I have a painful duty to perform in acknowledging the receipt of your recent work, which you have been so good as to send to me, and its dedication. The kind words which you have applied to me I accept as written in entire sincerity, however little I can lay claim to them.

Upon the subject of the work itself, and of its relation to your former one, it is perhaps better that I should not speak at large; but you will permit me, I hope, frankly to say, I had expected it would have been in the nature of a reply to the former book, which, instead of answering, it appears to me wholly to pass by.

I know that in the numerous references to fact and testimony, in which I am quite unable to put you to the test, you may not be open to the remarks I should certainly feel bound to apply to those of your statements in which I have cognizance of the subject-matter; such as those in pages 147 and 148. There is one of them, indeed, upon which I think it my duty to assure you, on my own authority, that you are in entire error. It is in page 148, respecting an "intermediate metropolitan." It was my duty as a Minister, in 1846, to assent on the part of the Crown to that measure *at the instance* of the late Archbishop of

Canterbury. I am sure that if you have the opportunity it will give you pleasure to rectify the mistake. Had the matter been one entrusted to any record generally accessible, I should not have thought it my duty to trouble you upon it.

You will, I am sure, sometimes think kindly even of the "Anglo-German" religionists whom you have left; and I assure you I earnestly desire to reciprocate such feelings.

And I remain always, my dear Sir, very truly yours,

W. E. GLADSTONE.'

The book was called *The See of St. Peter*, and though he waited till he had sent the book to press before leaving the Church of England, it did not appear till a fortnight or so after he was received. He appends favourable criticisms from Newman and also from Manning; besides kind letters of welcome to the Catholic Church written by Montalembert and Père de Ravignan on hearing of his conversion.

He 'preached as usual, twice, without book' on September 8, baptised an infant brought to him after the service, and left Launton next day, Monday, September 9, with his wife and two children. The children were left with friends in Buckingham; and Allies and his wife went to Birmingham; but failed to find Newman at the Oratory that day.

However, 'on Wednesday, September 11th,' he tells us, 'after general confession and absolution, I was received by conditional baptism into the Catholic Church by Father Newman, at St. Wilfrid's,' and on Friday, September 13, was given Holy Communion by Père Labbé, 'who had so kindly accompanied me from Launton, and watched over me as a parent over a child.' He remained at the Oratory for a fortnight after his reception, where once more, with no break to fear in future, he was 'supported continually by Father Newman's advice. He was my polar star, which never set.'

. . . . . .

Three years later, Allies summed up 'the grand lesson' taught him in the thirteen years (1837 to 1850) of which this little sketch gives an account. He says:

'Entrance into the Church of God of any living creature is a mere act of sovereign grace. It is in the power of our wills to put an *obex* to this grace; it is in the power of our wills to decline at any moment [its] gentle, delicate yet unfailing guidance; not to follow our partner in the dance; but it is not in the power of the most steadfast will, or of the clearest intellect, or of the most honest purpose all united, to make its own way into the Church of God, like a conqueror, by the triumphant conclusions of the reason. God keeps the thread which guides through that labyrinth in His own Hands: we may break it or cast it aside, but we cannot do without it. And as He opens the door at last, so He keeps the time when He will open the door at His disposal.'

CHAPTER III

HENRY EDWARD MANNING

A REMARKABLE proof of Newman's wise foresight is to be found in the care he took to secure a sympathetic chronicler of his life as an Anglican. When he 'came to the conclusion that if a memoir was to be published . . . a Protestant Editor must take the Protestant part,' he provided an efficient solvent for the 'varnish' applied to certain sketches of him, drawn by those in whose minds resentment at his loss to the Movement obscures the true reason of his departure.

In Cardinal Manning's case such precautions as he took were rendered useless by unforeseen events. Newman's contention that 'Biographers varnish, they assign motives, they conjecture feelings, they interpret Lord Burleigh's nods,' is borne out only too well by Purcell's *Life of Manning*, which for a long while was the standard history of his career. Far from being a safeguard of his reputation, it is largely responsible for the disagreeable and unfair impression of his character given by Mr. Lytton Strachey and his imitators.

Miss Mozley knew the Tractarian mind from within. Her two brothers were prominent members of the Oxford Movement; one of them played that part in rallying its ranks after Newman's conversion which Purcell's imaginative pen ascribes to Manning. Both were Newman's special friends and became his brothers-in-law ; so that Miss Mozley's intimate acquaintance with him extended over many years. She thus had every qualification for gauging his motives accurately and fairly ; whereas Purcell had neither the insight nor the experience necessary to interpret Manning's motives during the ten years between 1841 and 1851 which preceded his conversion. The varnish splashed on some of Newman's portraits is therefore very easily removed by the solvent he himself took care to provide ; but the thick coats which Purcell spread so lavishly over the picture of Manning are far harder to take away.

Purcell's variety of biographers' varnish has had a corroding effect on his canvas. Much acid conjecture has entered into its composition ; and little care has been taken to find evidence for the motives assigned. It is not surprising that Cardinal Vaughan's comment was : ' I do not recognise the portrait of him with whom I was in constant communication during forty years.'

This apparent desire to bury Cæsar, not to praise him (except with that faint praise which damns its subject by never acknowledging a quality without hinting at the presence of its complementary fault), is responsible for much prejudice against Manning. Men who dislike any form of ecclesiasticism find much to justify their antagonism in the picture given of his self-importance, his ' double voice,' the lack of human feeling which his silence regarding those who in their life-time had been dear to him is supposed to show. And those who contend that ' among those of his [Newman's] disciples who went beyond their great leader, one did so probably from ambition,' find their justification for this charge in Purcell's pages.

But the makers of such an accusation forget two things ; its gravity, and its unlikelihood.

Those who wish to discount the loss of the great Tractarian converts do so as a rule by ascribing reasons for their going which may be inadequate or petty but are not dishonest or dishonourable. But this cannot be said of the motive of self-seeking ambition which they tell us caused Archdeacon Manning to enter the Catholic Church. And why should a man whose prudence is insisted on *ad nauseam* by Purcell have expected to find full scope for his ambition in the Church, which, so we are told, had from the very first broken Newman's spirit, by her shabby treatment of him and by her neglect of his great gifts ?

By 1851 Archdeacon Manning had had six years in which to observe and take warning by Newman's shelving. Yet we are asked to believe that he threw to the winds his prudence and his common sense, not to speak of all notions of truth and honour and honesty, because, in spite of her treatment of Newman, Rome seemed to him to offer such dazzling prospects of temporal advancement that to obtain it he sold his soul.

Which alternative seems the more likely ? Did he perjure himself, and enter the Roman Church for the place and power he expected her to give him ? Or did he seek admittance because he believed her to be the One True Church established on earth by Jesus Christ ? On Passion Sunday, 1851, in Hill Street Chapel, 'having before his eyes the Holy Gospels which he touched with his hands,' he made his profession of faith in the Holy Catholic, Apostolic Roman Church. 'Grieving that he had erred in that he had held and believed doctrines opposed to her teaching, he abjured every heresy and sect opposed to her, and submitted to her with his whole heart.' Did he sell what he secretly believed to be his birthright, and enter the Church with a lie on his lips, 'probably from ambition' ? Henri

Quatre said that Paris was worth a Mass, but his standards were different in many ways from those of the Archdeacon of Chichester.

The charge is so monstrous that if it were not often repeated one would pass it over in contempt. But just as when any well-known preacher becomes a Catholic, Newman's fate after his conversion is deplored in Anglican church papers 'pour encourager les autres,' those known to be 'unsettled' are often told: 'Of course Manning would never have left the Church of England if he had been offered a Bishopric.' As one does not refrain from marrying for love because some-one else is alleged to have married for money, it is hard to see why such a statement, even if true, should hinder other conversions.

There is another flaw in the contention. To say that Manning was among those who went *beyond* their great leader (as it cannot mean that they became Catholics while Newman stopped short) must imply that he entered the Church before Newman; for if one's objective is Rome one cannot go *beyond*. If Manning had really outstripped Newman on the road to Rome, the ambition theory would have lost one ridiculous element. But if, as is the stubborn fact, Manning did not become a Catholic till he had seen Newman's candlestick put firmly under a bushel (according to one school of biography) for six years, how he could have done so from ambition is hard to imagine. Unless of course he was so vain as well as so ambitious as to think he might go beyond his great leader in a different sense, and be highly appreciated by those who held Newman in low esteem. Fortunately the specific recommended by Newman as a solvent for biographers' varnish is amply provided in Manning's case too. 'Contemporary letters,' and extracts from his private diary which go far to neutralise Purcell's impression of him, are extensively quoted in his Life.

Three incidents in particular disprove the 'from ambition' slander entirely.

First of all, the offer of the Sub-Almonership in 1845, six years before he became a Catholic; which makes it quite clear that he had no reason to despair of getting high preferment where he was, and that he knew this. At the comparatively early age of thirty-eight, he, now Archdeacon of Chichester, was offered the post of Sub-Almoner to the Queen, which was known to be the certain prelude to a Bishopric. His brother-in-law, Samuel Wilberforce, had just vacated it on being given the See of Oxford. Yet this offer, with all that it promised, he declined, for reasons which should satisfy the most critical.

His diary shows the careful consideration he gave to it and how much its rejection cost him. An entry on December 4, 1845, gives seven reasons for and against its acceptance, which reveal his disinterestedness and self-discipline.

His reasons for accepting are as follows. First, that it comes unsought. This, he says, does not make it 'therefore to be accepted—such things are trials as well as leadings.' Secondly, 'it is honourable—but then,' he feels, 'being what I am, ought I not therefore to decline it (*a*) as a humiliation, (*b*) as a revenge on myself for Lincoln's Inn,[1] (*c*) as a testimony?' A third reason is that it affords 'an opening to usefulness'; but on the other hand 'all his usefulness is pre-engaged.' The fourth, 'that it may lead to more,' deters him when he thinks of his special weaknesses; and decides him that it is 'therefore, at least for that reason, not to

[1] i.e. for his attempt to secure the vacant Preachership in 1841 by allowing his legal friends to canvass the Benchers on his behalf.

be accepted. It is a sphere of temptation to which I am akin, and have been.' (Ambition here seems well in hand.) Though 'it has emolument,' he considers 'this is dearly bought with five sacred days,[1] and anything ethically wrong.' The last two reasons (vi) 'that I owe it to my friends' and (vii) 'that it is due to the Archbishop' he considers to apply only if his other reasons for accepting are good, and not otherwise.

A week later, after anxious deliberation, he writes: 'I have made up my mind, and will put down my reasons to-night, and, please God, write to-morrow to decline the honour.' One reason is for the sake of his flock, of his brethren, and of himself; and another, showing how he fought against his ambitious tendencies, is: 'I am afraid of venturing out of the Church into the Court. . . . If I am to go then I shall be called again, not less surely for having now refused.' The last words show clearly that he not only felt that a bishopric might lawfully be accepted later on, but that he was quite confident that his refusal, from conscientious scruples, to take this step towards one now would in no way prejudice another such offer being made him in God's own time.

This incident is a complete answer to the motives for conversion imputed to him by his detractors. The man who wrote in his private diary on February 15, 1846, 'Certainly I would rather choose to be stayed on God than be on the thrones of the world and the Church' did not throw all scruples to the wind and swear falsely before God's altar, with his hand on the Holy Gospels, on Passion Sunday, 1851. To bring against him the charge that, to gratify his ambition he abjured the faith of a Church in which he would willingly have been

[1] The Church festivals which the new office would oblige him to spend away from his flock at Lavington.

made Bishop, and professed his belief in another, shows either a complete lack of any sense of its gravity, or an unfairness and cruelty which cannot be excused.

'Contemporary letters are facts,' and from them and from Manning's private diary the following extracts prove the fierceness of the struggle he fought against this speedy fulfilment of his ambitions in the Church of England, and the victory he won.

He writes in his diary (January 25, 1846): 'I am ashamed of myself for having allowed the return of so many doubts and disappointed feelings. I have, since I left home, been deprived of my supports; have not found others confirm my view. The associations of the world came about me, and made me feel that I had played the fool and lost a great opportunity, etc. I cannot deny that in the region of the world, even of the fair, not irreligious, view of self-advancement, also of command and precepts, I have made a mistake. But in the region of counsels, self-chastisement, humiliation, self-discipline, penance, and of the Cross, I think I have done right. Yet great humility alone can keep me from being robbed of all this.

To learn to say no, to disappoint myself, to choose the harder side, to deny my inclinations, to prefer to be less thought of, and to have fewer gifts of the world, this is no mistake, and is most like the Cross. Only with humility. God grant it to me.

Feast of St. Paul.'

Five days later, on January 30, he makes this entry: 'Therefore, mistake or no, it is a good thing I have mortified my vanity. It is good I am susceptible of vexation, and regret that I should feel it; without trying to bolster myself up by expectations or complacency with myself. I have been both ambitious and designing, and it is good for me to be disappointed by the act of others as in Lincoln's Inn, and by my own as now.

It is hard to know exactly what is *the*, or the chief, motive on which we act. I believe I did refuse it on the reasons I wrote down. Yet something tells me I should not have refused it if I had not been alone. Yet I ought, if that reason be good now.

Could I be content to live and die no more than I am ? I doubt it. And yet in some ways I feel more so now than in time past. But that is because I am complacent over my books.'

And again, on February 15 he writes : . . . 'Have been really resting on other props, stays, and comforts, either present or to come. The great question is : Is God enough for you *now ?* And if you are as now, even to the end of life, will it suffice you ? I do hope I am feeling my way to more perfect deadness. No doubt this is one thing God is teaching me by this event.

It is difficult exactly to say what I am resting upon. I think it is partly the esteem of others, chiefly founded on what I have written ; and on expectation of something to come.

Suppose I were left here alone, or with an uncomfortable neighbour ; that my books were to leave off selling, and I were publicly attacked ; that the prospect of elevation were at an end, and that nothing were left me but to stay myself on God in prayer and parish work—should I feel as I do now ? If God were really my stay now, I should. But I think I should not do so, and therefore I doubt whether He is so. It is very hard to try this question when things prosper round us. Certainly I would rather choose to be stayed on God, than to be in the thrones of the world and the Church. Nothing else will go into eternity.'

A little later he refers to this incident as follows :

'I came home from London last night after three weeks very ill spent. My life there was irregular, indiscreet, and self-indulgent. . . . Somehow I had thought before I went to London that the prospects of elevation would have drawn me under their power. But I came home more estranged from the thought of being raised to any higher place than I went.

This is the *first year* I have found this to be so. Usually I have been powerfully drawn into the whirl of the actual.'

Another fact which his detractors on the score of ambition ignore is this. As he and James Hope walked together on the day before both were received into the Church, Manning said to him: 'Now my career is ended.' When he walked into the Chapel in Hill Street on that Passion Sunday, he knew quite well that an English mitre was well within sight if he remained an Anglican; and unless insincerity is to be laid at his door as well as ambition, he had no visions of a Cardinal's Hat awaiting him in the future. If he had, an ambitious man who knew he would be a Catholic on the morrow would never have said, 'Now my career is ended,' but rather 'To-morrow my career begins.'

A week later, when the news of his reception became known, the Duke of Newcastle wrote to Manning: 'I mourn over what I must think the great error of a pure and noble mind seeking the true light, but I cannot cease to love and admire the man who makes the sacrifice which I know you have in obedience to what he knows to be right.' And Mr. Gladstone wrote to Hope, at the same time: 'The pain, the wonder, the mystery is this, that you should have refused the higher vocation you had before you. The same words I should use of Manning too.' His friends, who were evidently confident that a brilliant future lay before him in the Church of England, obviously shared his belief that his career was over now that he had ceased to be an Anglican.

Thirdly, and to my mind conclusively, comes his magnificent act of self-abnegation in 1878. Thirty-three years earlier, Archdeacon Manning, after a fierce struggle with his ambitions, had declined an office which was a passport to the bishopric he naturally desired. He did so that the villagers in his parish of Lavington might not suffer any spiritual loss by his absence 'on the feasts, especially Passion Week and Easter.'

Now, after the death of Pius IX, Cardinal Manning 'for a glittering moment stood on the step of the Papal throne.' But he refused the Triple Crown, as once he had forgone the hope of an Anglican mitre, for the sake of the souls of others.

He had written just before to Lady Herbert: 'The next Pope must draw Italy to him as Pius drew the whole world. And none but an Italian who loves Italy and is loved by Italians can do this.' So he refused that great Office, which surely no man governed by ambition could have borne to see go past him when within his grasp; and, in spite of the Cardinal's courteous assurances that there had been foreign Popes, and that Manning was no stranger in Rome, was firm in his refusal. For the sake of the Church, the first Pope after the loss of the Temporal Power must be, he said, an Italian.

'One, probably from ambition.' Those who assign motives and conjecture feelings should make sure of their facts, before they give rein to their psychological fancies.

The one tiny incident which is their excuse is as follows. Many years after 1851, Cardinal Manning heard from an authoritative source that he would have been offered the bishopric of Salisbury, which fell vacant in 1854, if he had not become a Catholic three years earlier. His comment was: 'What an escape for my poor soul.' It seems clear that the remark simply means, 'What a mercy that the gift of Faith came to me before I was in a position which might have dulled my spiritual vision, or weakened my power to grasp it when seen.' To interpret it as: 'If I had known that in 1851, I should never have dreamt of losing such a chance by becoming a Catholic, *what* an escape for my poor soul' shows either crass stupidity or an unenviable ingenuity in making the better appear the worse.

The main interest of Manning's history, so far as this study goes, is the progress of his religious sympathies from a definite Evangelical standpoint in 1833, till 1851; when he trod down the last of his Protestant prejudices and submitted to the Catholic Church.

Bishop C. Wordsworth, writing in 1892, says that before 1833, when his old friend Henry Manning settled at Lavington, his religious opinions were quite unformed. It seems more correct to say that they were formed, but not crystallised enough to take permanent shape.

He went to Lavington, at the age of twenty-six, to be curate to the Rev. John Sargent; whose daughter Caroline he married in November of the same year, 1833, a few months after her father's death. The living was in the gift of her grandmother, Mrs. Sargent of Lavington House, and she presented it to her new grandson-in-law. Mrs. Henry Manning was one of four sisters, the eldest of whom married Samuel Wilberforce; who later became Bishop of Oxford, much harassed by 'Romanizers' in his diocese.

Four years after their marriage Manning's beautiful young wife died. So many unfair conjectures as to his silence regarding her after her death have found their way into print that it is perhaps permissible to quote some valuable evidence which Baron v. Hügel put on record against this slanderous attempt to make Manning's attitude seem unfeeling or hard.

In a letter to Professor Clement Webb (December 5, 1918) the Baron thanks him for having suggested he should answer an unfair statement made in Mr. Lytton Strachey's *Eminent Victorians* on 'Manning's dispositions towards his late wife.' A note in the margin explains this allusion thus :

'Mr. Lytton Strachey accused Cardinal Manning of a desire to bury the recollection of his early marriage. The Baron in a letter to *The Times* said, on Cardinal Vaughan's authority, that the old Cardinal, with eyes about to close for ever, feeling beneath his pillow, pulling out a small, worn volume, and handing it to his spiritual son and successor (Vaughan) said, "I know not to whom else to leave this—I leave it to you. Into this little book my dearest wife wrote her prayers and meditations. Not a day passed since her death on which I have not prayed and meditated from this book. All the good I may have done, all the good I may have been, I owe to her. Take precious care of it."'[1]

Purcell says that Mrs. Henry Manning's influence tended to the Evangelical side ; and that in 1835, when there was a struggle between High Church and Low over the management of the S.P.C.K., 'The voice of the Rector's wife pleaded, perhaps for the last time—for the shadow of death was already upon her—for the cause and traditions so dear to her heart.' He gives no evidence for this, but Mr. Gladstone states that when he asked Manning, whom he met in London just before the meeting, 'what had brought him, a country clergyman, up to town' he was told 'To defend the Evan-

[1] Baron von Hügel, *Selected Letters*, p. 256.

gelical cause against the attempts of the Archbishop.' Mr. Gladstone added: 'This shows that Manning belonged at that time to the section of the extreme Evangelicals.' It also makes one wonder what grounds Purcell had for other impressions he gives of the relations between Manning and his wife.

The following episode in 1836 is interesting, as it marks Manning's position at the moment; and shows that the claim to be a Catholic Priest, so common nowadays in the Anglican Communion, was anticipated by him, while still counting himself 'Evangelical,' nearly a hundred years ago.

The occasion arose from some lectures given by Dr. Wiseman in S. Mary's Moorfields on the difference between the Catholic Church and Protestantism. Manning wrote an article in *The British Magazine* charging Dr. Wiseman with unfairness, as he considered it was impossible that 'Dr. Wiseman with his high pretensions to learning was ignorant of the essential difference between the Church of England and other Protestant bodies. The assumption of the exclusive right to the name Catholic for the Church of Rome, and the confounding of the Church of England with other Protestant bodies was on the part of Dr. Wiseman an unworthy controversial artifice.'

He signed this article under the pseudonym, 'A Catholic Priest,' but his intimate friend, Mr. S. F. Wood (uncle of the present Lord Halifax), pierced the disguise, and wrote to him as follows:

'TEMPLE,
3rd November, 1836.

MY DEAR FRIEND,

. . . A letter in the last *British Magazine* on Wiseman, signed "A Catholic Priest," has just met my eye. From its clearness and ability, and from a little talk we had together in August, I have a slight suspicion of the *author*. If I am right, I know he will forgive and consider of thus much : Agreeing with him most fully that the Anglican Church's *idea* of the rule of faith is as he states, and earnestly longing for its actual development in our day, I still think, that viewing our Church as an *outward historical* fact, looking at its tendencies and connections for the last ten or twenty years, its living preachers and members, Dr. Wiseman had a right as a *controversialist*, with his principles, etc., to *group* it with Biblical Protestants. And that it would be more wise, more humble, more truthful, and more Xtianlike to confess our practical defection from our principles, and to warn and to recall men to them, than hastily to tax him with unfairness.

Ever, my dear Manning, your affectionate,

S. F. Wood.'

Manning resented this ; and (after publishing a second article against Dr. Wiseman in *The British Magazine*) wrote to remonstrate with his friend, who replied :

'Temple,
Saturday, 2nd Dec., 1836.

My dear Friend,

Not feeling the least vocation to defend Dr. Wiseman, and having but a low opinion of his personal truthfulness, I had much rather drop the subject altogether, but your kind reply calls for a few words, and they shall be as few as I can. I never denied (God forbid) the comparative Catholicity of our Mother the Anglican Church, in the general, and as to this very point, "the Rule of Faith," I consider her notion is practically modified by her reception of the Nicene and

Athanasian Creeds and by her Liturgy, and as expounded by her greatest Doctors, the best of any Church. But I still think there is sufficient ambiguity in her own symbolical and formal exhibition of the rule, and quite sufficient contrariety in the expounders of it, to justify an hostile controversialist, with the present temper of the living Church members before his eyes, in taking (more or less) Wiseman's line, and the very obvious irregularity of the witnesses he calls rather proves to me, that he thought *habemus confitentem reum* and I need not labour the point, for surely if he had wished to blind he might have got up a very respectable *catena* on his side. Take first, §§ 1, 2, and 3 of the *Dissuasive,* Pt. I, B. 1 (not in one or two detached places, which we owe to a more or less really Catholic ἦθος) but in their whole scope and line of argument; take Chillingworth's notorious axiom, take Tillotson and Burnet, and twenty other *low* people in *high* places, take lastly Bishop Mant's just come out *Churches of Rome and England Compared,* p. 12, where he distinctly lays down the Bible as the Rule, and I think candour will allow this.' ('Comparative Catholicity' is good.)

The next step towards avowing his Tractarian leanings was taken in 1838, when he preached a sermon, The Rule of Faith, which clearly defines his position midway between Catholicism, which he misunderstood and therefore hated, and the Evangelical party, with which the Rector of Lavington had so far identified himself. In it he accepts the rule of Bishop Ridley; whose works he considers a proof of Anglican continuity with the Primitive Church, and ranks with those of Cranmer and Latimer as of equal authority with the Fathers. His position now was that taken up in recent years by Anglicans who follow the late Dean Wace;

and by Bishop Knox. This school, opposed both to Catholic and Anglo-Catholic doctrines, appeals to 'the First Six Centuries;' and will accept nothing as Catholic truth which has been defined since this arbitrary point of time. Like Ridley, he preferred 'the antiquity of the Primitive Church before the novelty of the Church of Rome;' whose origin, following Ridley in this also, he post-dated considerably. 'Quod semper' did not then mean to him what it says.

But in 1838 Cardinal Wiseman, who put a spoke in the Tractarian wheel a year later by that article on Donatism which shook Newman to the core, published one equally challenging to the position now held by Manning. This position had changed a good deal since 1835. The sheer Protestantism which took him to London that year to oppose the High Church tendencies of the Bishops in the S.P.C.K. difficulty had been left behind; and by 1836 he had come to consider himself a Catholic Priest, though only to use the title as a pseudonym. And now, just after his Rule of Faith sermon, in July 1838 came Cardinal Wiseman's article in the *Dublin Review* which attacked the Tractarian position, on which the new Rule was based. Dr. Wiseman's arguments were directed against the views held by Keble, Newman, and Pusey on Private Judgement and on Article VI of the Thirty-nine Articles. Manning leapt to arms to defend a theory of Anglicanism which seemed to justify his new belief; and convinced him that the Fathers of the Church and the Anglican 'Reformers' saw eye to eye in all matters of doctrine in which the latter differed from 'the Church of Rome.'

His weapon was the Rule of Faith; which he expanded from the original sermon into a controversial treatise; by means of Notes and an Appendix intended to meet Dr. Wiseman's points and to defend his own view of the Church of England against Catholic and Low Churchman alike.

The Rule of Faith gives three opposing theories of religion: the doctrines he had held as an Evangelical Low Churchman in days now ending; the Catholic, as he terms the High Church views he was about to embrace; and 'the Rule of the Roman Church,' as deduced, he tells us 'from a work of great repute among the Roman Catholics in this country.' (*Faith of Catholics*, by Berington and Kirk.)

The Roman Rule, he says, supposes that:

'1. There is a living judge of interpretations, guided by an inspiration the same in kind with that which dictated the Holy Scriptures.

2. That the rule by which the judge shall proceed, is "what was anciently received."

3. That some points of *belief* which, if it means anything more than the sixth Article of the Church of England, must mean of *necessary faith*, were not committed to writing in Holy Scripture, but rest on *oral* tradition *alone*.

Acting on this rule, the Church of Rome, at the Council of Trent, added to the Nicene or Constantinopolitan creed many doctrines which cannot be proved from Holy Scripture; e.g. transubstantiation, purgatory, invocation of saints, veneration of images, indulgences.

4. A profession of this faith she requires as necessary for communion.'

He then contrasts it with the Catholic (by which he means the Anglican) thus:

'The Church of Rome asserts that *oral* tradition is a sufficient proof of points of necessary belief. The Church of England, that Scripture is the only sufficient proof of necessary faith.

The Church of Rome says, that the doctrinal articles added to Pope Pius's creed, may be proved from Scripture, but need not. The Church of England, that they ought to be proved from Scripture, but cannot.

The Church of Rome maintains that they are binding, because they are Apostolical traditions. The Church of England denies that they are Apostolical traditions, inasmuch as they will not stand the Catholic test; not being *primitive*, nor have they even been *universal*, nor held with consent of all Churches.'

He ends with The New Rule; which is so nearly identical with Evangelicalism that the hostile tone of his definition and comments naturally gave great offence to those with whom he had shared its 'fallacious' views so short a time before.

'The other fallacious rule is as follows:

That Holy Scripture needs no interpreter, but is plain to all.

But this is felt to be so evidently untenable, that it is generally stated in this form:

That the Holy Spirit, which dictated the Scripture, now guides all who seek the truth into a right understanding of it.

Now here is exactly the same fallacy as in the Roman rule above given. The Church of England carefully distinguishes between the immediate guidance of inspiration, and that guidance which leads men through the means God has ordained for the conveyance of truth.'

The Appendix to the original sermon made matters worse as regards the Evangelical party, already hurt and horrified by his previous publication; as, after quoting Chillingworth against the Catholic position, he contended that antiquity had been 'sacrificed by modern Protestants in order to establish the right of private judgement'; and that 'the rejection of universal tradition' has 'led to schism and Socinianism'; from both of which the Church of England as he now pictured it was triumphantly free.

Not only to Catholics but to present-day Anglicans, brought up either as Liberal-Evangelicals or as Anglo-Catholics, Manning's attitude at this time is almost impossible to imagine. Very few of the new generation have any of that horror of Rome to which the wills of some of their elders still testify; and probably few Anglicans, of any shade of belief, now hold the complacent view of Article XIX that not only 'the Church of Rome hath erred,' but also 'the Churches of Jerusalem, Alexandria, and Antioch'; while the Church of England alone is the 'visible Church of Christ.' Overtures to the Eastern Churches by one party, to the Nonconformists by another, and the adoption of many of the 'ceremonies' of 'the Church of Rome' by an increasing number of Anglicans make that attitude impossible any longer.

But till the late 'eighties and even the 'nineties, the descendants of the first Tractarians were brought up to look upon every sort of Dissent from the Established Church (including 'Romanism') as the sin of schism.[1] Some of the High Church clergy taught that an Anglican who took part in non-Anglican worship was guilty of spiritual unfaithfulness, and had therefore broken the Seventh (Sixth)[2] Commandment. To enter

[1] Canon Curteis's Bampton Lectures for 1866, 'Dissent in its Relation to the Church of England' takes 'Romanism' as the subject of his first Lecture. The second generation of Tractarians were brought up in the theory he inculcates, and the third generation, now middle-aged, still finds it hard to abandon it now that a truer view of history, from sources not readily available in the 'sixties, has modified some of his conclusions and rendered others untenable.

[2] The A.V. division of the Decalogue differs from that in the Vulgate.

a Catholic Church (except as a tourist) and hear Mass was as wrong as to go to a meeting in a Unitarian or Baptist chapel.

The following verses are taken from a Tractarian hymn which probably none of the present generation has ever heard sung; though up to the end of last century it was fairly well known. It exactly expresses the loyal devotion to the Church of England, and the belief in her unique position which the Oxford Movement brought about.

> 'What time the evening shadows fall
> Around the Church on earth,
> When darker forms of doubt appal
> And new false lights have birth.
> Then closer should her faithful band,
> For truth together hold,
> Hell's last devices to withstand
> And safely guard her fold.
>
> O Father, in that hour of fear,
> The Church of England keep,
> Thine Altar to the last to rear
> And feed Thy fainting sheep;
> May she the holy truths attest
> Apostles taught of yore,
> Nor quit the Faith by saints confest
> Though tempted ne'er so sore.'

It is hard for those brought up to love and defend the shadow to leave it for the substance. 'Lost causes and impossible loyalties,' their very weakness makes it hard to put them aside and rejoice in the triumphant and glorious certainty which at first seems too good to be true.

Manning sent his Rule of Faith to Newman and Keble, and the Appendix to Newman. Both approved in the main, with a few criticisms on Newman's part; but the tract gave great offence to many of Manning's earlier friends, and Keble's hope that his bishop had 'no dislike' to Manning's view was only partially fulfilled.

His next pamphlet, entitled 'The Principle of the Ecclesiastical Commission examined in a Letter to the Bishop of Chichester, 1838,' pleased Bishops and Tractarian leaders alike. The former approved it as a defence of the rights of the Anglican Episcopate to rule the Established Church against a claim made by the State to appoint Ecclesiastical Commissioners to enquire into and administer Church property. It was natural that the Bishops and their Chapters should resent the Commission, whatever their views of Supremacy might be; and the Tractarians opposed it with all their power as being against Catholic tradition. Manning's pamphlet is therefore very important. It shows that the crux is, and always must be, the Supremacy of the Church. And Newman's letter of approval—'I have nothing to find fault with but a few grammatical and other points which I have marked'—is a proof that in 1838 Manning was in complete accord with the Tractarians on the point which led Newman, Allies, and Manning to submit to the One Church within the next few years.

This passage is most significant:

'In our minds, your lordship is not only one of the Apostolical Body to whose united wisdom and equal authority the Church in this land is, by a divine commission, put in charge, but also the sole consecrated ruler and guardian of the Church,[1] and diocese to which we belong. Our bishop is to us the source of authority, and the centre of unity in order, deliberation, and discipline. In his suffrage our assent and dissent is virtually expressed. We believe that no power,

[1] This cannot be what he wrote. Probably it should read '*in the* diocese' etc., not '*and*.'

spiritual or ecclesiastical, excepting only collective authority of the whole Episcopal Order, to which supreme jurisdiction all bishops are severally subject, can reach us, unless it pass through his express permission Your lordship is therefore both the natural protector of our privileges, and the natural depository of our fears.'

The following passage shows the same divergence between Bishops and clergy regarding the scope of episcopal jurisdiction, as was seen lately in Convocation when the Bishops proposed to admit Nonconformists to communion, in accordance with the Lambeth decision on that point in 1930. Manning says:

'We have been told that the greater proportion of the clergy are in favour of the commission; that they have expressed their consent by their silence; that the cathedral bodies indeed as persons interested oppose, but that the parochial clergy tacitly approve the recommendation of the Ecclesiastical Commission.'

His keen political insight warns him that the Anglican Church now has 'another supremacy to beware of. The two swords have passed from the pope to the king, from the king to the people. The next patriarch of the English Church will be Parliament, and on its vote will hang our orders, mission, discipline, and faith; and the pontificate of Parliament is but the modern voluntary principle in disguise.' Justified many times since then, a crowning proof of the truth of this prediction was given in 1928, when the House of Commons rejected the Revised Prayer-book; submitted to Parliament by the Archbishops, all the Bishops but four, and a large majority in Convocation and in the Church Assembly. In spite of the Enabling Act, authority to use the book was considered by Parliament to 'hang on its vote'; and that vote was cast against it.

In the same year (1838) Manning joined with the Tractarian leaders in their resistance to a national system of secular education; but his activities were checked for a time in 1839, as he was obliged to winter in Rome on account of his health. He was in no way drawn to the Church by what he saw of it abroad; his first impressions, like those of Newman and Allies, were in that respect neither true nor lasting.

Nothing of moment happened during 1840, which he spent, after his winter in Rome, in parish work at Lavington; but the following year, 1841, was for Manning, as well as for Newman and Allies, a year of destiny.

The bonds which bound him to the Established Church were tightened by his becoming Archdeacon of Chichester; and the condemnation of Tract 90, which, as we have seen, shook Newman's belief in the Catholicity of the Bishops' views and dislodged Allies from his place as chaplain to the Bishop of London, made it difficult for him in his new official position to support the leaders of the Tractarian school (to whose views his bishop was opposed) as whole-heartedly as, according to Purcell, they expected.

Purcell, whose *Life* is the main source where the letters which deal with this period of Manning's career are to be found, is far from being a trustworthy guide here. He 'assigns motives' in a way even the Strachey school might envy; so that it becomes even more difficult to disentangle the real from the legendary Manning than to see the real Newman through the fog created by unsympathetic or partially informed minds. The vigour and conviction with which Purcell's portrait is drawn almost compel belief in the artist's insight as well as admiration of his imaginative power.

Tract 90 gives him a wide field of conjecture as

regards Manning's nature, but he shifts his ground so often that only a strict confinement to contemporary letters can give us a standpoint from which to judge the true state of affairs.

He begins by stating that Manning broke with Newman and the Tractarians over Tract 90, and chose 'to take his stand by the protesting bishops' with a view to further preferment in the future. It seems as if Archdeacon Manning, according to Purcell, was incapable of taking any action for the simple, straightforward reason that he believed it to be right; and Purcell quotes his first Archidiaconal Charge, July 1841, as an example of his astuteness in facing both ways. He suggests that Manning's praise of the Reformers is specially intended to dissociate himself from Newman, whose dislike of their over-zealous work had been freely expressed: and compares Dr. Pusey's 'characteristic fervour and generosity' in throwing himself into the breach in defence of Tract 90 with the behaviour of 'the prudent and judicious Archdeacon of Chichester'; who, 'though disbelieving in popular Protestantism, did not stand in the face of such a storm by the side of the writers of the Tracts, but took his stand by the side of the Bishops.' He did so, Purcell says, 'not only in accordance with the natural bent of his temperament, but on the conviction that his being ticketed as a "Puseyite" would limit his influence and lame his right hand in defence of the Moderate High Church Party to which he now again inclined.'

This is a most characteristic passage. 'The natural bent of his temperament' in this context might fairly be said to be that of obedience to Episcopal authority, and therefore to his credit. Whether Purcell meant this, or had a less charitable thought in his mind, is open to conjecture. But the second motive thus suggested, without a shred of evidence to justify such an insinuation, is part and parcel of the character which so often 'fills the room up of the absent' Manning in this Life of him, and 'walks up and down' in the mind of his biographer.

Purcell's desire to create his own Manning blinds him to plain facts regarding the original. The praise heaped on the Reformers in the Charge of 1841 was simply the consistent expression of views which Manning had never changed. Newman's quite opposite estimate of their work had, in 1836, caused so much misgiving to Mr. S. F. Wood, who was otherwise greatly drawn to both Newman and his teaching, that he consulted Manning on the subject in the following letter, which puts the attitude of the Moderate High Church party clearly enough to be worth quoting in full.

'TEMPLE.

Wednesday, 29th January, 1836.

MY DEAR MANNING,

During part of last and of the present week I have enjoyed the great privilege of having Newman living in my chambers, and I believe you will receive a paper from him in this cover about the Oxford Tracts, and also about a plan of Dodsworth's for getting up a spring lecture on Church matters in London. Of course Newman and I have had a great deal of interesting talk together, one result of which has been to confirm certain points of the view about Church teaching, etc., etc., I lately sent you, and to convince and satisfy me that it is not mere matter of idle speculation, but involves practical consequences of very great weight in our present condition, and about which I earnestly wish to confer with you *above all other persons.* And in the outset I must beseech you not to communicate the sentiments herein contained to anyone in their present shape: (1st) because, though I am confident I state the substance of tendency of Newman's opinion accurately, I would not pledge him to anything thrown out to a friend; and (2nd) because I am most anxious to avoid the semblance of a difference between those who hold so much in common, and who may so usefully co-operate together.

I will begin by professing my entire and cordial and active assent to all the great features of their system—to the apostolical succession, to the virtue and efficiency derived therefrom in the sacraments, to their view of the sacraments themselves, to the reverence due to antiquity and Catholicism; and by owning that the times require the most prominent assertion of them. But I had hoped that the high Evangelical doctrines, delivered from the exaggerated and distorted guise in which some had dressed them, and reduced to their true position in the system, would have been allowed a place therein.

I grieve to think that I have discovered in one person at least a violent repugnance to them, and to justify this an adoption of principles which go so far (as to be available they must) that they have at least this advantage, viz. they open one's eyes to their unsoundness. I will first state what they are, (1) Newman holds that from the time the Church ceased to be one, the right of any part of it to propound *articles of faith*, as such, is suspended; all that remains to them is to impose terms of communion, articles of peace, etc. Further, he says that before the Reformation the Church never deduced any doctrine from Scripture, and by inference blames our reformers for doing so, moreover he objects to their doctrine in itself as to justification by faith, and complains of their attempt to prove it from the Fathers, as a perversion of their meaning. Generally, his result is, not merely to refer us to antiquity but to *shut us up* in it, and to deprive, not only individuals but the Church of all those doctrines of Scripture not fully commented on by the Fathers ; and he seems to consider that our Reformed Church has erred as much in one direction as the Council of Trent in another ; and that the fact of other churches holding different views—e.g. on justification—requires the suspension of our judgment, or at least prevents full acceptance of our own doctrine concerning it.

Surely in thoughts like these one may see glimpses of a beautiful and comprehensive system, which, holding fast primitive antiquity on the one hand, does not reject the later teaching of the Church on the other, but bringing out of its stores things new and old, is eminently calculated to break up existing parties in the Church, and unite the children of light against those of darkness.

I have endeavoured in vain to gain an entrance into Newman's mind on this subject, and have tried each joint of his intellectual panoply, but its hard and polished temper glances off all my arrows. Still I feel so fully the truth and importance of all the *positive* parts of his system, that it does not at all damp my devotion to it. And I try not to be restless or anxious about such difficulties, but wait calmly in the sure trust that if any of us be otherwise minded, God will reveal this also unto us. You cannot conceive what satisfaction it will give me to know your sentiments and hear your counsel on this matter. I trust and believe that what I object to in Newman is merely owing to his resiliency from opposite error, and that

Pusey and others do not share it. And I am sure he will not seek to put forward such views: and this is another reason why I earnestly entreat this subject may be confined to our two selves.

Ever your affectionate friend,

S. F. Wood.'

Purcell tells us that Manning, who 'had a profound belief in the divine origin of the Reformation and in the apostolic work of the first Reformers,' laid down in his reply (not given) such strong arguments in their favour that Wood was completely satisfied, at any rate for a time. In a subsequent letter he thanks Manning for his admirable explanations, and ends by declaring that, 'I will knock under to the advice given.'

There is no evidence whatever to show that Manning's views on the Reformers had changed in 1841 from those which he held in 1838, when he cited Cranmer, Ridley, and Latimer as witnesses to that theory of 'the rule of faith of the Reformed Church of England and of the Church of primitive times' which Cardinal Wiseman challenged.

It is hard to see why the re-affirmation of these views in his first Charge should be considered a hit against Newman, or to find anything contrary to Tractarian belief in his conviction that the Church of England's destiny was, 'if true to her heavenly Lord', to be 'made glorious in His earthly kingdom as the regenerator of the Christendom which now seems dissolving and the centre of a new Catholic world.' Not only was this conviction the whole foundation of the Oxford Movement, but it is held by the Tractarians' successors to-day. Year after year each Anglo-Catholic Congress Anniversary meeting acclaims views identical with Manning's prophecy as to the destiny of the Bridge

Church, though the Reformers are now looked upon with Newman's juster estimate.

Purcell gives no extracts from the Charge to support his view that it was aimed at the Tractarians. What he quotes from it as regards the destiny of the Church of England tallies with Newman's letters on the same subject at that date, though Manning takes a more optimistic view of her position and progress in the Middle Way than Newman was able to do. Manning's praise of the Reformers is not quoted by Purcell, merely hinted at; and the distrust of Rome, expressed in the passage given from the Charge, is no more stressed than in Newman's own writings up to that time. Surely the truth is that Manning's first Charge was intended to profess a belief in the Church of England similar to that summed up in the hymn quoted a few pages back, not to disavow Tract 90. That seems to have been the view taken at the time, as Purcell tells us that in the following year 'not by the Record only . . . Archdeacon Manning's name was coupled with the unpopular party.'

In a characteristic passage he adds: 'To vindicate himself from this imputation, to throw cold water—he was not a bad hand at that chilling process—on the hot-headed defenders of Tract 90, Pusey, Ward, and the rest of them, the Archdeacon, in his Charge[1] says:

"This then, is no season for controversy. . . . All things about us are too living and real, too full of trial and of responsibility and of the judgments to come to suffer us to be men of arguments and replies and rejoinders. In the bitterest age of controversy we may be safe if we will, for there can be no fight where there is only one combatant. We have our safety in our own hands. Let each man speak the truth as he believes

[1] His second Charge—July 1842.

it : if we agree, God be praised ; if not, let us 'speak it in love' : quick tempers, keen tongues, sharp sayings, are not of God." '

'Did he mean all that by shaking his head ?' Newman might well charge biographers with interpreting Lord Burleigh's nods. It is hard to read any very scathing rebuke to 'Pusey, Ward and the rest of them,' into the above passage. No wonder that 'as time went on sharp sayings were repeated and tongues grew keener, and the name of Archdeacon Manning was again and again bracketed with that of Pusey.'

Purcell goes on : 'In his Charge of 1843, Manning repudiated still more emphatically connection with Newman or Pusey in the following significant passage :

"Be it that there are heard sharp and discordant voices, even among our teachers. What matters it to us, who are called by no man's name ; to us who have no rule of truth, but 'the faith once delivered to the saints ?' 'Nemo me dicat, O quid dixit Donatus, O quid dixit Parmenianus, aut Pontius, aut quilibet illorum : quia nec Catholicis Episcopis consentiendum est, sicubi forte fallantur, ut contra Canonicas Dei Scripturas aliquid sentiant.'" What do these words of St. Augustine mean in the mouth of Archdeacon Manning but virtually this : "Let no man call me a follower of Newman, a follower of Pusey, or of Ward, or of any other of them ; for did I not take my stand by the side of the protesting bishops in condemning Tract 90, as contrary to the sacred Scriptures and to the Thirty-nine Articles ?" '

As an example of free translation this can hardly be bettered. No wonder that the *Record* failed to pierce Manning's meaning, and spoke of him in 1834 as 'one of the most noted and determined of the Tractarians.'

The truth really seems to be this. Dr. Pusey saw eye to eye with Newman in every line of Tract 90, Manning did not. Naturally the former defended Newman when attacked for proclaiming tenets which both held to be true. It was not his 'characteristic fervour and generosity,' but his love of truth which made him take his stand by Newman; to be generous in defence of a personal friend who is teaching heresy is no virtue in a Doctor of Divinity. Faith unfaithful did not keep Pusey falsely true; he really believed Newman was right!

And 'the prudent and judicious Archdeacon' seems simply to have thought it right to stand by the Bishops, whom he had, three years before Tract 90 was published, declared to be 'the Apostolical Body to whose united wisdom and equal authority the Church in this land is, by a divine commission, put in charge.' A bishop to him was 'the source of authority, and the centre of unity in order, deliberation, and discipline.' Why the writer of these words should be accused of a mean, self-seeking motive because he did not range himself against the Bishops in defence of a tract they had declared to contain unsound doctrine, seems incomprehensible. One cannot help feeling that if he *had* done so, Purcell would have made great play with the words just quoted to prove inconsistency on that score.

His bias is very difficult to understand. A Presbyterian biographer might be excused for thinking it unnatural that an Anglican clergyman should put the allegiance sworn to his Bishop above his private judgement, when by disregarding it he might help a friend. But as a matter of fact Manning had never been a very close friend of Newman; and unlike Pusey and Keble did not hold Newman's views on the Articles, which the whole Episcopate had just condemned. Why Purcell, a Catholic, should have thought a disinterested loyalty to the Bishops on Manning's part an impossible reason for his conduct, it is hard to see. Unless, of course, he took so cynical a view of Anglican loyalty to Episcopal authority as to believe that a proof of its existence could not occur.

Purcell seems to have been unable to grasp that Manning sincerely believed that Episcopacy meant government by Bishops ; and that it was his duty not to question their views publicly, even if they differed from his own or that of his friends.

His position at this time seems to have been almost that of Keble, Newman and Pusey, except for two essential points of difference.

'For eight years,' Purcell says, 'the writers of the *Tracts for the Times* at Oxford had been labouring, heart and soul, in infusing a new spirit into the Anglican Church, in reviving doctrines which it had long since forgotten to hold, far less to preach and teach ; devotions it had ceased to practise or even to remember. For eight years they had been unsettling and disturbing minds by enlarging—in spite of the Thirty-nine Articles, or by putting, as Ward and only a few others did, a non-natural interpretation on them—the boundaries of the hitherto accepted or current faith of the Church of England. In leading the Church back to antiquity, in comparing its teaching with the faith of primitive times, they discovered that doctrines and devotions taught and practised in antiquity were wanting in the Anglican Church. With an honest zeal the Tractarians set to work to restore what they believed had been lost. They exalted the sacredness of the Eucharistic rite ; and a perpetual Sacrifice for the quick and the dead ; and insisted on formal repentance for sin after baptism ; made selections from the Roman breviary of devotional services; introduced in a modified form praying for the dead, invocation of saints, veneration of relics, and other Catholic doctrines and practices.'

Manning had followed them in these attributes of Catholicism, but he was not prepared to go as far as Newman in his strictures on the Reformers, nor in his attempt to interpret the Articles in accordance with the Council of Trent. And of course Newman far outstripped him in his clearing away of the stumbling-blocks of prejudice which kept both men back on the path to Rome. For six years longer than Newman he tolerated the principle that 'truth and error, the lion and the lamb, should be permitted to lie down together within the fold of the Church of England.' How that comprehensiveness became impossible to him we shall now see.

Many years later he summed up his beliefs in 1833; when, by an odd coincidence, he became Rector of Lavington shortly before Keble's famous Assize sermon inaugurated the Movement. He had at that time, he tells us, 'profound faith in the Holy Trinity and the Incarnation, in the Redemption by the Passion of our Lord, and in the work of the Holy Spirit, and the conversion of the soul, I believed in baptismal regeneration, and in a spiritual, but real, receiving of our Lord in Holy Communion. As to the Church, I had no definite conception. I had rejected the whole idea of the Established Church. Erastianism was hateful to me. The royal supremacy was, in my mind, an invasion of the Headship of our Lord. In truth, I had thought and read myself out of contact with every system known to me. Anglicanism was formal and dry, Evangelicalism illogical, and at variance with the New Testament, Nonconformity was to me mere disorder.

Two years after the famous sermon, when the embers of Anglicanism in the Established Church had been fanned into flame amongst those who followed Newman and Keble, Manning preached a sermon in Chichester Cathedral on 'The English Church, its Succession and Witness for Christ,' on July 7, 1835. The view of the Church to which the Movement had brought him is clear from this passage, which also shows the false elements which that view contained.

'For the first fifteen hundred years of Christian antiquity, Christ's earthly Church was one, and His ministry one, till apostolic unity of faith and practice withered away in the hollow sameness of the Roman ceremonial. Now, for three hundred years men have seemed to sicken of the very name of unity, and to contemplate the unhealthy self-production of sect and divisions within the bosom of the Church with a spurious charity, a cold indifference, and even a misguided satisfaction. At length it has come to pass that every one of the self-separated fragments of the body catholic has successfully preferred a claim for itself and its teachers to be regarded as the Church and ministry of Christ. Our commission to witness for Christ hangs on this question, Are the bishops of our Church the successors in lineal descent of the Lord's Apostles?' The other questions involved had not yet dawned on him.

In 1836 Dr. Hampden's appointment to the Regius Professorship of Divinity gave a proof of 'comprehensiveness' which created a great and justifiable indignation in both High and Low Churchmen. His Bampton Lectures, 'The Scholastic Theology: considered in its Relations to Christian Theology,' alarmed them by the Rationalism and Socinianism they found there: and an attempt to prevent his appointment by condemning his Lectures in Convocation was made.

This attempt was frustrated by 'a party of German Rationalists rising up in the University,' as Manning's friend Twisleton called the new Broad Church School; and Dr. Hampden became Regius Professor, thereby playing an unconscious part in Manning's conversion in years to come.

We have already seen something of the development in his opinions which took place under Tractarian influence during the first years of the Oxford Movement, and have tried to see how far Purcell's comments on the part he played in it are true to fact. Now we come to the critical stage, which set in when Newman's loss of faith in the Movement became more and more evident in 1843, and lasted for nine years longer. With a great sum Henry Edward Manning obtained his freedom; and Purcell (who was free-born) seems to find it equally hard to count its actual cost to him and to refrain from attempting to do so.

His comments on the Fifth of November sermon preached in 1843 give proof of his inveterate tendency to try to explain what he cannot understand. Having made up his mind, apparently, that everything Manning did was with a view to running with the Tractarian hare and hunting with the Low Church hounds, he seems to think that Manning's attack on the Roman Church in this sermon was not the expression of a sincere, though mistaken belief, but merely an effort to prove himself a genuine Protestant by blackening the Catholic Church.

A far different explanation of it is worth considering. By October 1843, the rumours about Newman's intended submission to the Church were widespread, and the fear of his loss lay heavy on the hearts of the many who had come to follow his leadership in the last ten years. Manning, anxious to be reassured, wrote to Newman, and received a reply which he sent to Mr. Gladstone enclosed with one of his own. Neither it nor Newman's letter are given, but their contents are easily inferred from Gladstone's reply. It gives such a vivid picture of Newman's mind in writing to those who had been his followers, and of the horror which filled them at the possibility of losing him, that I give it in full.

'WHITEHALL,
28th October, 1843.

MY DEAR MANNING,

Alas, alas, for your letter and inclosures of this morning! My first thought is "I stagger to and fro like a drunken man, and am at my wit's end." But even out of the enormity of the mischief arises some gleam of consolation. For between four and five years he has had this fatal conviction; he has waited probably in the hope of its being changed—perhaps he may still wait—and God's inexhaustible mercy may overflow upon him and us. It is impossible for me at the end of a long day and near the post time really to enter upon this subject, and indeed I am so bewildered and overthrown that I am otherwise wholly unfit. But I will address myself *briefly* to points which appear to me to *press*.

I cannot make his letter hang together. The licence to you at the end looks like saying "I cannot bring myself to reveal this—do you reveal it for me"—but surely this is contradicted by his aspiration that God "may keep him still from hasty acts or resolves with a doubtful conscience." This could have no meaning—would be worse than nonsense—if the interpretation of the concluding passage which I have suggested were adopted.

I cling to the hope that what he terms his conviction

is not a conclusion finally seated in his mind, but one which he sees advancing upon him without the means of resistance or escape. This is sad enough, more than enough; but something of this kind is absolutely required to make his conduct (I must speak succinctly) *honest.* I am strongly of opinion, and I venture to press it upon you, that you ought not to rest contented with the bare negation in your P.S., but to write to him again—he cannot be surprised at after-thoughts following upon such a letter. To tell him as you tell me that you cannot put his letter consistently together; that much more would be requisite in order to enable you to come at his real meaning—not to say at any such view of the chain of what precedes, as you could in justice to him adopt—that you believe he never could intend you to make any use, save the most confidential, of that letter—that if he could for one moment be out of himself and read it as another man does, he would see it in a moment. (The description of his proceedings in 1841, of his letter to the Bishop of Oxford, of his committing himself again, is, *as it stands there*, frightful—forgive me if I say it—more like the expressions of some Faust gambling for his soul, than the records of the inner life of a great Christian teacher.) Therefore you cannot take this letter as it stands to be his. Reflect upon the constructions which that passage would bear upon the mind of the country. It would lead men to say—He whom we have lost is not the man we thought. It certainly would damage and disparage his authority and character in the manner which one perhaps should desire as to a confirmed enemy to Truth, but which with respect to him it would be most wicked to do otherwise than deeply lament.

I do not know whether out of these confused chaotic elements you can make the ground note of a further note—or whether you will think it right—but I feel that there are such *imperative* reasons upon the face of his letter, reasons relative to himself and his own good name, for your keeping it secret, that I am very loath your refusal to divulge should stand without any reason; next I have the hope that he does not desire or contemplate abandonment of the Church; and lastly, I would to God you could throw in *one word*, glancing at the fatal results, which I may seriously illustrate by the effects that the horrors of the French Revolution produced in a most violent reaction against democratic principles in England. But even this, though a great historic truth, seems cold for the matter we are now dealing with.

I think you come to town next week—come to our house and take up your quarters there, that we may communicate freely. We may then, please God, talk of James Hope, and other matters.

I am compelled thus abruptly to close.

Ever yours affectionately,

W. E. GLADSTONE.'

Purcell's comments on this letter must be read to be believed. The only possible motive for them seems to be to cheapen a man for whom he so often expresses admiration. Nothing he quotes from letters to or from Manning or from his diary can be said to prove the charge of personal treachery to Newman at which Purcell more than hints.

He says: 'Manning, we may be sure, did not "stagger to and fro like a drunken man," at the thought of Newman's secession; nor, with Mr. Gladstone in the excitement of his intense grief, regard Newman as a "Faust gambling for his soul." Still less would prudence allow him, as Mr. Gladstone suggested, to enter into controversy with Newman. Supreme over private feelings was the public duty imposed upon the Archdeacon of Chichester by Newman's letter, or the construction put upon it, to break, and, on this occasion at all events, in an unmistakable fashion, with the Tractarian party and its illustrious leader. Manning knew better than Mr. Gladstone did "the fatal results to all Catholic progression in the Church which Newman's fall would produce." To-morrow, when the fatal tidings, which to-day he held locked in his breast, should become public, there would be, as Manning knew but too well, an end to all Catholic progress; an end to peace; an end to his own work and position. All alike would be tarred with the same brush. Time pressed: an opportunity was at hand: Manning was not the man, in the Church's interests or his own, to shrink, no matter at what sacrifice of personal friendship, from a public duty.

The necessity of things—a hard taskmaster, as he found out to his cost, and not on this occasion only—induced him once more at that period of acknowledged "declension," to take a new departure and make a fresh sacrifice. Archdeacon Manning was equal to the occasion; he was not afraid, in that evil day, to gratify the Ecclesiastical and Civil authorities, to respond to the popular "No Popery" outcry against Newman and the writers of the Tracts by preaching a Fifth of November sermon in the pulpit of St. Mary's, Oxford, but now abandoned by the illustrious recluse of Littlemore.'

Unless he wishes to discredit Manning, it is hard to see Purcell's aim in writing the above. He seems to have no clear picture of the situation in his mind. 'The thought of Newman's secession,' he says, did not trouble Manning, as it did Mr. Gladstone, because it might wreck the Movement; his one thought was to avoid any personal loss through it. If the Tractarian card was not a good one to play, he had the Protestant one also in his hand and could show himself a No-Popery champion by a violent 'Gunpowder, Treason, and Plot' sermon on the Fifth of November. Such a sermon would mark his distrust, not only of Newman, but of all 'Roman' tendencies in the Movement.

Yet we are asked to believe that it was this man whom the Tractarians trusted to rally them when their leader left them two years later! For it was not the Protestants who, in Purcell's epic (the Tractarian historians tell quite another story), flocked to the Archdeacon of Chichester in 1845 and implored him to drive Rome from the field. It was, we are told, 'the unsheltered and orphan children of the Oxford Movement' who sought the protecting wing of one who, barely two years earlier, had aroused their indignation by a sermon which disgusted them, Purcell tells us, not on account of its bad taste but because they considered it to be anti-Tractarian as well as anti-Catholic! Could there have been a more unlikely or unsuitable choice?

The true story of the Fifth of November episode seems to be this. Manning did desire, as he says in a letter to Dr. Pusey, to undo any harm that he might have done by his former assurances to 'clergymen and laymen all about him' that Newman's teaching was 'safe and sure' and that his system could not lead to Rome. The letter speaks for itself. There is no *personal* bias against Newman, but a plain dread (now that his conversion seems inevitable) that many others may follow him into what still seems to Manning a corrupt form of religion.

He writes:

'LAVINGTON,
22nd Sunday after Trinity, 1843.

. . . I can no longer deny that a tendency against which my whole soul turns has shown itself. It has precipitated those that are impelled by it into a position remote from that in which they stood, and from that in which I am. This has suddenly severed them (so far at least, alas !) from me. With the knowledge I communicated to you, it is an imperative duty for me to be plainly true to myself at all cost and hazard. It would be deceit to let them think I could feel anything but sorrow and dismay, or do anything but use the poor and small strength I have to save others from passing on blindfold and unawares into the same perplexities with them. I feel to have been for four years on the brink of I know not what ; all the while persuading myself and others that all was well ; and more that none were so true and steadfast to the English Church ; none so safe as guides. I feel as if I had been a deceiver speaking lies (God knows, not in hypocrisy), and this has caused a sort of shock in my mind that makes me tremble. Feel for me in my position. Day after day I have been pledging myself to clergymen and laymen all about me that all was safe and sure. I have been using his books, defending and endeavouring to spread the system which carried this dreadful secret at its heart. There remains for me nothing but to be plain henceforward on points which hitherto I have almost resented, or ridiculed the suspicion. I did so because I knew myself to be heartily true to the English Church, both affirmatively in her positive teaching, and negatively in her rejection of the Roman system and its differential points. I can do this no more. I am reduced to the painful, saddening, sickening necessity of saying what I feel about Rome.'

It is characteristic of Purcell to quote the following, with no comment, from two letters of the Rev. J. B. Mozley to his sister.

'OXFORD,
7th November.

Archdeacon Manning preached on Sunday. . . . I did not like either the matter or tone. He seems so really carried away by fear of Romanism that he almost took under his patronage the Puritans and the Whigs of 1688 because they had settled the matter against the Pope. . . . I suppose he wants to disconnect himself from the ultra party, and has taken this means. The Heads were immensely taken with the sermon, of course.'

The other quotation runs:

'Lincoln's Inn preachership is now in the field. Manning, I think, stands. They say Manning is too High for the Lincoln's Inn men; if so, it shows the inutility of men making demonstrations—for his sermon here was thought quite Low.' The inference Purcell wishes his readers to draw jumps to the eyes.

That Newman's refusal to see Manning the day after the sermon was preached was a sign of personal resentment seems open to question. His diatribe against the Church was equally distasteful to Pusey and Keble; as far as one can see on grounds of taste, not of personal offence. Any covert attack in it on Newman, such as Purcell detects, would be aimed equally at them, but there is no suggestion that *they* refused to see him. Newman probably expected, and wished to avoid, an explanation of the sermon which could only be controversial, and would do nothing to mend matters.

Keble seems chiefly to have been distressed by it as a sign that Manning was 'protesting too much.' He said many years later: 'I always feared what would become of Manning when I heard of his violent 5th of November sermon. Exaggerations of this kind provoke a Nemesis, and it did not surprise me so much as it pained me to hear that he had become a Roman Catholic.'

The following letter from Newman in reply to one not quoted in the Life, but plainly one of apology should the sermon have given pain, shows that *he* did not take it as an act of personal treachery:

'LITTLEMORE,
24th December, 1843.

MY DEAR MANNING,

How can I thank you enough for your most kind letter received last night, and what can have led you to entertain the thought that I could ever be crossed by the idea which you consider may have been suggested to me by the name of Orpah? Really, unless it were so very sad a matter, I should smile; the thought is as far from me as the antipodes. Rather, I am the person who to myself always seem, and reasonably, the criminal, I cannot afford to have hard thoughts which can more plausibly be exercised against myself.

And yet, to speak of myself, how could I have done otherwise than I have done, or better? I own, indeed, to great presumption and recklessness in my mode of writing on ecclesiastical subjects on various occasions; yet still I have honestly trusted our Church and wished to defend her as she wished to be defended. I was not surely wrong in defending her on that basis on which our divines have ever built, and on which alone they could pretend to build. And how could I foresee that, when I examined that basis, I should feel it to require a system different from hers, and that the Fathers to which she had led me would lead me from her? I do not, then, see that I have been to blame, yet it would be strange if I had the heart to blame others, who are honest in maintaining what I am abandoning.

It is no pleasure to me to differ from friends, no comfort to be estranged from them, no satisfaction or boast to have said things which I must unsay. Surely I will remain where I am as long as I can. I think it right to do so. If my misgivings are from above I shall be carried on in spite of my resistance. I cannot regret in time to come having struggled to remain where I found myself placed. And, believe me, the circumstance of such men as yourself being contented to remain is the strongest argument in favour of my own remaining. It is my constant prayer that if others are right I may be drawn back, that nothing may part us.

I am, my dear Manning, ever yours affectionately,

JOHN H. NEWMAN.'

It is quite clear that Newman's future was a matter of engrossing interest to both Gladstone and Manning in the months which followed, and the bitterness against the Church which deepened in them both, in Gladstone's case permanently, is probably due to their chagrin at its power to draw and to hold him in spite of all their efforts.

The above letter was sent with two others from Newman (not given by Purcell) to Mr. Gladstone; whose reply contains clear proof that it was the Protestantism of the bishops, not pique at their censure, which drove Newman to despair of the position of Anglicanism. The suggested excursus on 'the word "contented"' would do credit to Polonius Malvolio.

'HAWARDEN, N.W.,
Sunday, 31*st Dec.*, 1843.

MY DEAR MANNING,

I return the interesting and kind but painful letter which you forwarded for my perusal. It shows that a most formidable contingency is in the distance, more or less remote. It may be indefinitely near, or indefinitely far. Can the degree of remoteness be affected by anything in your power, under God, to do or to forbear?

From the second of the three letters, taken alone, it would be a legitimate inference that any particular act or decision, and bishops' Charges this way or that, would have no influence upon his mind. But from the first letter—from the note in his new volume where he declares that the Church of England has lately by the mouth of her rulers been taking the Protestant side, evidently a *preparation*, conscious or not—and from his conduct the reverse is clearly the case. It is manifestly in the power of bishops and others, though the degree may be uncertain, to impel or retard his fatal course, and it should be deeply pondered whether, by a discreet use of your knowledge, any beneficial exercise of this power might be brought about.

Looking at the bishops' Charges *as a whole*, it seems to me that, through timidity, they have overshot their mark, in the Protestant sense, and that if there be no fresh sores opened, the Charges of the next year or two will be much above those of the last. This will be so far well.

Are there, however, any bishops—I think there must be many—who believe that the event we know to be possible would be to the Church an inexpressible calamity? These are the men whom to contemplate in any practical measure.

By one word he gives you an excellent ground of approach—the word "contented." Starting from that word you may, though with a light touch, avow that you are—(1) Not contented, but obliged; perhaps it might be dangerous to add, (2) Not contented, but thankful. Such writing might be a parable to him.

Is he aware of the immense consequence that may hang upon his movements? His letters do not show it. If he is not either now or at some future time he ought to have his eyes opened.

What is wanted is that cords of silk should one by one be thrown over him to bind him to the Church. Every manifestation of sympathy, and confidence in him as a man, must have some small effect. I am even tempted myself (for he made me an opening by kindly sending me his sermons) to ask him to converse with me at some time on a passage in which he speaks of the present temper of statesmen with regard to the Church. What say you to this?

Whatever you do, may God prosper your counsels. With kindest remembrances, ever affectionately yours,

W. E. Gladstone.'

Nearly a year later, November 8, 1844, Mr. Gladstone wrote that 'again the rumour about Newman seems to have blown over,' but a letter which Manning forwarded to him about a fortnight after dashed his hopes once more.

'Littlemore,
16*th November*, 1844.

My dear Manning,

I am going through what must be gone through, and my trust only is that every day of pain is so much from the necessary draught which must be exhausted. There is no fear (humanly speaking) of my moving for a long time yet. This has got out without my intending it, but it is as well.

As far as I know myself, my one great distress is the perplexity, unsettlement, alarm, scepticism, which I am causing to so many, and the loss of kind feeling and good opinion on the part of so many, known and unknown, who have wished well to me. And of those two sources of pain, it is the former is the constant, urgent, unmitigated one. I had for days a literal ache all about my heart, and from time to time all the complaints of the Psalmist seemed to belong to me.

And, as far as I know myself, my one paramount reason for contemplating a change in my deep, unvarying conviction that our Church is in schism and my salvation depends on my joining the Church of Rome. I may use *argumenta ad hominem* to this person or that, but I am not conscious of resentment, or disgust, at anything that has happened to me. I have no visions whatever of hope, no schemes of action, in any other sphere more suited to me; I have no existing sympathies with Roman Catholics; I hardly ever, even abroad, was at one of their services; I know none of them; I do not like what I hear of them.

And then, how much I am giving up in so many ways, and to me sacrifices irreparable, not only from my age, when people hate changing, but from my especial love of old associations and the pleasure of memory.

Nor am I conscious of any feeling, enthusiastic or heroic, of pleasure in the sacrifice; I have nothing to support me here.

What keeps me yet is what has kept me long—a fear that I am under a delusion; but the conviction remains firm under all circumstances, in all frames of mind. And this most serious feeling is growing on me, viz. that the reasons for which I believe *as much* as our system teaches, must lead me to believe more, and not to believe more, is to fall back into scepticism.

A thousand thanks for your most kind and consoling letter, though I have not yet spoken of it. It was a great gift.

Ever yours affectionately,

JOHN H. NEWMAN.'

It marked, Mr. Gladstone said, 'a step in advance towards the precipice; yet it still remains impossible to say how many more paces may remain between it and its edge.'

In 1845 came Ward's degradation, against which Manning recorded his *non placet*. In a letter to Robert Wilberforce, advising him as to his action, he shows a spirit utterly unlike that which Purcell continually attributes to him. He says:

'If you feel a desire to protect yourself against being supposed to hold Ward's principles, sign the declaration lying at Burns's. I do not sign it, because I have no fear or care about it. It is to me a clear and straightforward case of *fiat justitia, ruat cœlum*.'

The prudent and judicious Archdeacon of Chichester has 'no fear or care' about what may be thought of an action taken to prevent, so far as his vote can do so, 'a high moral wrong.' At the same date he wrote a letter of sympathy to Newman, whose enemies, Purcell says, were again becoming active; but his Charge in July was again disfigured by a bitterness against the Catholic Church for which Dr. Pusey rebuked him in a letter acknowledging a copy of the Charge. On August 8, 1845, Manning replied to this rebuke as follows:

'We owe to the Church of Rome a pure Christian charity as to a member of the Catholic body; we owe the same also to the churches of the east. I do not find you expressing the latter feeling, and that seems to me the cause why you are misunderstood to have not a charity to the whole Body of Christ, but a partial fondness and leaning to the Roman Church . . . will you forgive me if I say it ? (the tone you have adopted towards the Church of Rome) seems to me to breathe not charity, but want of decision. . . .

The Church of Rome for three hundred years has desired our extinction. It is now undermining us. Suppose your own brother to believe that he was divinely inspired to destroy you. The highest duties would bind you to decisive, firm, and circumspect precaution. Now a tone of love, such as you speak of, seems to me to bind you also to speak plainly of the broad and glaring evils of the Roman system. Are you prepared to do this ? If not, it seems to me that the most powerful warnings of charity forbid you to use a tone which cannot but lay asleep the consciences of many for whom by writing and publishing you make yourself responsible.'

Two months later, to the very day, Newman sat in his study at Littlemore writing those thirty letters, each worded almost alike, which were to tell his most intimate friends of his immediate reception into the Church. One was sent to Manning, who replied as follows :

'London,
14*th October*, 1845.

My dear Newman,

I have only this evening received your letter dated the 8th.

If I knew what words would express my heartfelt love of you, and keep my own conscience pure, I would use them. Believe me I accept the letter you wrote me, at such a moment, as a pledge of your affection. I shall keep it among many memorials of past days and lasting sorrows.

Only believe always that I love you. If we may never meet again in life at the same altar, may our intercessions for each other, day by day, meet in the court of Heaven. And if it be possible for such as I am, may we all, who are parted now, be there at last united.

It is a time that admits but a few words ; and I will say no more than that I am, my dear Newman, most affectionately yours,

H. E. Manning.'

Now comes a marvellous piece of imagination on Purcell's part, which is very hard to square with his earlier sneers (no other word is adequate) at Manning's cautious ' break with the Tractarian Party,' of which, incidentally, he gives no convincing proof. He now expects us to believe him when, unsupported by the historians of the Movement, or by any contemporary letters, he claims him as its re-organiser !

So far as I know he is quite alone in making this claim. The ' official ' tract on Newman published by the organisers of the Centenary celebrations speaks of ' the heroic efforts by which Keble, Pusey and Charles Marriott rallied and re-organised the shattered forces of the Movement.' Prebendary Mackay, an authority on that period, speaks of ' 1846, when Dr. Pusey took charge of the Movement,' and says that ' Keble, Pusey, Marriott, Church, and James Mozley remained to hold the fort.' Dean Church says : ' The only two facts of the time were that Pusey and Keble did not move, and that James Mozley showed that there was one strong mind and soul still left in Oxford.'

Where Purcell got his dramatic and contradictory

picture of Manning's action after Newman went, it is hard to discover. The fact that Newman became a Catholic later does not deter the Anglican historians of the Oxford Movement from doing justice to the great part he played in its launching. Why then (if he ever exercised it) have they all failed to acknowledge that 'saving office' of Manning's, which Purcell says kept it from being wrecked by Newman's departure? And if it is true that 'Archdeacon Manning had no lot or part, beyond that of a witness at a distance' in the Oxford Movement, after he took fright in 1841 at the bishops' condemnation of Tract 90, why did the 'broken hosts' turn to him in 1845? The passage is its own refutation. Broken hosts who have lost their leader look to the officers who fought under him to rally them; not to a neutral observer, once an ally, who has already failed them in face of the enemy.

Yet Purcell expects us to believe the following:

'Since the condemnation of Tract 90—that critical turning-point in the Tractarian Movement—Archdeacon Manning had no lot or part, beyond that of a witness at a distance, in the greatest moral revolution—greater by far and more far-reaching and abiding than the struggle of Laud and the Non-jurors—which has ever befallen the Anglican Church and the religious life of England. He held aloof from, even if he did not look askance at, men whose zeal he considered was not tempered by discretion, or at all events by the prudence and tact which governed his own conduct. On Newman's conversion, Manning stepped forward, not to carry on Newman's work, but to undo it; to put a stop to the results of his teaching, and still more to the force of his example. No one was better adapted for such a saving office than the Archdeacon of Chichester. He rallied the broken hosts, discomforted and disunited in the first instance by the retirement of their illustrious leader from the battlefield into silent Littlemore. He took under his protecting wing the unsheltered and orphaned children of the Oxford Movement. He inspired the timid with courage; brought back hope to the despairing; lifted up the hearts of the downcast and dismayed. He inspired the souls of them that came to him in doubt, with their faces already turned towards Rome, with all the confidence in the Church of England which filled his own heart. Yet, when the shock of Newman's departure from out of the Anglican Church, though long expected, came at last, like a sudden surprise, men's minds reeled and their hearts sank within them; they knew not what to do, whom to look to, whither to go. And as week after week, month after month, the long procession of them that went out with Newman in the year 1845, that *annus mirabilis*, passed before their saddened eyes, they, who had not the faith, the hope, the heart to follow him—the scattered remnant of the Tractarian vanguard—turned instinctively to Manning. His voice was heard like that of one crying in the wilderness. He spoke, as one inspired, of the divine certitude of his faith in the Anglican Church. To the afflicted of heart, the troubled in conscience, to those tortured by doubt, he presented the Anglican Church, "primitive yet purified," possessed "of purities in doctrine and practice wanting in the Western Churches, whither in their impatience men had gone, seeking what was not to be found." One thing alone was wanting to the absolute perfectibility of the Church of England; and that was her liberation from the bondage imposed upon her by the usurpation of the Civil Power. He directed their energies to this end, not only as good in itself, but as serving to divert their minds from doubts or controversial difficulties. His austere zeal, his earnestness, his personal piety and his dogmatic assurances attracted the hearts of men in that day of unrest. His confidence was contagious. He became a tower of strength to the weak or the wavering. The timid, almost frightened out of their wits by Newman's secession, were reassured; for such men instinctively felt that, under Manning's guidance, they were walking on the ways of safety and in the path of peace.'

The only basis for all this is the fact that Mr. Gladstone was very anxious that Manning should write an answer to The Essay on Development; and that a certain number of people (naturally his own penitents would do so) looked to him to quiet any doubts raised in their minds by the reasons that book gave for Newman's conversion, as well as by the state of the Anglican Church compared with the unity of Rome.

Purcell does not, however, produce one scrap of evidence to show that Manning now seized the helm of the Tractarian Movement and diverted its course into anti-Roman channels. The few contemporary letters he quotes, and the extracts from Manning's Diary given in the Life, give an entirely opposite impression.

A month after Newman's reception, in November 1845, Manning writes in his Diary: 'I feel I have taken my last act in concert with those who are moving in Oxford. Henceforward I shall endeavour, by God's help, to act by myself, as I have done hitherto, without any alliance.' Even Purcell does not suggest that he formed a new party out of the broken hosts, which was the only alternative to what actually happened. Those who believed they could be 'Catholic without being Roman Catholic,' as the modern slogan has it, remained under the leadership of Pusey and Keble in the paths which had led Newman to Rome ; those who saw its impossibility followed him there.

Purcell tells us that many of Manning's penitents in his Anglican days gave him the benefit of their memory of the Archdeacon's help and guidance. It is strange that not one of them seems to have provided even one letter from their guide intended to strengthen the recipient's faith in the Anglican position after Newman left.

In a letter written in June 1845 to Robert Wilberforce, four months before Newman went, Manning speaks of 'not less than seven cases' of unsettlement with which he is concerned. He expressly states his inability to deal with 'the merely intellectual questions which are coming upon us,' and in another letter to him, written two days before Father Dominic went to Littlemore, he speaks of what he wants 'to see either done or shown to be impossible or needless,' implying that he has no idea of undertaking it himself.

The letters show his mind on the matter so clearly that it seems best to quote them in full.

'LAVINGTON,
30th June, 1845.

MY DEAR ROBERT,

I have longed greatly to see you in quiet, and to have the help and benefit of your judgment on some of the heavy events which are hanging over us.

The extent to which unsettlement has extended itself is a serious matter. At this moment (let this be kept to yourself) I am directly or indirectly in communication with not less than seven cases, I might make the number larger.

And I deeply feel that, with my little reasoning and constant active work, it is impossible for me, even if I were by nature able, to deal with the merely intellectual questions which are coming upon us.

I especially desire to join with you in this because some of the ablest and dearest of those round us fail to satisfy me in some of the conditions necessary for dealing fairly and solidly with the realities of our relation to the Roman Church. Whenever we have compared our thoughts I have felt that we feel the same points to be weak and strong.

You will find in the enclosed all I can offer on our last meeting. You have placed me in a position of great rebuke and humiliation, and I thank you for this at least.

Ever yours very affectionately,

H. E. MANNING.'

'LAVINGTON,

6th October, 1845.

. . . Everything, my dear Robert, has conspired to draw us together in brotherly love. . . . Our meetings have been so few and hurried, and I long for a time when we can, without interruption and alone, really weigh some of the matters which are now forced upon us.

I was glad some time ago to see by your answer that you are less anxious about the theological questions now afloat than I am. It makes me believe that I am over-sensitive to them, or that I do not yet feel the force of some answers which are really sufficient.

But my anxiety does not extend to doubts, for nothing can shake my belief of the presence of Christ in our Church and sacrament. I feel incapable of doubting it: again, the saints who have ripened round our altars for 300 years make it impossible for me to feel it a question of safety.

But it seems to me that our theology is a chaos, we have no principles, no form, no order, or structure, or science. It seems to me inevitable that there must be a true and exact *intellectual* tradition of the Gospel, and that the scholastic theology is (more or less) such a tradition, we have rejected it and substituted nothing in its room. Surely divine truth is susceptible, within the limits of revelation, of an expression and a proof as exact as the inductive sciences. Theology must be equally capable of a " history and a philosophy " if we had a Master of Trinity to write them.

That is what I want to see either done or shown to be impossible or needless.

With all kind and brotherly wishes, my dear Robert, yours very affectionately,

H. E. M.'

On November 3, after the news they had been dreading had come, he writes :

'My dear Robert,

. . . What shall I say of our dear friend Newman ? My heart is very heavy. I still seem to see great difficulties before us ; and wish I could read and talk with you, for we shall have to give plain answers and form to many hard questions. Not the least part of the difficulty will be to show why principles are safe so far and no farther.

Ever yours very affectionately,

H. E. Manning.'

In a letter dated December 30 he gives his views on Newman's Essay on Development, which he considers 'a wonderful intellectual work,' but says that after reading the book he 'was left where he was found by it.' Its influence, however, as a letter to Laprimaudaye will show later, was to prove a seed growing in secret in his mind.

Gladstone writes from Baden-Baden on October 20, probably directly he heard the news :

'My dear Manning,

A few words in this day of trouble must pass from me to you ; for your own sake I wish you had been with me here at the time of Newman's secession. To see the Roman Church on the defensive against Ronge,[1] rationalism, and thought tending towards rationalism within its own pale, is in the nature of a corrective to that half-heartedness and despondency which is almost forced upon us at home by the contemplation of our own difficulties.'

He says that almost all he sees in Germany drives his sympathy 'into the Roman camp—that is *quoad* German matters'—and in the following paragraph shows that he does not think Pusey's counterblast likely to be sufficiently pro-Anglican :

'Is there to be any firm and intelligible declaration from Pusey ? . . . I at one time thought of enclosing to you, for you to use or not . . . a letter to him [Pusey] expressing a very strong hope that it was his intention upon the occasion of Newman's secession to make some declaration of such a kind as will settle and compose men's minds, or at least tend that way, with a view to the future. No such effect as this is produced by showing that after infinite question one can just make out a case for remaining in the Church of England. I do desire and pray that the trumpet shall not give an uncertain sound, inasmuch as men are certainly called

[1] The attempt made by Ronge, an apostate priest in Germany, to 'cast off the yoke of Rome' did not keep the Roman Church on the defensive for very long. Ronge and his followers were quickly discomfited.

upon to prepare themselves for the battle. It is possible that you may be at work on this subject with him—if you are, pray say so much of this to him in my name as you like, or as little, or none at all.

It may appear strange, but I have almost a feeling of disappointment at not seeing more secessions with Newman ; because it looks as if they were to *follow*. . . . However, I suppose and hope that Newman's book will bring all this to a head ; and that persons are waiting for that in order to declare themselves. It is sad and bitter ; but a sweep now, and after that some repose, is the choice of evils—that which we should seek from the mercy of God.

Your affectionate friend,

W. E. GLADSTONE.'

A month later (November 21, 1845), Mr. Gladstone, obviously still dissatisfied, suggests that Manning should take up the cudgels against Newman's theory of Development. He writes :

'MY DEAR MANNING,

My chief object in writing is to suggest to you the possibility that you may have to entertain the idea of answering Newman's book. . . . After reading it I may have to write to you again on the subject. It will probably be a real and subtle argument, backed by great knowledge, and it must not, if so, be allowed to pass unnoticed, nor should the task be left to those who will do mischief.

All I will now say is this : if, upon reading it, you entertain the notion that you can do it, do not lose a moment in making known your intention among friends, and let it appear to the public as soon as you have made any progress that will warrant an advertisement. Oakeley's is a sad production, very unworthy of him, except in the spirit, which seems to me gentle and good. I grieve much over the loss of Faber. He was evidently a man who understood working the popular *side* of this religious movement, which has for the most part been left to shift for itself.

I have no doubt that many persons are waiting for Newman's book, and mean to say Aye or No, after reading it.

In haste, I am, always affectionately yours,

W. E. G.'

Again on December 23 he repeats his request thus :

'My dear Manning,

I had been long on the point of writing to you. Newman's book interests me deeply, shakes me not at all. I think he places Christianity on the edge of a precipice ; from whence a bold and strong hand would throw it over. Your mind, I am sure, has been at work upon it ; but do not hurry to tell me the results. I trust to see them ripen. Many thanks for your sermons, which I have just received. A blessed Christmas to you, you will not have this until that happy morning.

Ever yours affectionately,

W. E. Gladstone.'

The reply, which Purcell does not give, shows that the task had been begun. We shall see that the insuperable difficulties which Manning found in answering the book played their part in his submission to the Church six years later.

'Hawarden,

Sunday, 28*th December*, 1845.

My dear Manning,

I have got your note about Newman's book, on which I shall be very brief. First, I am more sanguine than you about the ultimate issue ; I am persuaded that Bishop Butler, if he were alive, would in his quiet way tear the whole argument into shreds—wonderful as is the *book*—so that one should wonder where it had been. Secondly, I am heartily glad you are at work upon it, and I augur that you will find your confidence grow as you proceed. May God be with you in the task. I have myself put down certain notes upon it; if I can connect them sufficiently, on some Sunday or Sundays, to give a hope of their being any use to you, they shall be sent to you.'

But in August 1846 Mr. Gladstone's standard-bearer shows signs of fainting. 'I have a fear, amounting to a belief,' Manning writes to him, 'that the Church of England must split asunder.' Gladstone's horror and surprise are shown in his reply.

'Nothing can be more firm in my mind than the opposite idea, that the Church of England has not been marked out in this way and that way for nought, that she will live through her struggles, and that she has a *great* providential destiny before her. I will say little in the way of argument, but I will more rely on reminding you that your present impressions are entirely at variance with those of six or seven months ago. I begin now to think that on a matter of magnitude I cannot differ from you; so I have the most immediate interest in your opinion, as I have a presentiment of its proving to be mine too, if it be indeed yours—hence this intolerance on my part.'

It is strange to reflect that by being so insistent that he should answer Newman's book, Mr. Gladstone helped to undermine that loyalty to the Anglican Church which had till then such complete hold on Manning.

The first shock, however, was a very faint tremor,

making no more (perhaps much less) impression than that caused in Newman's mind by Cardinal Wiseman's essay in 1839. In each case, six years elapsed before the house built on sand fell in ruins round its inhabitant.

Apart from the projected reply to Newman's book, which never took shape, Purcell gives two instances of Manning's success when 'he stepped forward, not to carry on Newman's work, but to undo it' by putting 'a stop to the results of his teaching.' They seem hardly adequate material for his glowing account of this campaign, but he provides no others.

It seems that Mr. John Giles, 'a stockbroker and a man of high culture,' Purcell explains, was sent to Lavington by his friends, who were alarmed to hear that he intended to seek instruction in the Catholic Faith. Manning did not disappoint them, and 'without a day's delay carried poor John Giles off to the Bishop of London, who confirmed him and administered communion.' The story of this fell swoop depends on the authority of Richmond who painted Manning's portrait in 1844. Purcell does not say when the incident took place; he merely says: 'Mr. Richmond told me [this] of a friend of his,' etc.; how long after the event he does not say. It must have been some years later, as Mr. Richmond also describes Manning's efforts to reverse his undoing of Newman's work, and says 'he was continually nibbling after John Giles, but he was too wise a man to come within Manning's reach.' No wonder, if the story is true! All Cardinal Manning found to say of the affair sounds as if it had been repeated to him in his extreme old age. He said, 'Yes, I remember poor John Giles very well; he was a good man; he was afraid of me!'

The only other instance given is one of 'those unique appeals addressed by his penitents to their spiritual director for guidance ' which, Purcell thinks, helped to make Manning feel it his duty to remain an Anglican. His answer is not recorded, nor the writer's subsequent history, so if her ' unhappy, unsettled ' mind found rest we do not know. I quote her letter in full, as its confusion is a pathetic instance of the harm which the tactics of May Blunt and the Vicar, unhappily by no means confined to them or to their day, can do.

' *15th October*, 1850.

MY DEAR FATHER IN CHRIST,

I am venturing to ask a great favour of you, it is that you will allow me to read and copy for my *own good, and quiet thought,* your answer to D. Dodsworth's attack on the Apocryphal books—and Rome as Babylon. Of course it is from May Blunt that I know anything about it, and she would not, if she knew, like my speaking of it again to you. I *think* you won't refuse me, and I am sure you would pity me, and like to help me, if you knew the unhappy, unsettled state my mind is in, and the misery of being *entirely, wherever I am,* with those who look upon joining the Church of Rome as the most awful " fall " conceivable to any one, and are devoid of the smallest *comprehension* of how any enlightened person can do it. I have had one kind short letter from Mr. Richards, but I feel as if he could do little good to me, so long as I am so completely alone and *forced* into thinking over things for myself, and the way in which the subject is brought before me.

My old Evangelical friends, with all my deep, deep love for them, do not succeed in shaking me in the least. I would add in asking you the favour to let me see what you sent May Blunt, that I am really cautious on one point, if on no other, i.e. about not saying to others (for one reason lest I should misstate it myself) what may be quoted or *garbled* and misstated *again at the cost of another.*

May says she will tell me all the heads of the argument when we meet, but I can't help exceedingly shrinking from the whole subject with her, because she makes up her mind not to believe things, and out-talks things so provokingly that I entirely lose the whole sense.

My brother has just published a book called *Regeneration* which all my friends are reading and highly extolling ; it has a very contrary effect to what he would desire *on my mind.* I can read and understand it all in an altogether different sense, and the facts which he quotes about the articles as drawn up in 1536, and again in 1552, and of the Irish articles of 1615 and 1634, *startle* and *shake* me about the Reformed Church in England far more than anything else, and have done ever since I first saw them in Mr. Maskell's pamphlet (as quoted from Mr. Dodsworth's).

I do hope you have sometimes just time and thought to pray for me still. Mr. Galton's letter long ago grew into short formal notes, which hurt me and annoyed me particularly, and I never answered his last, so, literally, I have no one to say things to and get help from, which in one sense is a comfort, when my convictions seem to be leading me *on* and *on* and gaining strength in spite of all the dreariness of my lot.

Do you know I can't help being very anxious and unhappy about poor Sister Harriet. I am afraid of her GOING OUT OF HER MIND. She comforts herself by an occasional outpour of everything to me, and I had a letter this morning.

This is what she says of herself in one part. "Oh how I wish I could run away from myself. Sometimes I am obliged to go out, and I walk and run till I feel I can go no farther, then I sit down and cry, then I set off again."

She longs for more "active work," but if she leaves St. Mary's Home she does not know where to go, she says; in short she describes herself as almost beside herself. She says Sister May has promised the Vicar never to talk to her or allow her to talk on the subject with her, and I doubt whether this can be good for her, because though she has lost her faith, she says, in the Church of England, yet she never thinks of what she could have faith in, and resolutely without inquiring into the question determines not to be a Roman Catholic, so that really you see she is allowing her mind to run adrift, and yet perfectly powerless. Forgive my troubling you with this letter, and believe me to be always your faithful, grateful, and affectionate daughter,

EMMA RYLE.

I wish I could see you once more so very much.'

As an offset to these cases of Manning's success in keeping enquirers from the Church, we are told that in May 1846 his wife's sister Sophia and her husband, the Rev. George Dudley Ryder, Newman's disciple, became Catholics; and both Mrs. Lockhart and her son, much to Manning's regret and in spite of his efforts, took the same step that year. Miss Lockhart remained an Anglican till Manning's own conversion, so there seems to be no doubt that she was kept back from the Church on the 'Trusty's here' principle which, as we have already seen, made many of Newman's Anglican disciples also feel safe where they were so long as he remained. But these few instances of Manning's power to prevent conversions to Rome give little foundation for the part Purcell assigns to him as a substitute for the Movement's lost leader.

Yet unless he really played that part the theory of 'the Double Voice' falls to the ground. If 'from unconscious self-deception he believed that he singly and solely knew how best to extend the work and will of God upon earth' there must surely have been some outstanding success to cause such megalomania. Unless 'his self-will, self-confidence, self-seeking, even,' so turned his brain as to make him fancy that a desire for his own advancement in a Church he believed to be in schism was 'willing and seeking the things which God willed' there is no excuse whatever for his remaining one of the leaders of the Church of England so long after he had lost all faith in her. If he acted as he did from the motives Purcell attributes to him at this juncture, he must either have been a megalomaniac or a fraud.

It is at this stage of their respective journeys that Newman's advantage over Manning as regards a biographer becomes manifest.

Miss Mozley's mind was definitely Anglican and she could never share the Catholic outlook to which Newman's struggles brought him. But her sympathy with those struggles and her knowledge of his character made her fully aware of his sincerity during the transition period; and enabled her to understand his motives. Every stage through which he passed, every vacillation, she recognised as part of the naturally slow, painful, and uncertain process inseparable from an honest search for truth in the mind of a scrupulously sincere and honourable man.

But Purcell had never known Manning's Anglican mind as Miss Mozley had Newman's. He never met Archdeacon Manning before his conversion, so neither personal observation during the years of change nor a similar outlook before they began helped him in his attempt to explain Manning's conduct during that difficult period. He particularly fails to understand his desire to hurt no one by crying 'Wolf' before he was certain there was danger in the Anglican sheep-fold; and he evidently cannot credit him with good faith in his relations to his penitents and the Anglican public; though Manning's own confidential papers show that he acted as he did from a sincere and disinterested belief that it was the right course.

To say he spoke with a double voice implies that he knowingly taught what he knew to be untrue. The truth seems to be that he taught what he had always believed to be true, even though the consensus of opinion on which he had rested was losing its power to assure him of its truth, until he was perfectly certain that it was false. That is, he dared not teach those promptings of his divided mind which led him to the Roman position, or say anything which might throw others into his own unsettled state, until he felt quite certain that the Church of England was not part of the Catholic Church, and that no reforms in her method of government, no freedom from State interference, could make her so.

But Purcell takes a very different view of him. In his opinion 'a curious difficulty, almost startling at first,' crops up between 1846 and 1851; during which period we find Manning 'speaking concurrently for years with a double voice. One voice proclaims in public, in sermons, charges, and tracts, and, in a tone still more absolute, to those who sought his advice in confession, his profound and unwavering belief in the Church of England as the divine witness to the Truth, appointed by Christ and guided by the Holy Spirit. The other voice, as the following confessions and documents under his own handwriting bear ample witness, speaks in almost heartbroken accents of despair at being no longer able in conscience to defend the teaching and position of the Church of England; whilst acknowledging at the same time, if not in his confession to Laprimaudaye, at any rate in his letters to Robert Wilberforce, the drawing he felt towards the infallible teaching of the Church of Rome. . . .

The simplest solution that can be offered to a difficulty is for the most part the truest. In the trying period between 1847–51 Manning's mind was in a state of transition in regard to his religious belief. The struggle was as prolonged as it was severe. Until his mind had grasped the reality of things; had probed his doubts to the bottom; had reached solid ground, consistency or coherency of statement was perhaps scarcely to be expected. To see things in one light to-day, in another to-morrow, is but natural in such a transition-state of mind. To make statements on grave matters of faith to one person or set of persons in contradiction of statements made to others, is only a still stronger proof of a sensitive mind, perplexed by doubt, losing for the time being its balance.

In Manning's mind there was a superadded difficulty: he was by nature, if not absolutely incapable, unwilling in the extreme to confess his inability to answer a question or solve a difficulty or doubt. As an accepted teacher in religion, the habit had grown upon him of speaking always on all points of faith with an absolute assurance of certitude. In a letter to Robert Wilberforce of this date, Manning confesses that "people are rising up all over the country and appealing to me to solve doubts and difficulties which, as you know, perplex my own mind. But if I leave their appeals unanswered, they will think that I am as they are." For him, a spiritual teacher, in whom his penitents put their trust, to whom they come for counsel and guidance, to confess to his doubts would give scandal and do grave harm. Hence it came to pass that he had to speak, considering it under the circumstances his duty to do so, with a double voice. . . .

Manning had, to put it broadly, two sets of people to deal with; the one set those who put their trust in him—the ecclesiastical authorities and his own penitents; the other set, those in whom he put his trust—his intimate friends and confessors. He dealt with each set from different standpoints: from the one he considered it his duty to conceal his religious doubts and difficulties; to the other he laid bare, as in conscience bound, the secrets of his soul.

On this principle, the double voice in Archdeacon Manning is easy of explanation. He had a deep sense of responsibility as an accepted teacher in the Church, and a still deeper in regard to those who came to him as penitents for spiritual guidance. The Archdeacon of Chichester knew that he was regarded by his bishop and the clergy, not only in his own archdeaconry, but in the neighbouring archdeaconry of Lewes—where his orthodoxy had been vouched for by Archdeacon Hare—as a faithful son of the Established Church. Other bishops as well as his own consulted his judgment with deference. It was not in his nature lightly to forfeit such a position. As long as his conscience permitted him to keep silence, he never uttered a word in public as to his doubts and difficulties, never gave a hint even to those nearest to him, or most dependent on his spiritual guidance, of the changes which had taken place and were still going on in his religious opinions. On the contrary, he regarded it as a duty which he owed, on the one hand, to his office in the diocese, on the other, to his penitents, to exalt on every public occasion the claims and defend the position of the Church of England, as a living portion of the Church of Christ.'

If two words of the foregoing long extract from the 'Life' were different, it would change what seems a stigma on Manning's conduct into a truer estimate of it. If for 'voice' we could read 'mind,' and if in the sentence 'As long as his conscience permitted him to keep silence' Purcell had said 'obliged' instead of 'permitted,' a more charitable and, to judge from Manning's own letters at the time, a truer impression would have been given.

Fortunately for the truth, Purcell considered himself at liberty to print large extracts from Cardinal Manning's diaries and many of his most private letters. Whatever may be thought of his delicacy of feeling in doing so, he thereby provided a complete answer to his own 'Double Voice' insinuations. Those marked 'Under the Seal,' written to Laprimaudaye (Manning's confessor as an Anglican), and to Robert Wilberforce, under whose direction he seems latterly to have acted, are particularly valuable in showing the true state of affairs.

One, which Cardinal Manning endorsed in 1887, 'To my Confessor in the Church of England.'[1] gives much useful information as to his religious opinions in 1847, and to the part he had played in the Movement. It begins:

'*Under the Seal.*

44 CADOGAN PLACE,

16*th June*, 1847.

MY DEAR FRIEND,

. . . I must first do what I have not done before, and unwillingly; I mean, say something about myself.

[1] Laprimaudaye, his curate at Lavington.

Our *intimacy* began with last year, up to that time you could only know of me in a general way. Since that time I have never gone into what it is necessary you should know if you are to have any real knowledge of my thoughts on some points which have seemed to give you uneasiness. And my purpose in giving you that knowledge is only because I feel it to be due to us both, that you should not misunderstand, nor I to be misunderstood.

For 14 years I have lived the life of a parish priest—nearly half the time without a curate. Upon this has been added for 6½ years the work of the Archdeaconry and a most burdensome correspondence. The *active* work of the last four or five years has been so great that my stable and travelling expenses nearly equal my *whole household* expenses. I pass over many other things because these are enough to show that mine has been a life of *overwork*, and all my temptations and dangers the very reverse of those which attend a retired, reading, and speculative life such as some of our friends have lived.

For the last eight years I have been labouring to keep people from the Roman Church. In 1839, one person who was all but gone, was settled and has stood to this day, though a favourite brother went two years after. From 1842 to 1846 Mrs. Lockhart was held back. Miss Lockhart till now. In the beginning of 1846, a man who had seceded and received Roman baptism, was received back again in Lavington church. Six persons at this moment, I believe, have either laid aside the thought or suspended it, with relation to myself. Many men I could name in various degrees of nearness during the last five or six years. My whole labour has been this way.

. . . During the last four years the effort and

anxiety to retain friends in the English Church has *perceptibly* affected my health ; and I can trace, I think, the beginning of illness last year to that cause. So wholly and sincerely from my soul has all my heart and strength been given against the Roman tendencies and temptations to them.

I have never indulged in the habit of speaking against the Church of England or her writers living or dead, or allowed anyone to do so to me. The sort of footing on which I have lived with the clergy round me made it impossible for such a tone to pass.

In the year 1835, I preached a visitation sermon on the succession of the English Church, which led me into the question of Unity, and which I printed in the year 1841, having in the meantime continually kept the subject before me so far as I could find time for reading. That book was the substance of a correspondence by which I tried to keep a man from Rome, enlarged. In 1838 I preached another visitation sermon on Tradition. Both these books I believe have been used in keeping people from Rome, and I also believe successfully. They are both strongly and plainly Anglican, and in parts positively and by statement anti-Roman.

. . . I will endeavour to tell you *exactly* the state of my thoughts. Two subjects have been in my mind for the last ten or twelve years. The one is Unity, beginning in 1835 ; the other Infallibility, beginning in 1837–38. To these two points all the reading I could give has been given. On both I came to conclusions which uphold as [*sic*] against Rome ; and these conclusions, after long examination and re-examination, I printed. I can say, without fear, that the examination of these two subjects was as unexcited, calm, and practical as I could make it. They came before me as involved in the baptismal creed, as you will find if you care to see.

When Newman's book was published, Gladstone urged me to answer it. I declined pledging myself; but it forced me again into the two same subjects. To which I have continued to give all the thought and reading I can.

And I am bound to say that I could not republish either of the two books as they stand. They are inaccurate in some *facts;* incomplete as compared with the truth of the case; and concede some of the main *points* I intended to deny. The Anglican ground is, I believe, this.

1. To stand upon the text of St. Vincent of Lerins, *quod semper, etc.*

2. To interpret Scripture by antiquity as expressed in the canon of 1562.

3. To hold the faith of the Church before the division of the East and West as Bishop Ken said.

4. To show that the Roman points cannot be proved in the first 6 centuries as Bishop Jewel declared.

In the course of the last few years I have read the Apostolical Fathers, Justin Martyr's *Dialogue*—a good deal of Tertullian, St. Cyprian, St. Cyril of Jerusalem; St. Chrysostom, and a good deal more of St. Augustine, including the *de Civitate Dei*. The whole of St. Optatus, and St. Leo, besides habitually referring to parts for facts and quotations. The result is that I should be afraid of undertaking the defence of either Jewel's or Ken's positions.

. . . I wish it were possible to lay the whole aside. But it is in vain to dream of it. If I could do it myself, duty to others would make it impossible. Within the last month I have declined to enter upon these points with five men (three clergymen) and all (four especially) men of high excellence and value to us. Even if I could satisfy my own mind, I could not help others without seeing a clearer solution of the two following points :

First. Is not the infallibility of the Church a necessary consequence of the presence of the third Person of the Blessed Trinity ; and of His perpetual office, beginning from the Day of Pentecost ? This seems to me to be revealed in Scripture.

A perpetual presence, perpetual office, and perpetual *infallibility*—that is, a living voice witnessing for truth and against error under the guidance of the Spirit of Christ—seem inseparable.

Secondly. It it not a part of the revealed will and ordinance of our Lord Jesus Christ, that the Church should be under an episcopate united with a visible head, as the apostles were united with St. Peter ? It is not the question of primacy with me so much as *unity of the episcopate.* "*Episcopatus unus est.*"

I take St. Peter to have been the first of apostles, as the Primate of Christendom is the first of bishops ; in spiritual order or power all being equal.

Now these two questions are two principles, which involve all details. And the course of examination which has led me to them is the canon of 1562, i.e. Scripture interpreted by antiquity. .The Council of Chalcedon, which the Church of England recognises, exhibits them both in a form and distinctness which I cannot at present reconcile with what I have hitherto believed to be tenable.

I have now given you, as far as is possible in the fewest words, the sum of my meaning.

All bonds of birth, blood, memory, love, happiness, interest, every inducement which can sway and bias my will, bind me to my published belief. To doubt it is to call in question all that is dear to me. If I were to give it up I should feel that it would be like death ;

as if all my life had become extinct. Believe me then, that nothing short of a mass of evidence inspired and uninspired all going one way, and this evidence I have before me—could make me hesitate to shut my eyes, and take the Church of England on trust for ever as I have done with a loving heart in times past.

But the Church of England herself sends me by canon to antiquity, and in obeying it I find what I cannot solve. For this cause I must seek help. Now let me add a word on a subject I noticed in the beginning —I mean your fear of my going to Italy. "He that trusteth his own heart is a fool," but I may say that I have passed through all this before, having been much abroad, and already six months in Italy—three in Rome. The effect of this has always been *highly repulsive*. But I can say, I think, without fear, that no seductions of devotional books or the like have the least effect in this matter. I have been for years familiar with them. My difficulties are two definite and distinct questions, in which I am ready with a willing mind to be guided.

But I feel them to be too definite and distinct to be laid aside—and no treatment but such as is definite and distinct gives rest to my conscience. I would not have written all this about myself were it not that I feel too much love for you to bear, without an attempt to satisfy you, the pain of being thought to use lightness in a matter of Eternity. I do not ask you to go into these questions. I only wish you to see that my difficulties are neither from excitement nor imagination, nor from want of love to the Church of England, nor from trifling and fanciful causes. They lie deep in Holy Scripture and in the mind of the Spirit and the appointments of our Lord Jesus Christ. Only believe me to be as real and earnest in this as you think me capable of being in anything.

I have made this a long letter, willing if possible to make a second needless. Do not feel bound to answer it, as I shall not look for any reply. But give me your prayers against all the faults you see or think you see in me.

And do not imagine that I write this as any forward step or sign of moving one way or the other. I write because I resolved I would not even enter on these points in helping others till I had written to you. There are some about me whom I can hardly deny, and I could not much longer keep silence with them without making them fancy I was as they are.

Farewell, my dearest friend. Happy the day if through the precious blood of our Lord we attain that kingdom where light casts no shadow and all are one in the Eternal Truth. With my brotherly love and gratitude for all you have done for the least worthy.

Ever yours affectionately,

H. E. MANNING.'

Purcell now gives a letter from which the following extracts are taken. It was written three years later, he says, to 'a near relative, a lady, who had long desired to join the Catholic Church, and who, since the Gorham Judgement, was more pressing than ever. Manning speaks, not in the voice of a penitent or, as he spoke to his confessor, acknowledging his doubts and misgivings, but in the voice of an authorised teacher upholding the claims of the Church of England on the conscience of his penitent.'

Purcell's idea seems to be that it proves his theory of the double voice. To others it may seem a strong and pathetic proof of the double mind—agonising to be fused into singleness on one side or the other.

'Lavington,

6th May, 1850.

My dearest ——

I will endeavour to give you the reasons which make me strive to subdue both haste and fear in the great probation which is upon me.

1. Judging by the evidence of the Primitive Church there are many, and they very grave and vital, points on which the Church of England seems more in harmony with Holy Scripture than the Church of Rome.

2. The political, social, domestic, state of foreign countries as compared with England is to me a perplexity and an alarm.

3. For three hundred years, the grace of sanctity and of penitence has visibly dwelt and wrought in the Church of England.

4. The most saintly and penitent for three centuries have lived and died in it, not only without fear, but with great thankfulness for their lot as compared with another which they have looked on with mistrust, and even more.

5. I must believe that the spiritual discernment of Andrewes, Leighton, Ken, and Wilson was purer and truer than mine.

6. I am sure that they and a multitude besides were more learned and of greater intellectual penetration.

7. At the present time the great majority of the holiest and the wisest of my brethren differ from me in the strongest way on the point before us. They may be God's warning voice to me.

. . . I know too well my own faults of intellect, heart, and will, the shallowness of my spiritual life, and the narrowness of my information, to come to such a conclusion without the deepest awe, and the longest and most patient delay.

The evidence before me in part inclines to show that this event [the Gorham Judgement] is a revelation, in part a change. But I need more than I have as yet to decide a question with such tremendous issues for time and for eternity. It would be like the one mistake upon a death-bed.

. . . I have not yet heard Him in my conscience saying, "Flee for thy life." Till then, I will die rather than run the risk of crossing His will.

I fear haste, and I fear to offend God, but I fear nothing else; and in that faith by His grace I will wait upon Him, humbling and chastening my own soul.

. . . It is hard to compress into a letter any answer to such questions; but I feel no doubt or fear in saying that your probation is in the life of the soul. Keep your heart and will united with God, and then shall no harm break through to touch you. Be jealous lest these intellectual questions draw your will from the spiritual life, especially from prayer, even though you do no more than kneel in silence before God. It calms and subdues the soul to a consciousness of what is and what is not real and eternal.

To Him I commend you as always. His peace be with you. For His sake always very affectionately yours,

H. E. M.'

Another letter dated July 11, 1850, after the Gorham Judgement, shows that though in his heart he despaired of the Church he had served and loved during the best part of his manhood, his head still provided him with soothing reasons why he, and therefore those under his guidance, might remain her children.

'Lavington,
11*th July*, 1850.

Dear Madam,

I will endeavour to give you some statement of the ground on which I think you may without fear trust yourself to the mercy of God through Jesus Christ in the Church of England at this time.

The Church of God upon earth has what I may call its inner and its outer sphere.

The inner sphere is the fellowship of the soul with God through Jesus Christ, and a life of faith, love, repentance, and devotion. The outer sphere is the visible order of succession, government, canonical discipline, and the like. I believe that your probation lies in the inner sphere, and there all is clear and infallible. We have no doubt that no penitent can perish, and that no soul that loves God can be lost; moreover, that God will give both love and penitence to all who pray for it. But in the outer sphere it is impossible to judge of controverted questions without so much of intellect and knowledge, and that knowledge so various and of such difficulty to attain and estimate, that I feel no doubt in saying that any errors you may there be in will be tenderly dealt with by Him "who spared not His own Son" that He might save our souls.

When I come to look at the Church of England, I see a living, continuous succession of Christian people under their pastors, descending from the earliest ages to this day; and although it has had to bear mutilations and breaches in its external order and in its relation to the other churches, yet it seems to me to possess the divine life of the Church, and the divine food of that life, the Word and Sacraments of Christians.

So I have been able to feel hitherto. Late events have called this in question, but it seems to me too soon yet to pass sentence upon it. No one can say how long or how short a time may decide it; for in these questions it is not *dial* time, but *moral* time—that is events, acts, and changes, that must decide it. In the meanwhile, I do not feel any fear of resting for salvation within that inner sphere which cannot be shaken; for there all is clear and divine.

As to the outer, the questions, always difficult, are now still more so, and I am therefore even more full of hope that God will deal tenderly with all who sincerely desire to do His will.

Catechumens dying without baptism are held to be baptised *in voto;* and persons desiring to be in the Church, if, through ignorance or error they be out of it, will nevertheless be reckoned in it by the mercy of God. All this I feel applies fully to you, and I have no doubt in saying that you may "rest in hope," waiting to see the way and will of God with this great and lifeful body, the Church of England, meanwhile giving yourself to a life of faith which is not an intellectual state, but a habit of grace in the soul, infused by the Holy Spirit, and nourished by meditation, prayer, and obedience.

I trust and pray that God may increase this in us all, and give you all solace that is for your good.

Believe me, dear madam, your faithful servant in Christ,

H. E. MANNING.'

Until he found it possible to decide the questions which he honestly acknowledges trouble him, it is hard to see how he could have written otherwise. Many of Newman's letters under similar circumstances strike the same note, but has anyone ever accused him of speaking with a double voice ? It seems as if Purcell expected a man not even on the threshold of the Church to testify of what so far he had not seen. He cannot realise that Manning's mind in July 1850 was still the kaleidoscope it had become some years before. It could not become fixed in a definite, unchanging pattern till conviction became certainty in 1851.

The first stage towards departure from the Anglican position is clearly seen in this entry, dated May 1846 :

'I am conscious to myself of an extensively changed feeling towards the Church of Rome. It seems to me nearer to the truth, and the Church of England in greater peril. Our divisions seem to me to be fatal as a token, and as a disease. If division do not unchurch us it will waste us away.

I am conscious of being less and less able to preach dogmatically. If I do so, I go beyond our formularies. Though not therefore Roman, I cease to be Anglican.

I am conscious that my sympathy and confidence are much lessened. There seems about the Church of England a want of antiquity, system, fulness, intelligibleness, order, strength, unity ; we have dogmas on paper ; a ritual almost universally abandoned ; no discipline, a divided episcopate, priesthood, and laity.'

His change of attitude towards Our Lady appears at the end of the entry when he says that 'by an impression of consciousness not to be reasoned out' he seems to feel 'that . . . if John the Baptist were sanctified from the womb, how much more the Blessed Virgin,' and that 'it is a strange way of loving the Son to slight the Mother !'

In August of the same year he gives the symptoms which strike him as dangerous to the health of his Church, but shows no sign of believing them incurable.

This optimism is a typical product of the Anglican mind which Purcell fails to understand, and his inability to do so causes him to lay against Manning that charge of a 'double voice' which other great converts have escaped. He had neither Miss Mozley's own experience of Tractarianism nor Wilfrid Ward's inherited power to understand it. Naturally he found it very hard to realise that to Manning, as to many others in his position, the Church of England seemed a diseased branch of the Catholic Church, into which the life-giving sap would once more flow abundantly after the Tractarian pruning knife had been freely used. He did not yet see her with Catholic eyes; as a branch lopped off and stuck into the ground; only able to live as long as the nourishment gained from the parent tree still lasts in the severed wood.

Purcell is, I think, as unfair as his metaphor is inapt when he speaks of Manning as 'dissecting the diseased body' when he makes his diagnosis; and complains 'that there is not a touch or sign of tenderness or regret' in the letters to Robert Wilberforce which record his gradual enlightenment as to the Anglican position. No surgeon would speak of 'dissecting' a diseased body; he would as soon talk of 'operating' on a corpse. The knife in his hands (fortunately both for himself and his patient) cannot be 'kind or ruthless' as in Purcell's strange metaphor; it is impersonal, like Manning's attitude towards those symptoms in the Church which he wished to diagnose and then to cure. He never seems to have satisfied Purcell's sense of fitness as regards emotional expression, whether in speaking of his individual sorrows or his spiritual disillusionments. Purcell forgets that a surgeon has to conquer any personal feelings of tenderness or regret during an operation. If he allowed them to take charge he would embarrass those helping him and gravely endanger the patient's chances.

The Church of England, Manning writes in this entry, seems to him diseased :

1. *Organically.*

1. Separation from Church *toto orbe diffusa and* from *Cathedra Petri*.
2. Subjection to civil power *without appeal*.
3. Abolition of penance.
4. Extinction of daily sacrifice.
5. Loss of minor orders.
6. Mutilated ritual.

2. *Functionally.*

1. Loss of daily service.
2. Loss of discipline.
3. Loss of unity.
   (i) Devotion.
   (ii) Ritual.
4. No education for priesthood.
5. Unsacerdotal life.
   (i) Bishops.
   (ii) Priests.
6. Church effaced from popular conscience.
7. Popular unbelief of mysteries. Insensibility of invisible world.

A little later, in the same month (August 1846), he writes :

'(1) We give up all Protestants, and stand alone and against East and West on a plea of deliverance from bondage, and a greater purity of doctrine and life. (2) Can we maintain this ? How has the experiment issued ? What are its phenomena past and present as to unity and belief of the Real Presence ? (3) The Lutheran, the Calvinist, and each would go upon the same theory excluding us. (4) It seems incoherent and inverted to talk of catholicising the Church : we are not means of grace to it, but it to us. The Church must catholicise itself, or rather cannot be uncatholic, though *we* may. (5) Wherever it seems healthy it approximates the system of Rome, e.g. Roman

Catholic Catechism, Confession, Guidance, Discipline. (6) These things are potentially ours, but actually we have forfeited them. Using is having, and the Roman Church has them. (7) The same is true of the monastic life. The dissolution of monasteries would not have extinguished the spirit of monasticism if it had existed. The orders were destroyed in France in 1790, but can now count 35,000 members. In England, the Roman Church has already formed 30 convents. If we had the life we should have the orders. (8) The Church of England, after 300 years, has failed:

(1) In unity of doctrine.
(2) In enforcement of discipline.
(3) In training to the higher life.
(4) In holding the *love* as distinct from the respect of the people.
(5) In guiding the rich.
(6) In folding the people.'

The steps by which he had reached this position are detailed in a long and minute self-scrutiny entered in his diary on July 5, 1846; where he says: 'Strange thoughts have visited me'; and recounts them under twenty-five headings. The most important are as follows.

As he now feels that the Anglican Episcopate is 'secularised and bound down beyond all hope,' with no authority to which it can 'appeal for its restoration'; he therefore finds 'a greater difficulty in arguing in favour of the English Church and against the Roman.' Then comes this important and (as those who have gone through his experience will recognise) most significant passage:

'I feel as if a light had fallen on me. My feeling about the Roman Church is not intellectual. I have intellectual difficulties, but the great moral difficulties seem melting. Something keeps rising and saying, "You will end in the Roman Church." And yet I do not feel at all as if my safety requires any change, and I do feel that a change might be a positive delusion.'

The thought of the 'new creation,'[1] he says, has been growing in him and justifying the Roman doctrine, which seems 'to hang on "The Incarnation; the Real Presence (i. Regeneration, ii. Eucharist); and the Exaltation of St. Mary and the Saints."' This 'family of doctrines, right or wrong,' he thinks is 'preserved by Rome and cut or regulated by Protestantism.' He adds, 'And I see that the *regula fidei* is held by those who hold them and lost by those who have lost them.'

Now come some of the misgivings which beset him. 'Is all this listening to the tempter? Are they clouds out of a declining heart? Is instability and love of novelty the set-off and counterpoise to ambition? . . . May not this be a feint of the tempter? I fearfully mistrust myself.'

He goes on:

'I do not feel that I should doubt a moment if the choice lay between Rome and any Protestant body. It is only because the English Church seems to me to be distant from all Protestant bodies that I have any doubt. If the Church of England were away there is nothing in Rome that would repel me with sufficient repulsion to keep me separate, and there is nothing in Protestantism that would attract me. Is the English Church enough to alter the whole case? I think so. Yet I am conscious that I am further from the English Church and nearer Rome than I ever was. How do I know where I may be two years hence? Where was Newman five years ago? May I not be in an analogous

[1] The Jerusalem bishopric.

place? Yet I have no positive doubts about the Church of England. I have difficulties—but the chief thing is the drawing of Rome. It satisfies the WHOLE of my intellect, sympathy, sentiment, and nature, in a way proper, and solely belonging to itself. The English Church is an approximate. And that by my own supplements, ideal, imagination, ritual.'

Then comes a pathetic bit of self-revelation, which puts a very different light from Purcell's on the anti-Roman sermons and charges. How can a double-minded man, as a convert *must* be in the preliminary stages of his conversion, avoid being unstable in his ways?

He writes: 'The meshes seem closing round me. I feel less able to say Rome is wrong, less able to retain our own, less able to regain[1] confidence to myself. I feel as if I had shaken the confidence of my people, and I am unable to restore it by any anti-Roman declarations.'

Ten days later comes:

'15th July. To-day is my birthday—38. This last year has opened a strange chapter in my life. I never thought to feel as I feel now, and with my foot upon the step of what I once desired'; another proof that it was not thwarted ambition, driving him to look further afield for place and power, which led him to the Church.

In April 1847, nearly a year later, he states the case to himself as follows:

'20th April, 1847. The two questions are: (1) Is it the will of our Lord Jesus Christ that His flock should be subject to Saint Peter and his successors? (2) Is it part of the mystery of Pentecost that the Church should be infallible? I have this difficulty. If I treat

[1] i.e. 'win back others confidence in me.'

infallibility as a principle, I meet with difficulties in detail, e.g. Transubstantiation. If I judge of the detail I can find no principle. As a principle, it is with Rome. Only details with us. Yet if it be a principle, private judgment in detail is shut out.

Admitting—

1. The Infallibility of the Church.
2. The Church of Rome that Church,

would the residual difficulties to be received on infallibility be so many as in the English Church, e.g. the Canon, the censure of antiquity, the change of the Eucharistic office, and the like ? '

After giving these extracts Purcell expresses his surprise regarding two points. First, that these misgivings began in 1846, two years before the Hampden appointment and four years before the Gorham Judgement ; and secondly, that there is no hint of them in Manning's sermons and charges. Yet the letters to and from Mr. Gladstone on the Essay on Development, and Manning's letter to Laprimaudaye, which Purcell has already given, seem to put it beyond doubt that Newman's going, and the reasons he gave for doing so, shook Manning very considerably. And surely to expect him to air his doubts and difficulties in the pulpit at a time when he was far from being sure they were not sent by the devil seems somewhat unreasonable.

Now come the letters to Robert Wilberforce in which the last stages of the long struggle are clearly seen. The following one, written in Rome at the end of 1847, alludes to his refusal of the Sub-Almonership in 1841. He makes it quite clear that doubts as to the Anglican position were already in his mind even then ; and that one reason for declining the post had been his fear lest it should bias him in weighing them.

The letter runs thus :

'*Under the Seal.*
ROME,
2nd Sunday after Christmas.

MY DEAR ROBERT,

. . . I look much to you and lean much upon you. For I know no one with whom I more sympathise. And I know you to be a candid and laborious student ; what is more, I believe that the expectations of a bishopric, with the hope of wide usefulness, would not warp your convictions. You have too much mastered your own will to be drawn aside even by the strong attractions which are around you. It has been my prayer that such may be my case lest I should have eyes and see not. Do you remember asking me at the time of the Sub-almoner affair whether I refused it from unwillingness to involve myself further in our system ? I said, No, because that was not my fear. I did fear, and put it down at the time, lest the sphere of attraction should bias me in weighing the great doubts which had then fully opened themselves to me. Now this is what I believe you to be free from, I confide in you because it is so, and lean on you. I have as far as possible done as you wished me, and set my mind free by reading German and Italian, and by living in the open air. But I cannot say that anything has made much difference. Things seem to me clearer, plainer, shapelier, and more harmonious ; things which were only in the head have got down into the heart ; hiatuses and gaps have bridged themselves over by obvious second thoughts, and I feel a sort of *processus* and expansion going on which consolidates all old convictions, and keeps throwing out the premisses of new ones. Still I can say I have never felt the fear of safety or pressure of conscience which alone justifies a change. I have endless matter I should like to have your thoughts upon.'

The Hampden case gave him further misgivings, and several letters are given by Purcell which were written on the subject to Robert Wilberforce 'under the seal.'

In the first of these, written from Rome on February 12, 1848, he asks his friend's help, as he feels his position is altered by the certainty that no protest will now avert Hampden's consecration; and unless his objections can 'be shown to be without force,' he is 'afraid of thinking of the future.' He writes:

'I am convinced (by my own reading of them) that Hampden's Bampton Lectures are heretical in *matter*. And still more, that they are heretical in *form*. His system is the science of heresy. The Church of England was hardly saved from partaking in his heterodoxy by the censure of the University in 1836 and 1842, he being left in full communion. The Episcopate is fully made partaker in his heterodoxy by his consecration, and the whole Church, priesthood, and laity in communion with the Episcopate.'

It seems to him worse than the scandal of Bishop Hoadley's episcopate, as Hampden is to be 'confirmed and consecrated being under positive suspension and censure,[1] and his soundness is the cardinal point in the contest. By consecration the Episcopate gives sentence in his favour, and invests him with the special custody and dispensation of doctrine.'

Then comes this trenchant summing up of the Anglican position:

'The great tradition of the world and of the Church is the knowledge of God; and Hampden's system

[1] His lectures had been censured, as we have seen, for the Socinianism both High and Low Churchmen found in them.

undermines this, both in its matter and form, in its substance and proof. This seems to me to be the capital offence of any branch of the Church, and fatal to its divine character.

The separation of the English episcopate from the whole episcopate under heaven, the denial of Catholic doctrine in substance by a large body of the English priesthood, e.g. the doctrine of the sacraments, the Christian sacrifice, the visible and divine polity of the Church (articles of the Baptismal Creed) and the rejection of Catholic doctrine in *form* by the rejection of Catholic tradition as the rule of faith, the historical fact that the Church of England has made common cause with Protestantism as a mass, even in its degeneracy, as in the Jerusalem Bishopric; all these have for a long time deprived me of the power of claiming for it the undoubted guidance of the Holy Spirit along the path of Catholic tradition. It is not from the Church we receive it, but from our own books and our own private judgement.

This last event exemplifies the same impotence and uncertainty of witness in the highest doctrine of the divine revelation. It is in vain to speak of the Church of England as a witness, except as an epitaph. Its living office and character are tampered with; and its living, speaking testimony is not trustworthy.

I am left without defence. I cannot rest the Church of England and its living witness on anything higher than an intellectual basis. I trust it, because I think it to be right, not because I believe it to be right. It is a subject of my reason, and not an object of my faith.'

Having stated the Anglican position as he sees it, he goes on to explain his own in words which surely make his sincerity as obvious as is his turmoil and distress of mind.

'This event has brought out,' he says, 'a miserable truth, namely, that civil power is the ultimate judge of doctrine in England, a principle which is not more heretical than atheistical. If it be not the ultimate judge, "when, if not now," shall the case arise for denying and resisting the claim?'

'Not to deny and resist it,' he points out, 'is to consent, or at least to suffer the claim, against which loyalty to our Divine Lord, the salvation of His people, the Christian rights of the Church's posterity, and our own soul-sake binds us to spend every day, and every power of our life. My dear Robert, you will not misunderstand me, as if I thought myself to be anything, God knows, what I am humbles and alarms me. And it is under this condition that I add, that I do not know how I can serve a body I cannot defend. I seem *reduced* to a choice between my faith and all its foundations on one side, and all that life has, which is dear to me, on the other. The grounds on which I have striven, and under God not without hope, to keep others in the Church of England, are falsified. And I dare not seek or retain any influence but that of Truth, and the influence over individuals which only Truth has given henceforward has no foundation. It must be either given up or kept by unfairness in spite of Truth, which is impossible.

Dear Robert, do not think I am under any effect of ill-health, or sensitiveness, or locality, or momentary provocation, or the like. What I have written has been steadily advancing in my mind these ten years, and outward events do but verify old fears, and project old convictions upon realities. I will, as I promised you, be guided by you, and lean my whole weight upon you, and I know you will not offer me shadows for truths.'

Three days later, February 15, 1848, he writes again :

'God knows, my dear Robert, that every bond and tie of friendship and love, and a kindred higher than blood, to say nothing of every lower affection, which makes up home to me, bribe me into a state next to blindness, in the great issue between England and Rome. But there are truths so primary and despotic that I cannot elude them. Such is the infallibility of the mystical body of Christ on earth through the indwelling of the Holy Spirit. I could as soon disbelieve the canon of Scripture or the perpetuity of the Church. Infallibility is not an accident, it is a property, as inseparable by the Divine Will as perpetuity. This is evident to me from holy Scripture, from Catholic tradition, from internal and necessary relations of divine Truth and divine acts, as well as from Reason which alone would prove nothing.

I cling to the Church of England, because, trusting that it is a portion of the visible Church, it partakes of this undoubted divine property.

If it does not partake of this property it affords no foundation for my faith. It is useless to offer me antiquity for my foundation. What do I know of antiquity ? At my next birthday, if I live, I shall be forty. I must rest on something which itself rests continuously on antiquity, whose consciousness is therefore continuous, running down from the Day of Pentecost to this hour.

I cannot hide from myself that the state of England alarms me in this point. It cannot be denied that we have two contradictory theologies. Our episcopate is divided even in articles of the Apostles' Creed, e.g. the Church and the Sacraments. I am afraid that Hampden, if consecrated, will force us to confess more. Our priesthood is, if possible, more divided than the episcopate; and our laity are driven different ways, till the whole belief of a Church, teaching in God's name and with a pledge of divine guidance, is wasted away.

Surely it is not enough to say that our formularies are sound. Suppose it; but what are doctrines on paper, when the living speaking Church contradicts, or permits contradiction, of its own definitions? If the articles had to be judged at the last day instead of our souls, their orthodoxy might cover our unbelief. How long is this to go on? I am ready to say—I do not say that the Church of England teaches the doctrine of the Real Presence, but I must say that either those that deny it or I ought not to be priests of the same Church.'

Yet, clearly as he sees that 'the Church of England before this Hampden affair and after it is not in the same state, and cannot be defended on the old lines,' he does not know 'how the only possible turn can be taken without breaking all terms with old traditions and beginning a new decade of conflict'; and says: 'When I think of this, and the end towards which our divergent line inevitably points, I am aware of something which says, a false position can never be really mended. You say I give you too much credit; I only believe you to be what I daily pray to become. God knows that I would rather stand in the lowest place within the Truth, than in the highest without it. Nay, outside the Truth the higher the worse.'

Robert Wilberforce seems to have tried to answer Manning's doubts, but not very successfully; as on March 11, he writes to thank him for his letter but tells him:

'Truly what you say does not come home to me.

1. It is no question whether any Anglican court would pronounce Hampden heretical, but whether he is so. I think you are probably right about the courts; so much the worse.

2. My recollection of this matter, refreshed by the extracts lately republished, satisfies me that both East and West, in all ages, would pronounce him heretical.

3. He has recanted nothing.'

The line Robert Wilberforce took in order to hold him back, and his objections to it, are clear from this passage:

'Do you know that I take no encouragement in the sense intended from the phrase that much good is resulting by reaction, and making men speak out, and the like. So much the better for them. But the question—and the only one—is, are we, or are we not, on a basis which is tenable in the sight of God, and by the laws of His Church? I told you in my last letter that we are in a position I cannot defend, and that is a new fact to me. I do believe Hampden to be heretical, in substance and principle. It makes it worse to me to find that fact palliated or doubted. Can anybody doubt what judgement would be formed of him and his book here or at Munich, or what would have been said of it by St. Augustine or St. Athanasius? And I cannot go by any other rule. But besides this, the Court of Queen's Bench, *plus* Hampden's consecration, declares the civil power to be ultimate and supreme, even in spiritual obligations. This overthrows the only defence I have ever been able to make of our position. If it be true, I am myself one of the foremost in believing it to be fatal to our claim as a member of the visible Church. I cannot evade this, and I cannot obey it. If it be finally confirmed, I am at an end.'

Nearly a year later, another letter 'under the seal' shows that his doubts are growing in spite of all that he or his advisers can do to stifle them.

'*Under Seal.*

LAVINGTON,

Holy Innocents, 1849.

. . . I have tried to hold my peace, to lose myself in work, to take in other subjects which I dearly love and delight in, but all in vain. My whole reason seems filled with one outline. The faith of the Holy Trinity and of the Incarnation subdues me into a belief of the indivisible unity and perpetual infallibility of the Body of Christ. Protestantism is not so much a rival system, which I reject, but no system, a chaos, a wreck of fragments, without idea, principle, or life. It is to me flesh, blood, unbelief, and the will of man. Anglicanism seems to me to be in essence the same, only elevated, constructed, and adorned by intellect, social and political order, and the fascinations of a national and domestic history. As a theology, still more as the Church or the faith, it has so faded out of my mind that I cannot say I reject it, but I know it no more. I simply do not believe it. I can form no basis, outline, or defence for it. Our articles and formularies, so far as they contain the Catholic tradition, I understand. But beyond that I feel to have no certainty, sometimes no perception of their meaning. I do not rest upon them ; they are no rule to me ; I do not know whether I contradict or strain them. My only foundation of faith is the infallibility of Christ in His Church, and they are not utterances of that voice.

I confess that I feel all this growing to an almost intolerable weight. And events are not so much changing as revealing the position and nature of the

English Church. The Hampden confirmation and the Gorham Appeal show me that the Church of England, supposing it to continue *in esse* a member of the visible Church, is in a position in which it is not safe to stay. But I have always felt that even these would not move me if I could by any means sincerely, and in the sight of God, justify the relation of the Church of England to the Presence of our Lord ruling and teaching upon earth. I am forced to believe that the unity of His Person prescribes the unity of His visible kingdom as one undivided whole, and that numbers are an accident. It was once contained in an Upper Chamber; it may be again; but it must always be one, and indivisible.

On this hangs the guidance of the Spirit of Truth. If in this you can help me by showing me my errors, I shall be guided with a docile and thankful heart. Both your books drive me to the same point. In truth everything as it ceases to be vague, unreal, and negative, as it becomes positive, real, and intelligible, rises up with the faith and infallibility of the Church, which is the Body of Christ and the Temple of the Holy Ghost.

It is in vain for you or for me to say that the English Church holds or teaches as you and I believe. It bears with us because we are silent, or because it is not its practice to guard its own oral doctrine. Does it teach what I have said of the Sacrifice? or will it censure me for so teaching?

These are not cheerful Christmas thoughts, but in the midst of all I find great peace, living in a sphere of faith, and amidst the thoughts and images of which our system gives no expression.'

His friends' influence could not stand for ever against the weight of evidence slowly accumulating, and 'The

Gorham [Judgement] was the Dirige,' as Manning wrote to Allies, for himself and for many others. Mr. Gorham had been ordained by the Bishop of Ely in 1811, though he was known to hold heterodox views of Baptismal Regeneration. In 1847, Henry Philpotts, Bishop of Exeter, a loyal and conscientious High Churchman, refused to institute him to the living of Brampford Speke in the diocese of Exeter, without first examining him as to his orthodoxy. In the course of the examination the Rev. George Gorham denied the doctrine of Baptismal Regeneration, whereupon the Bishop refused to institute him. He took his case to the Court of Arches, and lost it in August 1849. He then appealed from the spiritual authority to the civil, that is from the Court of Arches to the Judicial Committee of the Privy Council, a lay body, which upheld his right to hold his heretical views, and presumably to teach them, as a beneficed clergyman of the Church of England in the diocese of a Bishop who repudiated them.

As Purcell says, the Gorham Judgement, pronounced by the highest court in the land, inflicted on the High Church party and to the Church to which they belonged, a twofold blow. 'It struck out an article in the Creed, and asserted afresh, as an inherent right, the Royal Supremacy in matters of faith.'

The twofold blow broke Manning. Till then he had clung to the belief that the Royal Supremacy was a temporary usurpation, from which the Establishment would soon be freed. James Hope, however, proved to him in letters (from one of which the following extract is taken) that Erastianism is inherent in the Church of England since the Reformation ; a discovery which led to its logical end fifteen months later, when both were received into the Church on the same day by Father Brownbill.

Hope writes on January 29, 1850:

'. . . On what, then, you will ask does my submission rest? I answer, on the belief, weakened but not yet destroyed, that under these heavy burdens, in her solitude and in her bonds, she yet retains the grace of the sacraments and the power of the keys. But if you should ask further, how I am assured of this, I should hardly know what to tell you; and when others have consulted me as to remaining or going, my answer has been, that I dared not advise. How indeed should I: unless I accept the theory of development as fully as Newman? There are many things in the Church of Rome which offer difficulty—unless I turn purely Protestant, it is impossible to justify all that has occurred and does daily occur in England. Many holier and wiser men than I, have deliberated and gone, but many holier and better than I, deliberately remain. It is not, then, with me a matter which reasoning can decide. I have a conviction that I have the means of grace where I am, means far beyond the use I make of them, and till this conviction is removed I dare not venture on a change.

With these feelings my duty towards the Church of England seems to me this: To watch most jealously that her position be not made worse, and to strive, whenever there is an opportunity to improve it; but to conceal her defects, or to seek by theory to escape from the facts of her past and present history (whatever I may have thought formerly), is not a course which I should now pursue.'

His view seems to be that there is nothing new in the submission of the Church to the Crown in this latest case.

'. . . The Delegates sat under royal commission, and the Judicial Committee of the Privy Council represent the same authority. There may have been more bishops concerned as judges at one time than at the other, but the source of jurisdiction was in law the same. This appeal then in point of jurisdiction offers nothing new to my eyes. The subject of it may indeed develop more fully the scandal of the system, but the system has long existed and been an offence in the Church. On both these points then, I would have a change if I could get it, but neither of them disturbs materially the grounds of my allegiance, because that allegiance has for some time rested upon considerations, in which these difficulties had already played their part, and had allowance made for them.

But that the Church should submit to the imposition of heretical doctrine at the hands of the State, so that a heretical clergyman may occupy a benefice in despite of the Bishop under whose charge the souls in his parish have been placed, opens out a very different question.

. . . If a false judgement be pronounced in Gorham's case, and that judgement be acquiesced in by the Church of England, then indeed a new feature will arise for which I find no place; whatever be the mouthpiece which utters the judgement, if the Church does not repudiate it, there is an article of the Creed struck out, and then indeed there will be a weight thrown into the scale against my allegiance, which it would seem ought to prevail.'

The agreement with such a view was so general that a meeting was called together in March 1850, where Pusey, Keble, Dodsworth, and other Tractarian leaders met with Manning, Hope, and Mr. Gladstone in order to draw up a set of resolutions against the Judgement. It was at first found impossible to agree on the form this should take; but after a time a

Declaration was drawn up in Gladstone's house to which twelve of the thirteen present signed their names. Mr. Gladstone at the last moment refused, owing to his position as a Privy Councillor, to do so.

The Declaration ran as follows :

'1. That whatever at the present time be the force of the sentence delivered on appeal in the case of *Gorham v. the Bishop of Exeter*, the Church of England will eventually be bound by the said sentence, unless it shall openly and expressly reject the erroneous doctrine sanctioned thereby.

2. That the remission of original sin to all infants in and by the grace of baptism is an essential part of the article "One Baptism for the remission of sins."

3. That—to omit other questions raised by the said sentence—such sentence, while it does not deny the liberty of holding that article in the sense heretofore received, does equally sanction the assertion that original sin is a bar to the right reception of baptism, and is not remitted, except when God bestows regeneration beforehand by an act of prevenient grace (whereof Holy Scripture and the Church are wholly silent), thereby rendering the benefits of Holy Baptism altogether uncertain and precarious.

4. That to admit the lawfulness of holding an exposition of an article of the Creed contradictory of the essential meaning of that article, is, in truth and in fact, to abandon that article.

5. That, inasmuch as the faith is one and rests upon one principle of authority, the conscious, deliberate, and wilful abandonment of the essential meaning of an article of the Creed destroys the divine foundation upon which alone the entire faith is propounded by the Church.

6. That any portion of the Church which does so abandon the essential meaning of an article, forfeits, not only the Catholic doctrine in that article, but also the office and authority to witness and teach as a member of the universal Church.

7. That by such conscious, wilful, and deliberate act such portion of the Church becomes formally separated from the Catholic body, and can no longer assure to its members the grace of the sacraments and the remission of sins.

8. That all measures consistent with the present legal position of the Church ought to be taken without delay, to obtain an authoritative declaration by the Church of the doctrine of Holy Baptism, impugned by the recent sentence; as, for instance, by praying licence for the Church in Convocation to give legal effect to the decisions of the collective Episcopate on this and all other matters purely spiritual.

9. That, failing such measures, all efforts must be made to obtain from the said Episcopate, acting only in its spiritual character, a re-affirmation of the doctrine of Holy Baptism, impugned by the said sentence.

H. E. Manning, M.A., Archdeacon of Chichester.
Robert I. Wilberforce, M.A., Archdeacon of the East Riding.
Thomas Thorp, B.D., Archdeacon of Bristol.
W. H. Mill, D.D., Regius Professor of Hebrew, Cambridge.
E. B. Pusey, D.D., Regius Professor of Hebrew, Oxford.
John Keble, M.A., Vicar of Hursley.
W. Dodsworth, M.A., Perpetual Curate of Ch. Ch., St. Pancras.

W. J. E. BENNETT, M.A., Perpetual Curate of St. Paul's, Knightsbridge.
HY. W. WILBERFORCE, M.A., Vicar of East Farleigh.
JOHN G. TALBOT, M.A., Barrister-at-Law.
RICHARD CAVENDISH, M.A.
EDWARD BADELEY, M.A., Barrister-at-Law.
JAMES R. HOPE, D.C.L., Barrister-at-Law.'

Ninety-two out of a hundred clergy in the Archdeaconry of Chichester sent a protest against the Judgement to their bishop. Mr. Gladstone attempted to organise one to the Bishop of London, to be signed by laymen only. But the project failed, as it was intended to be a substitute for the joint declaration of clergy and laity which the other opponents of the Judgement considered essential. He and Manning both were desirous of a new Ecclesiastical Court of Appeal, and Gladstone was very anxious to bind all objectors to the Judgement in a covenant 'not to move without two months' notice.' This proposal Manning absolutely refused; in spite, apparently, of Robert Wilberforce's advice that he should accept it.

In a letter to him dated May 22, 1850, he says: 'I have answered that I can in no way accede. I object to all engagement; and I dread exceedingly the temptation to tamper with personal convictions and individual conscience and [to rely on] the support derived from numbers against our light before our Father which seeth in secret. These and many more reasons make my declining final.' He writes again, under date July 10: 'No human power, or persuasion, could induce me to put my hand to any such declaration, especially in combination with men who could sign it in a sense and with an animus so different from my own.'

On the contrary, a second Declaration was drawn up and signed by Manning, Robert Wilberforce, and W. H. Mill, defining and limiting the Royal Supremacy in accordance with what they believed to be Catholic truth. Pusey and Keble were not consulted on this occasion, probably owing to Dodsworth's advice. Dr. Pusey had advanced an argument to prove that the Gorham Judgement did not affect the Faith which, Dodsworth said, had carried 'a multitude of ignoramuses with him'; and he considered that 'if we mean to be faithful to Our Lord's Truth we must break with Pusey and Keble.'

The second Declaration ran:

'Whereas it is required of every person admitted to the order of deacon or priest, and likewise of persons admitted to ecclesiastical offices or academical degrees, to make oath that they abjure,[1] and to subscribe to the three articles of Canon XXXVI, one whereof touches the Royal Supremacy:

And whereas it is now made evident by the late appeal and sentence in the case *Gorham v. the Bishop of Exeter*, and by the judgement of all the courts of common law, that the Royal Supremacy, as defined and established by statute law, invests the Crown with a power of hearing and deciding in appeal all matters, however purely spiritual, of discipline and doctrine:

And whereas to give such power to the Crown is at variance with the divine office of the Universal Church, as prescribed by the law of Christ:

And whereas we, the undersigned clergy and laity of the Church of England, at the time of making the said oath and subscription, did not understand the Royal Supremacy in the sense now ascribed to it by the

[1] There seems to be an omission here.

courts of law, nor have until this present time so understood it, neither have believed that such authority was claimed on behalf of our Sovereign :

Now we do hereby declare :

1st. That we have hitherto acknowledged, and do now acknowledge, the supremacy of the Crown in ecclesiastical matters to be a supreme civil power over all persons and causes in temporal things, and over the temporal accidents of spiritual things.

2nd. That we do not, and in conscience cannot, acknowledge in the Crown the power recently exercised to hear and judge in appeal the internal state or merits of spiritual questions touching doctrine or discipline, the custody of which is committed to the Church alone by the law of Christ.

We therefore, for the sake of our consciences, hereby publicly declare that we acknowledge the Royal Supremacy in the sense above, and in no other.

HENRY EDWARD MANNING, Archdeacon of Chichester.

ROBERT ISAAC WILBERFORCE, Archdeacon of the East Riding.

WILLIAM HODGE MILL, D.D., Regius Professor of Hebrew, Cambridge.'

This is the Declaration on which, it may be remembered, Allies's last hope of remaining in the Church of England hung. It was sent to every beneficed clergyman; to all laymen who had taken the oath of Supremacy ; to colleges and to newspapers ; inviting signatures in the hope that the religious feeling of the country would be roused, and the Bishops forced to take action. The issue at the moment appeared to be : who is the Head of the Church of England ? But 'a much broader question,' as happened in Newman's case, soon presented itself to many minds. That question is : Who is the Head of the Holy Catholic and Apostolic Church throughout the world ?

On February 10, 1930, the *Morning Post*, a paper which no one can accuse of romanizing tendencies, published a leading article on the Pope's recent action in face of the Bolshevist attack on Christianity. It expresses its grateful recognition of the 'high authentic note' in the Papal pronouncement ; which it contrasts with those of the non-Catholic religious leaders. And the article is headed THE POPE LEADS CHRISTENDOM. That is the answer to the question of Supremacy which Manning was now given grace to find and to act upon.

But, save for a small minority, the answer of the clergy and laity of the Church of England was a silence that gave consent to the Royal jurisdiction in things spiritual. They acquiesced in the choice forced on their Elizabethan forefathers ; whose statesmen said, like the Israelites of old, 'Nay, but a king shall reign over us' ; and were content to give their consciences into the custody of His Majesty's Privy Council. Out of 20,000 clergymen, about 1800 signed the Declaration ; and Manning 'saw that the game was up. It was a fair test fully applied,' he said, 'and it received next to no response.' Purcell tells us that : 'The result of this appeal was a signal failure. The spirited Protest against the Royal Supremacy fell flat. The vast and overwhelming bulk of the clergy of the Church of England, like the bishops, by their silence or acquiescence acknowledged the supremacy of the Crown in matters of faith—the original sin of the Reformation.'

This was the beginning of the end for Manning. He had done his best to lull his own misgivings and those of his penitents all these years by arguments which grew less and less convincing. In his Charge after the Hampden appointment he had even attempted to justify the action of the Bishops on the impossibly weak ground that Hampden's Lectures had not been condemned by the whole Church. For eleven difficult years he had faithfully followed the advice Newman gave him in 1839, when for the first time it had become his duty to deal with 'the Roman problem' and he wrote to Newman for guidance in doing so. It seems unfair to criticise him for acting, not only as Newman himself did during a similar stage of progress but under his direction, so the letter containing Newman's advice is given below. The line he suggests is almost identical with that taken at the present day by those, often themselves uneasy, who feel it their duty to discourage Anglo-Catholic 'secessions to Rome.'

Newman writes: '. . . I am conscious that we are raising longings and tastes which we are not allowed to supply—and till our bishops and others give scope to the development of Catholicism externally and wisely, we *do* tend to make impatient minds seek it where it has ever been, in Rome. I think that, whenever the time comes that secession to Rome takes place, for which we must not be unprepared, we must boldly say to the Protestant section of our Church—"*You* are the cause of this; you must concede; you must conciliate; you must meet the age; you must make the Church more efficient, more suitable to the needs of the heart, more equal to the external. Give us more services, more vestments and decorations in worship; give us monasteries; give us the signs of an apostle, the pledges that the Spouse of Christ is among us." Till then you will have continual secessions to Rome. . . . This is, I confess, my view, I think nothing but *patience* and dutifulness can keep us in the

Church of England—and remaining in it is a test whether we have these graces. If then your friend is attracted to Rome by the exercise of devotion which it provides, I should press on her the duty of remaining in the calling in which God has found her ; and enlarge upon the doctrine of 1 Corinthians vii., also I think you must press on her the prospect of *benefiting* the poor Church, through which she has her baptism, by stopping in it. Does she not care for the souls all around her, steeped and stifled in Protestantism ? How will she best care for them : by indulging her own feelings in the communion of Rome, or in denying herself and staying in sackcloth and ashes to do them good ? Will she persuade more of her brethren by leaving them, or by continuing with them ? If, however, she takes the grounds of *distrusting* the English Church, doubting its catholicity, and the like, then I suppose you must retort with the denial of the Cup—the doctrine of purgatory as practically held—the non-proof of the Church's infallibility—the anathema, etc., with the additional reflection that she is *taking a step*, and, therefore, should have some abundant evidence on the side of that step (and ought one not seriously to consider whether accidental circumstances have not determined her—disgust at some particular thing, faith in some particular person, etc.?). The step is either a clear imperative duty, or it is a sin. On the other hand, can she deny that the hand of God is with our Church, even granting for *argument's sake* Rome has some things which we have not ? Is it dead ? has it the signs of death ? Has it more than the signs of disease ? Has it not lasted through very troublous times ? Has it not from time to time marvellously revived, when it seemed to be losing all faith in holiness ? Is it *to be given up ?*—for her step would be giving it up—would be saying, "I wish it swept away, and the Roman developed in its territory," not "I wish it reformed—I wish it corrected —I wish Rome and it to be one."'

But now that last and hardest question called for immediate answer from him, as it had in the end from Newman. Must it 'be given up'? Must he bring himself to say of the work which had so engrossed him and of the Church which he had loved and served: 'I wish it swept away?'

One loophole remained. This was to find out from history whether the Royal Supremacy was inherent in the Establishment or not. If not, he must strive to rouse others from their inertia, and unite with all loyal Churchmen to free the Established Church from the State's usurpation of her rights. But if his researches should prove that the majority against his views were obedient to the State's lawful Authority over the Church of England, then there was only one answer to the question, and that answer was 'Yes.'

The task lasted six months, as the letters he wrote and received during this period show. By May 1850 he had come to see that 'the Reformation was a Tudor statute carried by violence and upheld by political power; and now that the State is divorcing the Anglican Church, it is dissolving'; and to ask, 'What principle of unity, of coherence, do we possess? What principle do we recognise as Divine? The Bible, the Prayer-book, private judgment and parliamentary establishment seem to me to make up the English Church. It has no idea, principle, unity, theory, or living voice, or will.'

The attitude of Keble and Pusey, whom he once thought too iconoclastic as regards 'Reformed doctrine' now alarmed him into 'pressing onward.' They both seemed to him 'to have given up the Divine Tradition as the supreme authority, and to apply private judgement to antiquity, as Protestants do to Holy Scripture.'

On June 15, 1850, he writes to Robert Wilberforce: 'I seem to see a providential intention in all that is befalling. Our past work, founded on passive, wide-spread confidence in easy times, is gone, we are both mistrusted and marked; but I believe a greater weight is on us both. We are identified with a great doctrine, and a great principle; and all we can give, is given to spread and deepen their hold on people. Individuals in numbers are turning up, and coming to you and to me. . . . We are fairly released from Protestantism, Rationalism, Anglicanism, and the like. If unity is ever to be restored, and the influx of the universal authority of faith again to support truth, and the Church of England, we are making way for it. Unknown to ourselves, we are thrust into a position which in Tudor days would have been intermediate; who knows, but that in these it may be the condition of obtaining the object of our daily prayers?'

And on August 5 he writes:

'Dear Robert,

I am suffering much. I have no home sorrows, as you;[1] but the Church of England has from me what, if I had a home, would perhaps be there. And I see nothing before me. If I stay I shall end a simple mystic, like Leighton. God is a spirit, and has no visible kingdom, church, or sacraments. Nothing will ever entangle me again in Protestantism, Anglican or otherwise.

[1] Archdeacon Wilberforce's wife was so distressed at his possible conversion that her health was suffering very much in consequence.

But that is to reject Christendom—its history and its witness for God.

You will see from the enclosed that things seem near.

Ever yours very affectionately,

H. E. M.'

The next letter is of interest, as it was written to him by Allies three days before his own reception into the Church and Purcell says that 'Mr. Allies's work on the Papacy, clear, logical and learned,' was not without its effect on Manning.

Allies writes:

'LAUNTON,

5th September, 1850.

MY DEAR ARCHDEACON MANNING,

I have finished my book, of which I hope you will see the results, such as they are, next week. Tell me how the argument strikes you. It is the result of seven long years of perplexity, in which I can safely say that Anglicanism has never given me one thread of guidance or a little finger of support. Now, I feel that I am passing from the dead to the living—from her who would divide the child that was not hers in half, to the true mother who yearns for her offspring. I go, *D.V.*, to Birmingham on Monday, to put myself in the hands of J. H. N.

I was rather surprised to hear of Lord Feilding, but it has cheered me up immensely.

I am quite unable to make out what is the practical drift either of your pamphlet or your circular;[1] but if you have really the faintest hope of Anglicanism it astonishes me.

[1] Manning's Tract on the Judgement, 'Appellate Jurisdiction of the Crown in Matters Spiritual,' published as a Letter to the Bishop of Chichester, July 2, 1850; and the Declaration drawn up by Manning, R. Wilberforce, and Mill.

But do not forget to give me your prayers, especially in this last struggle. God has given me certainly the strongest, both intellectual and moral, conviction of the thorough dishonesty and unreality of Anglicanism as a Church system ; and He has turned, what long seemed an obstacle scarcely to be surmounted on the side of Rome, into the most assured proof. I should dread some great misfortune if I did not obey His calling.

Ever yours affectionately,

T. M. Allies.'

Manning's letter on September 19 to Robert Wilberforce shows how Allies earned the right to be called a leader in the path to Rome, and also how greatly Manning's apparent vacillation was due to the fears expressed by Robert Wilberforce, under whose direction he seems to have put himself.

'Kippington,

19*th September*, 1850.

My dearest Robert,

You have been much in my mind. I do not know how to resist the conviction—

1. That the Church of England is in schism.

2. That it has therefore lost its power to preserve its own internal unity of doctrine and discipline.

3. That it cannot define, judge, or pronounce with the authority of the universal Church, while it is separate and in collision with the universal Church.

4. That the late events have not changed our position, but *revealed it*, and that they who see it are bound to submit themselves to the universal Church. The utter weakness of all that it set up against their conclusions turns into positive argument in behalf of them.

Allies has just printed a mass of historical evidence

which it would be immoral to put aside. He has deformed his book by a few things, which will make such minds as our dear brother[1] treat it unfairly. So truth suffers, and schisms are perpetrated. My dear Robert, I feel as if my time were drawing near, and that, like death, it will be, if it must be, alone. But I shrink with all the love and fear of my soul. Pray for me.

Ever yours most affectionately,

H. E. M.'

A week later he reassures him.

'*Most Private.*

44 CADOGAN PLACE,
26th September, 1850.

MY DEAREST ROBERT,

I have no thought of a hasty step. All you say of the immoral effect of precipitation I feel, and will be guided by you, for your sake and for my own. If I knew that I should die this day six months I should speak as if life were over and death near. This was the meaning of my last letter.

The state of my mind is a settled conviction that it must end in only one way. I feel that the Church of England, by every principle of Scripture, tradition, and history, is a human society, more ecclesiastical and mediæval than the Kirk, but equally *separate* from the universal Church. This conviction grows on me continually, harmonising all phenomena of our state. I seem therefore to have no doubt how it must end. But six months would still be *soon* in such a death.

Now, dear Robert, advise me. I have thought of going abroad for the winter, as a means of withdrawing

[1] Samuel Wilberforce, Bishop of Oxford, Manning's brother-in-law.

from collision, and from embarrassing others. Gladstone's going, and the English winter would be reason *ad exteros*.

It would give me time for last reflections and dying thoughts, and a *locus penitentiæ*, if, "which God avert," I be deluded.

Tell me how this seems to you.

I have heard from our dearest Henry.[1] He writes calmly, and, I believe, his mind and character will be confirmed and raised by what he has done. Dearest Robert, to be parted from you would be one of my keenest trials; may it never be, and, I believe, it cannot. Surely we want faith, and do not trust ourselves enough to the kingdom which is not of this world. I seem to see how we are called to suffer for faith, and for the elect's sake. We have spoken for truth, and written for truth; we must now act for truth, and bear for truth. Nothing but the suffering of the many can save the Church of England from running down the inclined plane of all separate bodies. It is for it that we are testifying, though it will not see or know it. Newman's going has preserved life.'

The last paragraph shows that the idea which Newman had once suggested to him, that by staying in the Church of England her children could save her, still lingered in Manning's mind. But 'the suffering of the many' loyal to a wrong system will not put it right; and in a letter of October 18, which Feast in his confusion of mind he gives to SS. Simon and Jude instead of S. Luke, he says he not only believes that

[1] Henry Wilberforce, brother of Archdeacon Wilberforce and the Bishop of Oxford, who had just become a Catholic. After Mrs. R. Wilberforce's death, her husband was also received, but died within two years of his reception, just before his Ordination to the Priesthood, in 1856.

'nothing will be done, but that nothing can.' His reasons seem unanswerable.

'LAVINGTON,
Feast of SS. Simon and Jude,
18*th October*, 1850.

MY DEAREST ROBERT,

I hope my letter did not add to your distress. Unless some new and peremptory reason should arise, I will do as you desire. God grant that nothing may part us. It would be to me a great and lasting sorrow, and unspeakably increase the fear and anxiety with which I weigh the thoughts of our present trial. The pain I have to bear, which you have not equally, is the cruel imputations upon honesty and honour. These wound me. They could not move me if I were not conscious that I have no hope for the Church of England. I not only believe that nothing will be done, but that nothing can. The fault seems to me to be in the original position; suppose the Royal Supremacy reduced to our limits, and the Church of England empowered to judge, and declare finally in matter of faith: the Thirty-nine Articles declare local Churches to be fallible, and the English Church is not only fallible, but irreconcilably divided in doctrines of faith, e.g. Regeneration, the Real Presence, Sacrifice, Priesthood, the Church.

This seems to me to reduce us to the necessity and to the duty of acknowledging our original position to be false and wrong. But this acknowledgment who will make? Even Pusey's tone is otherwise.

I do not feel what you say of condemning a Church which has such men as Keble in it. *I must condemn it, whosoever be in it* [italics mine].

Postscript. Do you see the line of the *Guardian* in the

first leading article? It is dreary and deadly work. Insular Anglicanism and partisan movement seem to be their highest aim. Let me hear from you what you did yesterday. I had a few words with Keble. I said, "I fear we differ in this. I might feel myself bound to submit to the Roman Church; you would not." He said, "I could not. I could not say my prayers there." Does he mean that Rome is the synagogue of Satan? for that is the only place in which I should think we could not pray. Does he not believe our "fallen sister" to be a part of the Temple of God? And if so, does he believe that Rome has erred in matters *de fide?* And would anything less sustain his words? I mused over your strange medley yesterday. I suppose you had at least three elements which will never hold together.

Ever your very affectionate,

H. E. M.'

Dodsworth now strengthened Manning's doubts by disclosing the extent of his own. He most pertinently asks if it is defensible to subscribe to the Thirty-nine Articles, or to continue subscription 'substantially on the ground of their comprehensiveness or indefiniteness on the theory of Tract 90, or some kindred one.' The question which arises in his mind is this: 'When we come to think of what subscription is, and the *nature of those truths* which are dealt with, is it defensible so to deal with such truths—is it enough to say only, we *don't deny* the Real Presence—the guidance of the Holy Spirit, the Church Catholic? Are we not doing our part to make Christian verities open questions?'

This he wrote in August, just after hearing the news of Mrs. Henry Wilberforce's reception, which he was right in thinking would be followed by her husband's before long. Later on he writes: 'I really cannot subscribe these Articles again. Pray tell me, now that you know so much of my mind, whether you think that I ought to communicate any more in the Church of England. Is not the actual institution of Gorham a decisive point? Is it not a crisis in which our Lord's truth is in jeopardy?'

In October the Bishop of Oxford laments the result of Manning's historical study in a letter to Mr. Gladstone, in which he complains that: 'It is, as you say, the background of historical enquiry where our paths part.' This was not surprising, for to the Bishop's dismay Manning had 'gone back into those early times' when 'Catholic usages' began. He had moreover, as the Bishop further deplores, 'fully accustomed his mind to them till the system that wants them seems to him incomplete and uncatholic, and one that has them the wiser and holier and more Catholic for having them, until he can excuse to a great degree their practical corruptions, and justify all together their doctrinal rightness.'

Against this background of historical enquiry the post-Reformation Establishment stood out in a new light to him. In a long letter to Robert Wilberforce, dated October 22, 1850, he tells him: 'I fain would hold on for many reasons, but I feel to be in a false position. I am not afraid of seeming to fly from a storm. . . . The true and over-ruling reason is that I am so deeply convinced that the Church is infallible through the guidance of the Holy Spirit, and that the Church of England is not under that guidance, as to leave me day by day less choice. I will try to put shortly what I mean:

The present state of the Church of England is a proof to me that a local church in a state of separation from the universal Church, cannot declare or preserve the

Faith. For 300 years we have been in a position which, whether now changed or revealed, is no longer tenable on any laws of the Church of Christ. I believe it is a revelation of a position untenable *ab initio*. For this Royal Supremacy is in principle as old as Henry the VIII. Gladstone's view is to me a clever theory. But all facts and histories are against it. Goode is right, I believe, to the letter. The Crown is supreme judge. The authority of the living and universal Church has been shut out for 300 years ; we have fallen into a functional impotence, and the local Church has not, neither can have, any other guide or support. Be our paper doctrines what they may, we have had contradictory bishops, priests, and people, for 300 years on baptism, the real presence, the sacrifice, absolution, succession, priesthood, rule of faith, the very constitution, and authority and identity of the Church. All this is 300 years old, this is no change. It may be an aggravation, but no more.

Now, I confess that I feel that nothing short of the re-entrance of this authority of the living Church universal can restore the functions of the Church of England. We are in material heresy and that throws light on our separation, and I believe we are in schism. With this feeling, growing daily with a conscious variance of reason, faith, and conscience, against the Royal Supremacy as in our oath and subscription, and against the anti-Roman articles, I feel driven to believe that I can delay no longer without violation of truth towards God and man. Do, dearest Robert, weigh this more gravely. Do not argue of expediencies and effects, but look at the facts of the case. Take your own view of the Article against Transubstantiation. You do not condemn the truth. All the world does, and believes you do, so long as you continue under subscription.

I am full of dread lest the truth of conscience should be lost by waiting and listening to the suggestions of flesh and blood. May the Divine Spirit guide us in this hour of trial, that we may be true to Him and His inspirations.'

A fortnight later his duty was at last made clear to him; when as Archdeacon of Chichester he was required to convene his archdeaconry against the Papal Bull which restored the Catholic hierarchy in England. The two letters which follow explain the situation.

'LAVINGTON,
7th November, 1850.

MY DEAR ROBERT,

. . . My object in writing is to ask your prompt advice on an urgent difficulty this moment arisen.

I have two requisitions to convene this archdeaconry against the act of the Pope.

The course I think of is to do as I am required. To let the whole proceeding pass, and at the end, to say: That I felt bound to act ministerially in convening them, but that I could not unite [with them]. For, as a secular question, I thought the Acts of 1828–29 require this religious freedom; as in Ireland and the Colonies, so in England.

As against the Crown, no wrong is done; the Queen has no jurisdiction in spirituals. As against the Church of England, I admit that it is an aggression. But that I am convinced that the Royal Supremacy has for 300 years put the English episcopate in the wrong; and that it is to be righted, not by opposing the Universal Church, but by reconciliation on just and lawful terms. And that I cannot, therefore, join in any act which does not recognise that principle. But I feel this to be inconsistent with the whole Anglican position. Also it is asking for a condemnation of the Reformation.

Moreover I may be fairly asked to address our bishop, declaring adherence and obedience to his jurisdiction. This I cannot do. It is like subscribing the 39 Articles again. But if I cannot do this, how can I bear office under him, and over his clergy ?

All this constitutes a *peremptory* cause, such as my last letter supposed possible.

My own advice to another man would be this :

1. Resign, but ask the bishop to allow you to keep your purpose in silence, till the day of meeting.

2. Meet the clergy.

3. State openly, and in a manful way, your reasons for not acting with them.

4. Justify your reasons by declaring your resignation.

5. Take leave of them so far as your office is concerned with all affection.

Let me have your mind as soon as possible. *Non hoc sine Numine.* The moves on the check[1] board seem to me to speak with the voice of a man, or rather, with a voice mighty in operation.

Ever yours affectionately,

H. E. M.'

A week later he reports what actually took place.

'LAVINGTON,
15th November, 1850.

MY DEAR ROBERT,

Tuesday, I was obliged to see the bishop, time pressing, and the clergy.

I told the bishop—

[1] Chess ? or checks for draughts or backgammon ?

1. That I was convinced of the unlawfulness by Christ's law of the Royal Supremacy.

2. That I believed it to be the instrument which had severed the Church of England from the Church Universal, and still keeps it apart.

3. That this act of the Pope is the legitimate consequence—the English Episcopate being lost to the Universal Church.

4. That I could not oppose the Pope's act, on any principle which did not tend to restore the Church of England's communion with the Universal Church.

5. That I knew the views of the clergy to be different and that I could not share their proceedings.

I therefore requested—

1. Either to resign at once :

2. Or, to call the meeting ministerially, and to state my dissent and resignation.

He desired me to take the latter course, except declaring my resignation, and desired me to consider of it. So the case will proceed.

But I feel that my foot is in the river. It is cold, and my heart is sad. But where faith can act, I seem to feel that the world has subdued the Church of England to itself, and that the Kingdom of Our Lord is not from hence. I do not say one word to urge you, dearest Robert, God forbid ; I know your heart is as mine, and I have gone through your present state.

Only do nothing against what may be found at last to be the Will and Presence of Our Lord. Give me your prayers.

Ever your own affectionately,

H. E. M.'

Mr. Gladstone had already written several long letters in the hope of counteracting the effect of

Manning's historical study. He now made two more attempts to bring him back to the views they had once shared. Purcell uses them in support of the Double Voice theory, so it seems only fair to quote them here.

In the first, dated November 5, 1850, Gladstone expresses his surprise at the undermining of 'the historical and theological foundations' of Manning's Anglican belief which has taken place. He goes on to say: 'I do not know whether you have forgotten, I am certain that I never shall forget a conversation in which, after your return from the Continent, you detailed to me (between the Pimlico quarter and my house) what in communion with death, and the region beyond death, you had not newly but freshly learned. It was in conjunction with an increased disinclination to dwell on corruptions in the Church of Rome, an increased aversion to mere nationality in the Church of England, that you most fervently declared to me, how beyond expression solemn and firm was your assurance, brought from the region you had then been treading, not of the mercy of God to those in invincible ignorance, a mercy reaching to every religious profession, and to *none*, but of the unmoved and immovable title of the Church of England to her share in the one divine and catholic inheritance. Have you *really* unlearned those lessons? It cannot be; and if it were, I, for one, should have this mournful idea driven home upon me, as I have long felt it of Newman, the destiny of that man has been to do little comparatively for the Church of Rome, much against the whole ethical grounds and the constructure of belief in Divine Revelation.'

Manning evidently wrote to correct his memory of a conversation which had taken place two years before, and to state what he had really intended to convey to

Mr. Gladstone's mind. This attempt completely failed. The next letter, dated December 20, says:

'We are sadly, strangely at issue on the *facts* of the conversation soon after your illness. If I have any one clear recollection in my mind, it is that your assurances then did not relate at all to God's mercy to those who faithfully follow their light, be it what it may, but to your perfect sense of security in the Church of England from its objective character.'

He then attempts to recall him 'from sentiments which appear to me partial and (forgive me) even morbid, to former convictions singularly deliberate, singularly solemn, as entitled to exercise a higher authority over your conduct in this hour (as you truly call it) of trial.'

This letter also ends with a shaft aimed at Newman, whose influence he evidently blames for the many conversions to Rome which caused so many of the flower of the Movement to leave it about this time.

Mr. Gladstone persisted in believing his own impression of his friend's views, and did not keep the letter in which Manning attempted to refresh his memory and correct his mistaken impression. The result was that nearly fifty years later, after the Cardinal's death, Purcell relied upon Mr. Gladstone's unsupported memory of words spoken long ago, though it is clear that Manning tried to correct the impression they made on him as soon as he knew what it was. From this 'strong oral evidence' (as Gladstone himself chose to consider it) of Manning's view of the Anglican position in 1848, he drew a characteristic inference which those prejudiced against the Cardinal take as a proof of the 'double voice' theory. It is much to be regretted that Mr. Gladstone did not keep Manning's letter in support of the 'strong oral evidence' of his own memory on a point which he evidently considered of great importance in Manning's history. The one-sided account has been used by Purcell to Manning's disadvantage in a way which seems hardly fair.

Now come letters to Manning's own family, which ought to make the most suspicious of Purcell's readers believe in the honesty of his motives for the decisive action he had now resolved to take.

He writes to his sister Mrs. Austen, on November 18, 1850, telling her his intention of going abroad for the winter, as if he is not at Lavington (which he was now making up his mind to leave) he 'had better be fairly away'; and goes on:

'. . . My last letter, I fear, gave you no comfort. But, dearest Caroline, I dare not betray the truth. Come what may, let me only be faithful to Him whose faith and kingdom are wounded, and, what is worse, betrayed by those who love ease and this world—peace with men and popularity rather than to suffer for His sake. I do not say this to censure them, nor to ask your assent, but to express my own mind. Whether I be right or wrong in this great trial which has come upon the face of the land, He will know that my heart's desire is to be faithful to Him. And then all is well. "A little while," and in His light we shall see light. And all trouble and trial will be over.'

To his eldest brother he writes on November 21:

'My dearest Frederick,

Our last correspondence and conversation happily renders it needless for me to enter again into the subjects which gave to us both so much pain. No words will express what I have felt at the thought of distressing you whom I have loved from my earliest life. But where duties, especially of conscience and religion, come in, I can never forget the words, "He that loveth father or mother more than Me is not worthy of Me." It is this alone that has supported, and still does support, me in the trial I have had to go through.

I have weighed earthly happiness against what seems to me to be plain duty, and after great and prolonged suffering my deliberate choice is to do what I believe right, at the loss, if it must be so, of all I love best in life. I will enter into no details in which it might pain you to follow me, and will only say that I have requested the Bishop of Chichester to accept my resignation.

And now, dearest brother, I will ask of you one kindness. Do not write to me more than the words that you will pray for me. My love to you and to Edmunda make anything more a new pain to what I bear already. May God ever bless you both with His abundant grace, and unite us once more, where all are one, even as He is one.'

His request for no more in reply to his news than the assurance of prayers for him was not granted—far from it—so he writes again on November 26:

'My dearest Frederick,

May God reward you for all your brotherly love and sorrow for me conveyed in your two kind letters. He alone knows how I suffer in giving you pain; and if anything I could do would spare you I would refuse nothing except to act against conscience, which would grieve you more than any errors into which I might fall.

After our meeting in the summer I refrained from writing to you, believing that silence would be more acceptable to you than the pain of correspondence.

I would have written gladly if I had thought it would have been according to your wish.

And now, dearest brother, all my mind shall be open to you whensoever you desire it. And it would be a consolation to me that you should truly know what my convictions and reasons are. The reasons requiring the resignation of the archdeaconry involve also the resignation of all that I hold under the same oath and subscription. For my future I have made no decision. When I know what it will be you shall have an instant communication of it.'

With great patience he tries to carry out his promise of full and open explanation in a letter from 44 Cadogan Place, on December 5:

'My dearest Brother,

Our conversation last night was disconcerted [*sic*], it may be through my fault: if so, forgive me. Let me, however, ask you to put this note with the papers in your book of Extracts.

I believe that I shall satisfy you before long of the perfect identity of principle by which my belief has been governed from 1835 to 1850, and that what you thought to be inconsistency is in truth expansion. But I am so little concerned to defend myself, that I will, for this time, grant all you say and be held inconsistent. This would be a strong reason for self-mistrust and prolonged examination and re-examination. But in the *matter of fact* it proves nothing. It is simple *personality*.

The point to be proved is the point of *fact*, i.e. that whereas I was *right* in 1838–40, I am *wrong* in 1850. For instance—Suppose that in 1840 you had written a book to show that the Evening Hymn was not by Bishop Ken. And in 1850 to show that it was Bishop Ken. If I had said " You are inconsistent," you would have said "Granted; but look at the facts and the evidence. I was wrong in 1840. I am right in 1850."

If I had said "No; you are *inconsistent*, I won't look," you would say again "Granted; but look at the *fact*. My inconsistency cannot alter the *fact*. I mistook this and that proof; I was ignorant of this and that evidence. I did not perceive this or that error in my own statement. I did my sum *wrong*. Go over it and prove it. The fault is mine, but the sum bears proof now."

This is what I wished you to see. I was making no self-defence. You shall keep me under the harrow as a toad until I have convinced your calm sense. "Let God be true, and every man a liar," much more let me be scourged as inconsistent. But His Truth is not mine but His.'

His family's opposition, however, could do no more now than delay him. His mind was made up. A few months before, he had tried to hold Allies back after the Gorham Judgement, by saying to him: 'Samuel waited till God called him three times. This is not your third call,' a remark which may help to explain why he waited so long. But the third call, the 'anti-Roman uproar' raised against the Hierarchy, had succeeded the Hampden appointment and the Gorham Judgement; and the following letters written in the middle of December 1850, show that all he now needed was strength to make that plunge into the unknown from which the bravest may shrink. One to Robert Wilberforce has a note of persuasion running through it; to James Hope he speaks as to one literally in the same boat with him, waiting for courage to leap into the water to sink or swim.

In the first of these letters (December 14, 1850) he

tells Robert Wilberforce : ‘ Since we met I have done little but try to soothe my kindred. They are all most kind, except my eldest brother, who has a way of his own. I have taken no steps beyond writing to James Hope, who will, I trust, be with us through all. My wish has been to keep perfectly quiet, and, for reading, I have done little but *De Maistre* on the Pope—a wonderful book.

I must say that when human sorrow subsides and leaves my judgement clear, I seem to have no doubt that the Church of England is in schism, and that the final consequences of schism, misfortune, disorder, division, and loss of divine faith, are upon it.

We have either bravely or obstinately shut our eyes, and lived as if the history of the last three hundred years were either perished or in our favour. In truth it is notorious and against us. The reign of Edward the Sixth and Elizabeth, and the Protestant Settlement of 1688, ought to have opened our eyes.

Your book on the Incarnation stands alone among us, and you had to borrow and steal to make it. The true owner is over the water ; and all the consequences are living and real in his house, but in ours do not exist. To take one example—the altar, and all that issues from it and returns to it. . . . Indeed I think that if you and I had been born out of the English Church we should not have doubted for so much as a day where the one Church is. . . .

. . . It [Rome] has unity, continuity, harmony, integrity, and what have we ? Let me hear from you ; and believe me always yours very affectionately,

H. E. M.’

In the letter to James Hope he enters into no reasons for doing the duty which they both now see lies before them. As they 'both feel that the argument is complete,' there can be no doubt as to which of the two alternatives confronting them they must choose.

'*Private.*

44 Cadogan Place,
11*th December*, 1850.

My dear Hope,

I feel with you that the argument is complete. For a long time I nevertheless felt a fear lest I should be doing an act morally wrong.

This fear has passed away, because the Church of England has revealed itself in wrong to make one fear more on the other side. It remains therefore as an act of the will. But this, I suppose, it must be. And in making it, I am helped by the fact that to remain under our changed or revealed circumstances would also be an act of the will, and that not in conformity with, but in opposition to, intellectual real convictions; and the intellect is God's gift and our instrument in attaining knowledge of His will. . . . It would be to me a very great happiness if we could act together, and our names go together in the first publication of the fact.

The subject which has brought me to my present convictions is the perpetual office of the Church, under divine guidance, in expounding the faith and deciding controversies. And the book which forces this on me is Melchior Camus's *Loci Theologici*. It is a long book, but so orderly that you may get the whole outline with care. Mohler's *Symbolik* you know.

But, after all, Holy Scripture seems to me in a new light, as Ephes. iv. 4–17. This seems to preclude the notion of a divided unity, which is in fact Arianism in the matter of the Church.

I entirely feel what you say of the alternatives. It is Rome, or license of thought and will.

Ever yours affectionately,

H. E. M.'

Robert Wilberforce, probably hampered by his wife's distress at the alternative Manning and Hope contemplated, now planned a scheme with others like-minded to form a 'Free Church' in England, as the Presbyterians discontented with their Kirk had just done in Scotland. Manning's refusal to consider joining in it was put wittily and to the point. 'No, three hundred years ago we left a good ship for a boat; I am not going to leave the boat for a tub.'

Yet it now became more and more clear to him that his days in the boat were numbered. One by one his most trusted friends were leaving it; and those who remained were, as he plainly saw, unaware of its unseaworthiness. And close by, while the great waves which threatened to swamp his boat broke harmlessly against her impregnable sides, the Tall Ship rode at anchor; and the Star of Truth her captains had been given 'to steer her by,' nearly nineteen centuries ago, shone undimmed by mists of error. Several of those once in the boat with him had found courage to leap overboard and swim to her for safety. More and more he felt sure that they had done right. But the waves ran high between, and his courage left him when he thought of breasting them. It was Laprimaudaye, his curate in the past and his Anglican confessor, still his intimate friend, who now did him a crowning act of friendship by nerving him to take the plunge. Faith had given him courage to trust himself to the waves which so daunted Manning, and instead of overwhelming him they had swept him safely on board. In the letter of joy he wrote to Manning he begged him to take courage and follow him without delay.

Manning's reply was :

'44 Cadogan Place,
3rd January, 1851.

My dearest Friend,

What can I write to you? My heart is too full, for your sake, and for my own, I feel to have so much share in you, that your act seems mine. God grant it be His will! Let me hear from you, calmly and truly, as you have ever loved me, and been to me a brother indeed, be so now.

The world will censure you for reckless haste. I do not. I know the long, mature, and suffering preparation you have gone through; the haste is only external.

I long to hear how your dear wife is. Give her my love, pray write to me. . . .

Truly it is not in man that walketh to direct his steps. May God keep you both in His hands, from all evil; and unite you to Himself. Believe me, my dearest friend, yours in true love,

H. E. M.'

Laprimaudaye's answer evidently contained the encouragement and guidance which Manning asked and his experience entitled him to give. It is not quoted, but Manning's reply makes that clear. It also makes clear what Purcell seems never to have guessed at—that 'tout savoir, c'est tout comprendre.' Manning's own 'long long trial of mind' helped him 'not for a moment to feel what some may have hinted'; and 'whatsoever adverse appearances' may have presented themselves to others did not blind one who had dearly bought his power to see the true aspect beneath. The necessity for 'long, mature and suffering preparation' is clear to him who has undergone it; it is the world outside which sees and censures what appears to it as either 'reckless haste' or the double-voiced counsels of a vacillating guide.

The letter runs:

'KIPPINGTON,
28th January, 1851.

MY KIND AND LOVING FRIEND,

Your letter has just reached me and touched my heart. Be sure that I feel for you with all my heart and that your words are sacred. Long long trial of mind tells me all that you mean.

After all intellectual processes there remains a step which can be taken only by the will. And in this step the fears you speak of come in. Moreover, it is the nature (or caprice) of the human mind that the side to which we are actually moved seems for a time to be weakest; we know its weak points, and doubtful points by contact; and the opposite conceals its weak points under certain prominent points of strength. I can feel this even now ἐμεταιχμίω between the two hosts.

No, I do not for a moment feel what some may have hinted. I know your mind, its texture, and its convictions, and I believe that, under whatsoever adverse appearances, the mind and intellectual work has been continuous and mature. . . .

The words, that last Sunday night, I do indeed remember; and I believe they will never be forgotten. I am where you left me, at least outwardly. If I do not say more, it is only from a rule by which I have tried to govern myself—never to say what I am not prepared to do. But I may say to you, and you alone, that I cannot think to be long as I am now. I have been dealing one by one with the many bonds of duty which bind me on every side, unravelling some and breaking others. I owe still some acts of deliberation to particular persons. When they are discharged I shall believe that I stand before God all alone, with no responsibility but for my own soul. And then I trust I shall not be wanting to the inspirations of His will. Pray for me, dearest friend, I have been suffering deeply. But God's will be done. . . .

I have not much to say from our dear home and flock, they know what you have done. But Maria says they are very sorry, and speak very kindly. What tender affections, and visions of beauty and of peace move to and fro under that hillside where I see it rise in memory. Nothing in this life, except the Altar, can ever again be to me as Lavington. Poor old Scutt is at his rest, and I have a sort of craving to number him still, and the lingering old of my flock, among them that sleep before they count me as their pastor no more. But once more, God's will be done.

Give my true and affectionate love to your wife and to your children.

Ever yours, dear brother, in His love,

H. E. M.'

The reference to old Scutt shows a tenderheartedness which may help to neutralise some of Purcell's hints at a lack of it in Manning. Scutt was an old shepherd at Lavington who had greatly valued his ministrations, and the sort of craving which Manning felt, to wait till all 'the lingering old' of his flock were beyond hearing of what might distress them, could only be felt by one who loved the souls under his care.

A letter he wrote to Lord Campden[1] about this time,

[1] Later Earl of Gainsborough and a convert.

in answer to one telling Manning of his reception, throws more light on his reasons for delaying so long. He says: 'Since we parted I have been through deep sorrow. My convictions had long been formed that I could not continue to hold on, under oath and subscription, but obedience to others made me wait. When this anti-Roman uproar broke forth I resolved at once. I could lift no hand in so bad a quarrel either to defend the Royal Supremacy, which had proved itself indefensible, or against a supremacy which the Church for 600 years obeyed. I, therefore, at once went to the Bishop of Chichester and requested him to receive my resignation. He was most kind in desiring me to take time, but I, after a few days, wrote my final resignation. What my human affections have suffered in leaving my only home and flock, where for eighteen years my whole life as a man has been spent, no words can say; but God gave me grace to lay it all at the foot of the cross, where I am ready, if it be His will, to lay whatsoever yet remains to me. Let me have your prayers for light and strength.'

The 'obedience to others' which he says made him wait probably alludes to the pressure put upon him to remain by Robert Wilberforce. But a time comes when all human obstacles must be set aside. Only three months were now to pass before the letter of April 6, 1851, which told Robert Wilberforce that the step he half hoped, half feared, to avert had been taken. The letters to him which immediately preceded it describe the final stages of the long struggle.

The first written on January 7, 1851, tells of the conversions of Bellasis, Dodsworth and Laprimaudaye, and of their 'calm, happy, undoubting' attitude, which doubtless greatly encouraged him. He continues:

'I have been suffering more inward sorrow than anyone but God can ever know. My love to the Church of England is the strongest affection I have except the love of Truth. No one can say how I feel torn and fleshed on all sides, as people were with hooks in other days. But my reason stands clear and steadfast. If it were not that I feel bound to put no interval between conviction and action, and that I am still desiring to wait if haply an interposition of God should reveal to me that I am deluded—I should say "I am convinced that whatever is tenable or untenable, the Church of England cannot be defended in its doctrine, position, or principles." It seems to me in manifest schism from the Church of all lands and of all ages. And its rule of Faith seems as manifestly private reason, judging by way of historical criticism.

I have abstained, in conscience, from censuring or laying any stress upon the conduct of the living Church of England. But it seems to me that it has sold itself to the world for its endowments. And its pastors have betrayed the Divine authority of Faith—not one article alone, but the whole principle of Divine Authority in Faith. In truth, the more I dwell on the Anglican Reformation, Theology, and Church, the more it seems to me to be a revolt from the mind and will of our Divine Lord in the order and Faith of His Kingdom.'

The letter of January 22 is important. He says:

'My dear Robert,

Your kind and affectionate note is a real solace to me; for though, thank God, I am well in health, and have a clear calm assurance in my reason and conscience that I am in the way both of right and truth, yet my heart is, as it was after a great event many years ago,[1] sad and lonely.

I have abstained from all forward acts or communications, so that I am in a vacuum, the support of past work is gone, and the reality which stands out ever before me is not mine to rest upon. In this state of suspense, which I desire to keep until I shall have taken some time for a disengaged review of my convictions, I necessarily feel at times lonely and sad. Not, I thank God, in the higher sense; this region was never more steadfast and full of substance. And never less Anglican for that reason. . . .

You are right in the main about Newman's book. In 1837–8, I was working on the subject of the Rule of Faith; and was convinced, with a depth which has never changed, except to grow deeper, that Universal Tradition is the Divine Witness of Truth on Earth. On this I rested until 1845, but with increasing difficulty in bringing the Church of England within the sphere of that witness. In 1845 I read Newman's book on Development. It did not satisfy me; but it opened my eyes to one fact, namely, that I had laid down only half the subject. I had found the *Rule*, but not the *Judge*. It was evident that to put Scripture and Antiquity into the hands of the individual is as much private judgement as to put Scripture alone. . . . This consciousness of the Universal Church is something more than the common reason of Christendom. It is also the living and lineal illumination of the Divine Spirit, for "consensus Sanctorum est sensus Spiritus Sancti."

I remember saying this to you in St. James's Square about 1846: that the perpetuity of the Faith must have a higher basis than the individual or collective intellect

[1] This must refer to his wife's death.

of the Church. The book which drove this conviction home to me was Melchior Camus's *Loci Theologici*. From that day to this every line of inquiry has run up into the same conclusion.

1. The plain words of Scripture prove to me that the Church is One, Visible, and Perpetual. What is perpetuity in Faith but indefectibility, or, if you will, infallibility ? There never has been or ever will be a moment when the Church of Faith shall cease to be One, visible and ascertainable. Ephes. iv. 4–16 seems to me, as Bull says, *luce meridiana clarius*.

The advent and office of the Third Person of the Holy Trinity, as given in Scripture, is also to my mind conclusive. It appears to me that Protestants have found this so plain, and so fatal to their case, that they have *Socinianised* it away. The Church of England is Socinian in its practice as to Sacraments and the Rule of Faith. It sees that to be Scriptural is to be Roman. . . .

2. Next, Historical Tradition is even more plain.

The Universal Church of the first 700 years believed in divine, infallible guidance in its office. The Greek Church after the schism claims this as much as the Roman Catholic Church. No Christian denied it till Luther, after he was condemned by the Church.

Again, mere human history would suffice—Schlegel says that " the Catholic Church is the highest historical authority upon earth." What is this but the *maximum of evidence* as to what Our Lord and the Holy Spirit revealed ? This alone would convince me.

3. Lastly, what does Reason say, but that the *certitude* of revelation to succeeding ages demands a perpetual provision secure from error ? How else can I be certain of what was revealed 1800 years ago or even that there was a revelation at all ? What is

infallibility, but revelation perpetuated, and inspiration produced by illumination—the extraordinary by the ordinary—the immediate by the mediate action of the Holy Spirit ? The strange and sad words I have heard from good men about "craving for certainty," and "uncertainty being the utmost sphere of moral probation," are alarming for the faith of their followers. Is it the probation of Faith to be uncertain whether there be a True and proper Trinity of Persons—whether there be a Real Presence—or any Holy Ghost ? And if not in these, why in any truth whereby we must be saved ? . . .'

On February 4 he writes a long letter which contains little concerning his own state of mind, but throws light on his friend's difficulties and the way to meet them.

'James Hope is still in the north, minded much as I am. And now, dear Robert, for you I feel very sincerely. My chief anxiety for you is that you should not *re-commit* yourself in any word, deed, or way to the Anglican system. I have felt great help and light in the clear unbiased position I have at this time, and I wish you could keep yourself as near to it as your position allows. I am so afraid of the *idola tribus*, or species, or lest our *position* should become our *conscience*, which is evidently so with many. I trust you will always open your thoughts to me. You know it would always be under seal ; and I know from such long and deep experience what this trial is that I would never press you by the touch of a finger. I deeply feel that "*hæc mutatio a dextera Excelsi.*" What you say of your wife is a great sorrow ; but have *faith*.'

The next four letters are obviously written in answer to questions which are not given, so what the exact points raised were can only be inferred. The following passages from them may be of interest in showing his line of approach.

'As to Barrow, I seem to have no regard for destructive arguments. His book ought to be called "Historic doubts on the Primacy," which the Presbyterian avenges by "Historic doubts on Episcopacy," and Strauss by "Historic doubts on the Historical Christ." The utter weakness of Barrow is shown when he writes *constructively*, as in his "Unity of the Church," which in fact destroys all but the name. For this reason I feel the nibbling at details of no force. "Nothing can stand before envy."'

In a postscript to this letter (Feb. 18, 1851) he adds: 'Is not the Apostles' Creed the expansion of the baptismal formula?

Is not the Nicene the exposition and guard of the second division of the Apostles' Creed? Is not the Tridentine the exposition and guard of the third division? Is not the principle of authority divine and infallible, one and continuous throughout? And has not the Tridentine as the Nicene done its work permanently and clearly? What else has?'

The letter of February 27 is evidently in answer to a question which seems still to prove a stumbling-block, to judge by non-Catholic writers to-day. He says:

'My notion is:

1. That the Church *potentially* contained all its future decisions from the first.

2. That its decisions became binding only when they became *actual*.

3. That, until made actual, individual minds were

free to use their discernment upon the traditions of the Church.

In this way I understand St. Vincent's *Commentarium* as a guide for individuals, when the Church has not decided, and until it shall decide, but no longer. So I understand St. Augustine *De doctr. Christ.*, and the question of the canon. There was no canon, as we now understand it, when he wrote, for there were many. And this throws out into higher relief the office of the living Church, preserving and propounding the Faith by oral tradition.

Indeed, I know of no *final* treatment of the canon till *Trent*, when three classes of sacred books:

1. The Heb. canon.
2. The Hellenistic.
3. The Apostolical—were united in one Index. . . .

All these things warn me that the only power which overcomes the world is Faith. And I do not believe that the Church of England is established by faith but by the State.'

The letter of March 3 has one passage specially worth quoting, as the fallacy has not ceased to be employed.

He quotes from De Maistre's *Essai sur le principe générateur des constitutions politiques* as follows:

'1. Que les racines des constitutions politiques existent *avant* toute loi *écrite*.

2. Qu'une loi constitutionnelle n'est et ne peut être que le developpement ou la sanction d'un droit *pré-existant et non écrit*.

3. Que ce qu'il y a de plus essentiel, de plus intrinsèquement constitutionnel et de véritablement fondamental n'est jamais écrit, et même ne sauroit l'être, sans exposer l'état.

4. Que la faiblesse et la fragilité d'une constitution sont précisément en raison directe de la multiplicité des articles constitutionnels écrits (Lect. IX).

He quotes Tacitus's *pessimæ reipublicæ plurimæ leges*. This seems to me to be absolutely true, and to belong in its highest truth of application to the Catholic Church. And it seems to me to show the fallacy of Protestant controversial writers who make lists of Roman errors.

Supremacy . . .	A.D.	600
Transubstantiation . .	,,	1070
Confession	,,	,,

This is the reverse of fact and truth. The points were not then first *created*, but written. They were not first affirmed, but denied.'[1]

On March 8 he writes an important letter referring to the anniversary which dates it. On March 8, 1850, he had attended a meeting in London at which the decision to take common action against the Gorham Judgement was made. In a letter (also to Robert Wilberforce) dated May 10, 1850, he had summed up the effect of the meetings of which this was the crucial one upon his mind. To print it here may make the import of the anniversary letter clearer. He wrote it after two months' reflection on what had passed at those meetings in London, which had done much to unify the 'double mind.'

'. . . Now that I can review things from a distance, I seem to see one, and one only light, calm and clear, steadfast and expanding.

I seem to see that all Divine authority in England is at stake, all Divine law for the intellect and for the will;

[1] This is rather obscure, but seems to mean that these points were called in question, for the first time, at the dates given—thus necessitating the written definition of beliefs never before denied.

that to reinforce the Divine authority of the Catholic Church as it exists among us we must testify against the whole Reformation schism, which is a national and corporate private judgement; that we must testify for the Divine authority by suffering, sorrow, loss, and lifelong sacrifice; that in so doing we shall be not "injuring millions," but instructing, awakening, saving millions. All that we have taught is at stake; if we wish to rivet it we must suffer for it.

I did not find Pusey. He was not come. But I have read his book[1] with sadness. Does he believe that the Church is a Divine kingdom; that for three hundred years it exercised its Divine office, not only without but in spite of emperors? Can he fail to see that to concede the power of "giving judges" is to make the Church a clerical Westminster Hall? What does he mean by saying "doctrine is not touched, but discipline is?" Is not doctrine the *oral* teaching of 15,000 priests, 80,000 school teachers, two or three millions of heads of families? What is the doctrine of the Church but the *univoca methoda docendi*—the real and unanimous teaching of 1800 years? Can he confound "doctrine" and "dogma" or "fides"? I wish I could go on, but I must stop to-day.'

This was his position in May 1850. Now, ten months later, on the anniversary of the meeting at which the Declaration was drawn up, he reports further progress towards the truth. He has come to see that the question is not one of 'more or less submission' but of 'antagonist principles' which cannot be reconciled.

[1] This book, published so soon after Pusey had signed the Declaration of March 8 with them, caused Manning and Dodsworth to mistrust him and his followers in this important matter. It 'carried a multitude of ignoramuses with him,' as Dodsworth said, and probably did much to cause the complete failure of the second Declaration drawn up by Manning, Dodsworth, and Mill.

This makes 'Reunion' impossible; and entire submission, whether corporate or individual, to the Universal Church is essential if Unity is to be attained. He writes, therefore, on March 8, 1851:

'My dear Robert,

I must join with you in signalising this day. What a year this has been since the time when I came and found you all writing letters in Maskell's lodgings.

The effect of that day was, I think, to set us at a point of view from which the Church of England became an object, as it were, external to our minds, and out of which we seemed to be projected so as to see it from without. And the issue of this contemplation I think is, that if the Church have a divine polity and office, the Church of England has fallen from it: and that the Presbyterian Kirk of Scotland, and the Episcopal Church of England, are alike offspring of one and the same principle, of the private spirit in opposition to the Divine Tradition and lineal consciousness of the Universal Church.'

A letter of March 14 shows how soon the end must come:

'Do you remember last autumn bidding me to wait six months? I have done so morally, and now I find myself with no reason against acting but the shrinking of flesh and blood and the vague fear of making a mistake where my whole light tells me that there is no mistake. It is like the *feeling* of fear at passing a mountain road, of the safety of which I am by reason perfectly convinced.

1. First, I seem to be convinced beyond doubt of the nullity of Protestantism, and of Anglicanism. In point of spiritual and sacramental action upon souls, of

dogma, of unity, of certainty, the Church of England seems to me to be out of the sphere of the Catholic Church.

2. Next, granting for a moment your views of the small traces of certain prominent R.C. points in the first 500 years, yet traces there are, as in a portrait taken at five years old of a countenance at 50. And, waiving this, which is a question of details, the Divine institution of one organised, authoritative Witness is in those 500 years proved by every form of evidence of Scripture and tradition.'

A week later he not only makes his own intentions clear, but the relations between him and his adviser are reversed. He not only determines to act against his counsel, but predicts that he also will change.

'44 CADOGAN PLACE,
21*st March*, 1851.

MY DEAR ROBERT,

I write to you as a *solatium humanitatis*, which I need greatly. And your letters are among my chief comforts. I do not indeed think that we shall ever be otherwise than we are now. Life has been saddened for me down to the very root, the last thirteen or fourteen years of solitude, and the last five of mental trial have, I trust, broken me to a spirit which will keep fast by all affections. At this time I am suffering in my way as you in yours. The very atmosphere of this house with all its kindness is very trying ; and out of it I am fronting and bearing by anticipation what I used to forbode for the future. The measure of this is, I hope, being exhausted in part before the time. And it is less by far than I could have believed. Many kind friends have been raised up at this moment who, without agreeing, do not upbraid, and even enter into the justice and uprightness of what I have done and may do. So I believe it will be "As thy days, etc." I have so found this in time past that it is a sin in me if I doubt it now. And now it still is fulfilled to me. And I believe will be. It is God's way to veil His consolations till they are needed, that we may go onward and upward in faith, and then every wind and turn in the way brings out some new solace and even joy. So it will be with you, my dear Robert, I am well assured, and your fear and forebodings will be dispelled at the moment of meeting them.

As to Bramhall, he is very learned and copious, but seems to me, like Lord Coke, unscrupulous. His conclusions are broader than his premisses, as I found about the Royal Supremacy.

I send you the enclosed, which I should like to have back, to show the form into which I feel my thoughts to have settled down with a full conviction. You will see that it is only the *outer* not the *inner* way of treating the question, the latter being to me still more convincing as Mohler puts it. James Hope seems as fully satisfied with their line as I am, and we have tried it over and over to find a flaw. What a corroboration is given by the failure and functional impotence of the Anglican Church. I will mind [i.e. remember] what you tell me about letters.

Write to me when you can.

Ever yours, my dear Robert, very affectionately,

H. E. M.'

On March 29 he wrote a letter on the Real Presence, Transubstantiation, and the Mass; and added a postscript two days later which none who has shared the experience can read unmoved.

'Yesterday for the first time I went to what we are writing of: and no words can express the sense of its reality.

I know what you mean by saying that one sometimes feels as if all this might turn out to be only another "Land of Shadows." I have felt it in time past, but not now. Neither has it ever lasted a moment on reflection. The Θεολογία from Nice to St. Thomas Aquinas, and the Undivided unity diffused throughout the world of which the Cathedra Petri is the centre—now 1800 years old, mightier in every power now than ever, in intellect, in science, in separation from the world; and purer too, refined by 300 years of conflict with the modern infidel civilisation—all this is a fact more solid than the earth.'

Any other consideration after this seems an anti-climax, but it seems fair to show what pressure was brought to bear on him during the last three months of his struggle, pressure of a kind which must have tried Manning's pastoral love of souls, his ambitions good and bad alike, to the very utmost. Satan indeed must have desired to have him. It is hard to imagine a more thorough sifting of every motive than the appeal to every side of Manning's nature which beset him then. His greatest difficulty, as the letters of this time show, was to decide what was right; and the following letter, from a man he greatly respected, begging him to remain on the very plea which appealed most to him, his power to lead a measure to reform his Church, must have tried him to the uttermost.

The writer was the Rev. T. C. Carter, of Clewer, whose saintly life and teaching was an inspiration to many in the Anglican Communion, as his books of devotion still continue to be. Four months before Manning's reception he wrote as follows:

'Clewer.
(No date, but it must have been in
late December, 1850.)

My very dear Sir,

I thank you and our acknowledged benefactor most sincerely for the gift which I received this morning.

My heart most truly expands to what you express; it is the faith in which I have lived and would hope to cling to, till I can know as I am known. Oh that I may look to you onward as one that may ever strengthen us in this faith! I use no light or unmeaning word, God knows I feel we need such, and the more, as this Divine order which you truly describe is violated. But after earnest thought, though without such stores for thought as you have, I cannot see why the violence done may not yet be remedied, or why it is more than similar outrage and disturbance in past periods of the Church's sacred course: for the divine order I faithfully believe to be the Church of England's heritage, and to have been followed in her better days; and if so, will not a hopeful faith trust that yet a little while and it may be so again? I know not when I may express a hope to you again; I wonder how I can write to you as I do, but a thought burns within me that some one should now arise in a calm, simple, lofty spirit, to take a leading part in urging on our awakened brethren the solemn need of accomplishing the object of your Declaration, and in pointing the way to, and forming the kind of, synod, which might be in harmony with Catholic truth, and suiting the needs of our Church; and I cannot but feel why you should not be in God's grace an instrument of His hands, and do His work. Do not let such words as Bartie's sadden you. There are many hearts among us who do not feel so harshly and suspiciously—yet do not measure the sympathy you have by the number of names ; for numbers more are deterred from signing by such reasons as B.'s, and other reasons of different people opposed to you. I will pray humbly as I can heartily, that you may live and die in peaceful hope within the communion of the Church of England, wherein I know so large a part of your heart is, and where, I trust, it may be for ever. My deepest thanks are ever due to our common Master for his gift to you. Pardon all I have said I ought not.

Your very gratefully affectionate

T. C. Carter.'

Manning answers on January 3, 1851 :

'My dear kind Friend,

Among many letters which this time has brought me, none of them moved me more than yours. All our past thoughts of sorrow gave to its affectionate forbearance a force beyond words. But in this too I find a consolation. You have not shrunk from opening your grief to me, and that gives me the comfort and strength of opening my grief to you. In truth, my heart is almost broken. All human love, all that makes life precious to me, except one thing, is passing or past away. To add sharpness to this sorrow, I seem to others to be base, false, and a coward in the day of trial. I cannot seem otherwise. And what have I to answer ?

I cannot resist the conviction which forces itself upon me, like light, on every side, that the Church of England is in a position at variance with the Will of God : and that to uphold it in that position is to fight against God. When the thought, even the sight, of my home, flock, and church come over me my heart breaks, and no human solace so much as touches me. The only one thing left is a conscience clear and at peace.

I could no longer continue under oath and subscription binding me to the Royal Supremacy in Ecclesiastical causes, being convinced:

1. That it is a violation of the Divine Office of the Church.

2. That it has involved the Church of England in a separation from the universal Church, which separation I cannot clear of the character of schism.

3. That it has thereby suspended and prevented the functions of the Church of England so as to efface from the faith and mind of its people the divine laws of unity and authority in Faith and discipline.

But I will not attempt in a letter to detail my reasons on so large a subject. I did so in a printed letter to the Bishop of Chichester last July which I will desire Murray to send you, I have only said this much to show why I could no longer without violence to conscience and truth continue to hold under an oath the matter of which I believe to be at variance with the divine order of the Church. Beyond resigning I have taken no step; neither am I, either by nature or habit, inclined to precipitation. But the tendency of my belief is manifest: and yet nothing but a necessity laid upon me as by the will of God will move me.

I can find no words to thank you, my dear friend, for your affection of which I am most unworthy. And yet if human love, or sorrow, or any other lower motive, had held me when truth and conscience bade me decide, I should have been more unworthy still. This makes me trust that I shall not forget your affection, and that you will remember me in your prayers.

What a life is this, and how full of griefs which go through the soul! Thank God it is not our rest, and that we shall soon be beyond the reach of sin.

My purpose is to stay in London (except a few visits

to my family) till Gladstone's return. If you are in London in the week after next I could call and see you.

Once more my thanks, and may all consolation be with you and your children.

Believe me, ever yours most affectionately,

H. E. Manning.'

Mr. Carter's further letters are not given, but Manning's are here printed in full, as the light they throw on the sincerity of his convictions is almost more illuminating than any written to Laprimaudaye or Wilberforce. It is hard to see how his arguments can be refuted historically, or his caution before taking the final step blamed, in the light of these letters.

He writes :

'Pendell Court,
Bletchingley,
14*th January*, 1851.

My dear Friend,

On my return here to-day I read your kind letter which reached me this morning.

Many and sincere thanks to you and your wife for all the affection it breathes to me. Indeed, I return it from my heart, and do not forget you. You say right. I have been in a deep ; and human sorrow has all but broken my heart. No one but God only knows what it has been ; what my only home and flock were to me. But my reason has never doubted of what was my duty, and through all I have had a calm which is enough.

You kindly desire to know my future, yet I feel unwilling to speak of what I have not decided. But this I may say : Nothing could ever move me from the Church of England except the conviction that it is no part of the Catholic Church.

If this conviction be confirmed, I see only one path. I say this to show why the events of this time, prosperous or adverse, seem to me to be secondary. The question is deeper ; though they tend to illustrate and therefore to decide it.

What you have heard of Laprimaudaye is true. And now, dear friend, let me have your prayers that I may have no will of my own, no leaning on self ; no following my own light ; but that I may be led by the one only light which never errs.

Give my Christian love to your wife and trust it for yourself. Believe me, always very affectionately yours,

H. E. M.'

A fortnight later he sends the following :

'Kippington,
Sevenoaks,
29th January, 1851.

My dear Friend,

Thank you from my heart for your affectionate letter. It is very soothing to receive such tokens of brotherly love.

It would need more than a letter to answer the points you raise in any such way as is due to your kindness. I can therefore only beg you to do me justice by believing that I am not hasty or precipitate, or swayed by affections, or drawn away by the fascinations of devotions. My whole heart and mind for twelve years has laboured in the endeavour to justify the Church of England on its own grounds. I am not conscious of any desire deeper or more controlling than the desire to believe our position to be defensible. All that makes or ever has made life dear to me is on this side.

On the other, plain facts, evidences which no one has

endeavoured to meet, appear to me to convict the Reformation of schism.

I cannot say that the argument you draw from Andrewes and the many good men of the Anglican Church weighs with me more than as a caution and warning. Because on the other side, I see at once, More, Fisher, and Pole. And if a *consensus Sanctorum* is to weigh, the line from St. Gregory the Great to St. Vincent of Paul turns the scale.

But this is not the proper evidence. For twelve years the subject of unity has been my chief employment. I could with difficulty clear our position at any time. And the grounds on which I have rested in time past are now simply destroyed.

Long before I knew you I found them failing. Believe me, therefore, that I write under no hasty or recent feeling.

For long years my mind has not been as you imply that yours is on Roman points. There is nothing in them which would disquiet me. Your affection has drawn me to write this—more than I intended. Believe me, my dear kind friend, always affectionately yours,

H. E. M.'

These letters to Canon Carter seem a fitting close to those which have, I hope, shown 'the true life of a man' during a long period of trial such as the majority never experience. They were written almost at the end of that 'long, mature and suffering preparation' during which he got up the case for the defence of his Church's position like the able lawyer he would have made. Now, after years of hard work on the evidence, he was forced to throw up his brief; as honesty compelled him to see that right lay with the other side.

The position is historically the same now as it has

been for nearly four hundred years. The State has the same power to interfere in spiritual matters as it had under the Tudors and the Stuarts ; and exercises it, even since the Enabling Act, in an equally arbitrary manner. The House of Lords' veto (by one vote) of the Bill to divide the diocese of Hereford, grown too large for efficient supervision by one Bishop, is one instance of this ; the rejection of the Prayer-book in 1928 another. The Test Act at least ensured that an Anglican should appoint bishops to vacant Anglican sees. That safeguard has gone. At the present moment many English bishoprics are filled by bishops appointed to them by a Welsh Baptist or a Scottish Presbyterian Prime Minister.

The Public Worship Regulation Act of 1874, under which several clergy who refused to obey it were sent to prison, in one case for over a year, was in principle as tyrannical an act of usurpation of Church government as the Acts of Supremacy and Uniformity in 1559 ; though, mercifully, the savage cruelty and wickedness wrought, in the name of the State and with its sanction, in the Penal Days would never be tolerated now. But its right to rule 'the Church of England established by law' under the Tudors is as impossible to gainsay now as it was then ; and a Church which, even under protest, acknowledges such Supremacy cannot claim to be part of the Catholic Church.

His Majesty's Declaration, prefixed to the Thirty-nine Articles at the end of the Book of Common Prayer, leaves no doubt as to the Supremacy. It will repay the study which it is seldom given.

This Declaration every Sovereign since the days of Elizabeth has had to make on his Accession. It asserts his claim to be Supreme Governor of the Church of England and pledges him to see that 'there shall be due Execution upon those ' who shall attempt ' any varying or departing in the least degree from the doctrine and discipline of the Church of England now established,' as set forth ' in the Articles agreed upon at the Convocation Holden in London in the year 1562.'

Just before the Declaration comes an Order for the discontinuance of one Form of Prayer and the institution of another. It is ' given at Our Court at St. James's the Twenty-third Day of June, 1910,' and it is signed, not by the Archbishops of Canterbury and York, but (' By His Majesty's Command ') by Winston Spencer Churchill, then Home Secretary.

So even if all the bishops, clergy, and laity were unanimous in their demand for a Revised Prayer-book embodying Anglo-Catholic doctrines, it is clear that Parliament could—in fact must—veto their demand unless a majority of the electors, of whom only a minority are Anglicans, should give assent.

Manning, as we have seen, predicted this in his *Letter to the Bishop of Chichester ;* but the historical reason for this humiliating state of affairs did not become clear to him till after the Gorham Judgement. Then, greatly helped by the arguments of Hope and Dodsworth, he came to see that even Disestablishment, proposed as a remedy by Gladstone and other High Churchmen, could not cure the weakness which had sapped their Church's vitality since its very start. The same remedy has been demanded by many since a crisis as grave as the Gorham Judgement, and very similar to it, occurred in 1928. The reasons why it cannot do any good are the same now as in 1850, when Hope and Dodsworth and Manning saw them so clearly and expressed them so well. The letters on that point seem therefore especially useful to-day, when the same cure for the same troubles is being suggested once more.

Disestablishment would be equally unavailing now as then. It might free the Church of England from many disadvantages, but it cannot make her the One Church. As Manning wrote in 1851, soon after his conversion: 'Surely the question is not how man has marred the Church, but what God made it. No sin of man can destroy what is indestructible, and no human purity can make a human society to be God's Church.' This was the point to which his efforts after the truth had brought him, and nothing could now avert the necessity of a step which to him seemed the end of his career.

Dodsworth, Laprimaudaye, Allies, Maskell, and others who had hoped with him to free the Church of England from subservience to Parliament and thus make her Catholic once more, had left the ranks of the Anglican clergy and become Catholics. His friends and penitents among the laity were rapidly following them. He could no longer 'indulge' (as Purcell strangely describes his final struggle) 'in the painful luxury of making up his mind.'

The considerations which had been working in their minds for months at last determined both him and James Hope, who had reached certainty by the same lines, that the Church of England had 'severed itself from the rest of Christendom' at the Reformation and 'that the Church of Rome is the only true Church of God.'

The following letters which conclude this study need little comment. That from Dodsworth, dated July 20, 1850, seems unanswerable regarding the inherent Erastianism of the Church of England and the impossibility of endowing a 'new creation' with antiquity.

I quote it in full ; it may show others the new light which it threw on Manning's problems.

'I quite agree that no remedy goes to the root of the matter which does not repeal the statutes of Henry VIII. But this gives rise to a serious question. Is it *fair* and *right* to ask for such a repeal ? Put yourself in the place of an Erastian. He says, "I knew what I was pledging myself to when I took my oath. Does this new discovery of yours entitle you to bind me in a way different from that by which I have already bound myself ?" In other words, is it not an element in the Church of England, made so when it severed itself from the rest of Christendom, to acknowledge this spiritual supremacy ? *Then* our plain duty would have been to abide in the old religion *rather than accept this innovation.* Does the lapse of 300 years make our duty different ? I have thought the same as you of the Royal Supremacy. But we have been mistaken, and our opponents have thought more correctly of the status of the English Church. Can we in fairness avail ourselves of our mistake (for without it we could not be where we are) to oust them ? I must say this seems to me at least *questionable.*

But dearest friend, is there in these days the remotest *possibility* of getting liberty for the Church by the repeal of the statutes of Henry VIII ? Would one-half of the people of your meeting go with you in this ? and think what chance you would have in the House of Commons or with the people of England, who think more of a farthing in the pound than of the whole body of statutes affecting the Church. Only, if they have a strong feeling, it is against priestcraft and exercise of spiritual power. No, IT CAN NEVER BE ; and with this conviction have I any *right* to be where I am ? . . .

To me it will be a trial to *act* without you. I have long expected only to follow, or at most accompany you. But things seem brought to a crisis with me. . . .

Ever yours most affectionately,

W. Dodsworth.'

As its present Vicar states in a recent article on the history of his Church, Dodsworth ' built up ' the congregation of Margaret Chapel, now All Saints, Margaret Street, before ' going on to the larger work ' of Christ Church, Albany Street. But now, as his successor at Margaret Chapel, Frederick Oakeley, did after him, he had answered the questions his letter raises in the negative, and had gone on farther still.

Those questions, and the italics in Dodsworth's letter, are as pertinent in 1932 as in 1850. To us even more than to Manning and his contemporaries, the following words, written by him in September 1851, to Robert Wilberforce, apply :

' Surely it is the hand of God which has reproduced under our eyes in the last two years the acts of the Reformation. We see now what we should have seen then. We have seen the Reformation as if we had lived in the reigns of Edward VI and Elizabeth. Surely the Gorham case is no *change*. It is a revelation. And Anglicanism is but Episcopal Protestantism, a human society with human opinions.'

The struggles of Anglican bishops to enforce their views on clergy and laity who dissent from them are almost as unedifying, from the Catholic standpoint, as their discomfiture at the hands of Parliament. Spain, Mexico, and Russia have shown us how a powerful minority can rob the faithful of their spiritual privileges at this time, exactly as the fines and butchery of the Penal Days coerced the people of England into Protestantism under Elizabeth and the Stuarts, except for the heroic handful who kept the Faith, 'in spite of dungeon, fire and sword.'

Not only are the acts of the Reformation reproduced under our eyes, but a more accurate knowledge of history than was available to most people till this century enables us to form a truer judgement of them. Unlike Kingsley, we do not go 'to Froude for history' but to the contemporary documents which are becoming more and more accessible. Foxe's *Book of Martyrs* no longer has the field to itself as a source of historical tracts and novels with an anti-Catholic bias.

We know that though three hundred Protestants were burnt for their religious opinions under Queen Mary, many times that number of Catholics suffered cruel deaths for the same cause under the Tudors before and after her, and the first three Stuart kings. In an Anglican account of the Reformation we read:

'A hideous persecution of the Roman Catholics in the North of England followed in the latter part of Elizabeth's reign. The Gunpowder Plot was manipulated from abroad, but Guy Fawkes and the Yorkshire gentlemen who helped in his desperate adventure had bitter memories to goad them into crime. The story of the bishops whom Mary burnt in Oxford is indeed terrible. But for a hundred Englishmen who have read that story there is perhaps hardly one who has read the tale of the execution of Robert Bickerdike of Farnham, or of Margaret Clitheroe of York, who was slowly crushed to death naked on the bridge across the Ouse.'[1]

[1] *Religion since the Reformation,* by Dr. Leighton Pullan—his Bampton Lectures, 1922.

Henry's persecution of Catholics who refused to break Church laws at his bidding was as hideous as Elizabeth's and more hideous than Mary's. Latimer's end was merciful compared with that of Father John Forrest, Catharine of Aragon's confessor, who had 'seen sixty-four years of life, and forty of those had worn the habit of St. Francis' before he was slung in a cradle of chains over a slow fire and roasted alive while Latimer preached at him by the hour, because he would not break the Seal of Confession at the bidding of Henry VIII. The King did not pronounce that savage sentence out of Protestant wrath at 'a Romish error' which had crept into the pre-Reformation Church. Those who spoke against the Sacrament of Penance felt the lash of his Six-stringed Whip. But when the laws of the Church conflicted with the will of her self-appointed Head in England, the priest who obeyed the former died the most cruel death the offended tyrant could devise.

We no longer accept the picture of the Jesuits' work in England which Kingsley painted in *Westward Ho!* We know from the accounts of those who witnessed their martyrdoms what constituted the treason of the priests who were hanged, drawn, and quartered for saying Mass, 'a treasonable act' which at least a third of the Anglican clergy now claim to perform—in many Anglo-Catholic churches every day. We know that Margaret Clitheroe was pressed to death, and Mary Ward scourged and then hanged, for no other crime than trying to save hunted priests from the gallows and its awful sequel. The men who committed that compassionate form of treason were given even harder measure; they suffered the same terrible fate as the priests they tried to save. Their names may be read, with their occupations—'Thames waterman—gentleman's servant—farmer—gentleman—nobleman '—and so forth, with those of the priests whom they failed to rescue, on the rails of the beautiful Altar to the English Martyrs in S. James's, Spanish Place.

Those who were brought up to 'think Kingsley a divine,' like Froude in Bishop Stubbs's epigram, are fewer than they were. At least a third of the Church of England now shares the beliefs which Henry VIII not only himself continued to hold, but ordered his subjects to profess under pain of death should they speak against them. His Whip with Six Strings, as its victims called the Statute of the Six Articles, obtained the willing consent of both Houses in 1539. It upheld (i) The Real Presence of the 'natural Body and Blood of Christ' in the Mass, (ii) The sufficiency of Communion in one kind, (iii) The celibacy of the priesthood, (iv) The perpetual obligation of religious vows, (v) Private Masses, (vi) Auricular confession. Those who spoke against the first were to be burnt; the penalty for contradicting any of the other five was to be fined and imprisoned for the first offence, and hanged for the second. Few of the Protestants who date the Church of England from the reign of Henry VIII realise that if they had been members of that Church under *his* rule, Spiritual and Temporal, they would have had to have kept their opinions very much to themselves.

Ever since the Reformation there have been two parties in the Church of England, who claim a totally different ancestry from each other. The Anglo-Catholics say that they are sons of the ancient Church, the Ecclesia Anglicana. But that Church claimed the Pope as its Head; not a Tudor whose father's lucky marriage with the White Rose of York had set him firmly on the Throne of England. The Protestants say they descend from the Reformers, Cranmer,

Ridley, Latimer; and if they date the Reformation from 1562, they are probably right. But as Cranmer managed to escape the Six-Stringed Whip, and Latimer was Henry's Court preacher, their forefathers must have professed the errors of Rome for some years after they were freed from the Papal yoke by the new Head of the Church of England. Still, as 'the doctrine and discipline of the Reformers' were enforced on the Church of England by Statutes still unrepealed, they have a distinct claim to be their legal heirs. When the Wycliffe preachers sing at their meetings:

> 'Ye Protestants of England
> Baptized in Martyrs' blood,'

there is no doubt at all as to what martyrs they mean.

But what of the Anglo-Catholics? They also accept 'the innovation,' as Dodsworth calls it, which our ancestors, if they were loyal Catholics, resisted even to death. Yet at their Congresses they sing 'Faith of our Fathers, holy Faith,' a hymn which Faber wrote after his conversion, when he had returned to the Old Religion. We know what *he* meant in that hymn. When Anglo-Catholics sing it, whose memory do they honour? From 1539 or so onwards, whose Faith did their Fathers share? The Faith of Thomas More and John Fisher who died in defence of 'the Papal claims,' or of the King who had them beheaded? Of John Forrest who died in agony because he offended the King by his refusal to break the Seal of Confession at his bidding, or of Hugh Latimer, who spoke so lightly to his friends of 'the roasting of the Friar'?

When Latimer in his turn burnt at Oxford, in Mary's reign, gunpowder placed on the pile for that purpose ended his sufferings with merciful quickness. He was condemned to death for denying the Real Presence, and other ‘ blasphemous fables,’—words which, in such a context, rightly shock Anglo-Catholics, whose clergy are still forced to subscribe to the Article in which they occur.[1] Some hailed him as a martyr to the truth, others looked upon him as a heretic paying the price of his errors. Which of these views was held by the fathers whose memory Anglo-Catholics remember with pride and affection when they sing that hymn at their Congresses to-day ?

If they themselves had lived in those days, would they have upheld Henry VIII when he claimed to be Head of the Church ? Would they have thought Cranmer right to deny the Sacrifice of the Mass ? Would they have followed John Knox when he shamed his Priesthood and tore down the Tabernacle in S. John's Cathedral at Perth, desecrating the Blessed Sacrament in his hatred of the Mass and his desire to inflame the mob against It ?

When they say ‘ Blessed be Jesus in the Most Holy Sacrament of the Altar,’ and speak of the Sacrifice of the Mass as being part of the Prayer-book's teaching, do they ever wonder if that was really the faith of the English Church after the Reformation ? If so, why was Article XXXI, still in the Prayer-book, drawn up in 1562 ? Why were the priests who offered that Sacrifice butchered as traitors when they did so under Tudors and Stuarts in the Penal Days ? And finally why do more than half of the Anglican clergy and laity deny it to-day ? When they quote Laud and Andrewes in support of the Catholicity of the Church of England under the Stuarts, do they realise that priests were executed for saying Mass as late as 1679 ? How can they blind themselves to these definite proofs that the Sacrifice of the Mass is a marked ‘ departing ’ from

[1] Article XXXI, Note 4.

'the doctrine and discipline of the Church of England,' as laid down in the Articles agreed upon 'by the Archbishops, Bishops, and members of the Convocation holden in London in 1562?'

To these Articles every Anglican clergyman must still subscribe. Many still believe them. To those who do not, Dodsworth's way out of the difficulty seems to afford a solution. His question hit the nail on the head eighty years ago, and it is still in the place where he hammered it in. 'The lapse of three hundred years,' as he saw, can make no difference to our duty. Where we would have been then we ought to be now. If our fathers quitted their posts, we must man them once more. Where they sold the pass, we must win it back. If we agree with the Reformers we must accept 'the innovation' of their doctrines; if we do not we must go back to the Rock from which we were hewn.

The point at issue is still the same. Our Lord said: 'And there shall be One Fold under One Shepherd.' Where is that Fold, and who is its Shepherd? Who is the Head, not merely of the Provinces of Canterbury and York, nor even of the Anglican Communion, but of the Holy Church throughout all the world? More and Fisher did not die to uphold the dogma of Transubstantiation, King Henry would have burnt them if they had denied it. It must surely be clear to all who study the Tudor period carefully that the Church of England owes its existence to the question of the Supremacy. Henry VIII believed in the Mass, the Seven Sacraments, auricular confession, clerical celibacy, all the 'errors' against which the Articles were framed by the Reformers after the Authority of the Pope had been cast off. Elizabeth most certainly believed in the Mass, so far as she believed in religion at all. The crux was the Supremacy then; as it was to the Tractarians in 1850, and to their successors to-day.

If the Pope was the Head of the Church in the sixteenth century, he is Head of it now. If Henry VIII was right in his act of usurpation, the Church of England must take Parliament, as the King's representative, for her Supreme Governor.

Anglicans who believe that the Church of England has been always Catholic, and attempt to prove it by extracts from the writings of Anglican post-Reformation divines,[1] account for her separation from the Catholic Church by saying that at the Reformation the Church of England kept the ancient Faith intact, and merely got rid of wrong doctrines added to it in mediæval times by Rome. What those 'wrong doctrines' were can be seen by reading Articles XXII, XXV, XXVIII, and XXXI at the end of the Book of Common Prayer. They are being taught to-day, in spite of those Articles, by the Anglo-Catholic clergy, who are trying now to put back the pearls which fell from the string when King Henry cut off the clasp which held all safe.

If they are right to teach those doctrines now, why was it wrong to teach them then? Since the State, as the House of Commons showed by its action in 1928, still vetoes them, ought they not to repudiate its Headship now as More and Fisher and the English Martyrs repudiated it then?

The Catholic Faith they claim to teach would have been lost four hundred years ago but for the Papacy they repudiate. In repudiating it they nullify their claim to hold 'the full Faith.' Some of the truths of

[1] 'The English Church always Catholic,' a tract published some years ago by the Anglo-Catholic Society of SS. Peter and Paul.

that Faith the State which established their Church still forbids them to hold. So, as Dodsworth asked eighty years ago, have they any right to be where they are ?

. . . . . .

By the end of March 1851 Manning had taken his first practical step in answer to that question. He formally resigned his office and benefice ; and soon after, on March 23, went to an Anglican Church, with Mr. Gladstone, for the last time. The following Sunday he assisted at Mass, as he tells Robert Wilberforce in the letter dated March 31, already given.

Mr. Gladstone, to the very last, tried to keep him back, just as Manning did his utmost to bring his old friend with him. The end of a letter dated April 1, in answer to Manning's suggestion of a meeting, is very sad.

'*Valeat quantum.* My present point is to show that you simply go past me now, as you did in my reference to the conversation of some years back. Oh ! look well whither you are going and what work you are marring, but most of all for God's sake look whether you are dispassionately using the means given you of holding fast or reaching the truth. Forgive haste, and believe me affectionately yours,

W. E. G.'

On April 6, Passion Sunday, in Hill Street Chapel Father Brownbill received him into the Church with James Hope, who, as he had so much desired, was 'with him' through all. Two letters to Robert Wilberforce recount the event. The first, dated the same day, says :

'14 Queen Street,
Mayfair,
6th April, 1851.

My dear Robert,

You will not be surprised that I now tell you of the step James Hope and I have this day taken. With the fullest conviction, both of reason and of conscience, we have sought admittance into what we alike believe to be the one true fold and Church of God on earth. Pray for me that I may be thankful for the peace which overflows even in the midst of human sorrow. So it must be, for so He foretold ; but all is well if we may do His will and see His face at last. Give my Christian love to your wife. And may God be with you, my dear Robert.

Ever yours most affectionately,
H. E. Manning.'

In the second, dated Tuesday in Holy Week, he gives fuller details, and speaks of his future :

'My dearest Robert,

I have wished to write to you but have been much hindered.

The thought of seeing you again is much comfort to me. And remember my promise ; I will not say a word of argument to you. Even I will not (for I feel I cannot) write as I did a few weeks ago, partly because my own mind is at rest ; and partly because I so respect the trial of yours that I shall only follow your leading.

You will, perhaps, wish to hear somewhat that has befallen me.

On Passion Sunday, after Sacramental Confession, Profession of Faith, conditional Baptism, and Absolution, I went to the High Mass. Hope was received at about 3 o'clock the same afternoon. Palm Sunday we were confirmed, and communicated in the Cardinal's private chapel; and by his desire I received the tonsure. He has expressed his wish and intention to proceed without delay, and at Whitsuntide to admit me to the Priesthood. He said that it was his decision and act on his own responsibility, not at mine or my seeking. I requested that I might afterwards take a full time for exact study, and abstain for some while from any responsible employment. To this he assented.

I am much impressed by the *hard work* which is going on in the Roman Catholic Church; and the hold it has on people of all degrees is beyond all I thought.

I am living alone here, near the Jesuits' Church; the services of which are most consoling.

And now I will say nothing yet of my own mind, except that I have more than I ever asked or thought. A letter I wrote a month ago about a sort of overflow, different in kind from argument was more true than I then thought. May God keep me watchful in His holy fear. Pray for me, dear Robert, that I may be kept in His grace, and not lose it by my own sin, then all is well, and more. May every one dear to me share this gift.

Let me hear from you. I think you will find Badeley glad to see you.

May God ever bless you and reward you for all your love to me.

Ever yours affectionately,

H. E. MANNING.'

. . . . . .

Thirty-eight years later, nearly three years before his death, on Passion Sunday, April 7, 1889, Cardinal Manning writes of his past.

'6th April in 1851 was Passion Sunday. On that day, before High Mass, I submitted to the Church, and heard Mass for the first time in its unity. Since then, London has been my home and place of work for eight and thirty years, that is in four periods: (1) over three years in Rome; (2) about three years without a fixed place; (3) eight years at Bayswater; (4) twenty-four years as I am now. I am thankful that I have only been in two places during fifty-five years, from 1833 to 1889, Lavington and London. Moving to and fro seems to me to leave little behind it. I hope that a lasting work has been left at least in London. I have not lived in society, but among my priests, and for my people; open on all days and at all hours when they needed me or liked to come to me. If I had gone out into society I could have done little. My time would have been wasted. My evenings lost. I should have pleased a few and offended many. A Society bishop, like a Society paper, is the centre of gossip and in perpetual risk of scandal. I have no doubt that I have been unpopular, and have disappointed many, but I believe they would have trusted me less, and in their troubles would not come to me as they do now. And I feel sure that my priests would have felt that I was less to them, and my poor would have thought me less their friend and pastor. My only contacts with the world have been public and for work, and especially for the poor and the people. Looking back I am conscious how little I have done, partly from want of courage, partly from over-caution. And yet caution is not cowardice. For the highly sensitive state of England and of London, one step too fast is worse than ten steps too slow, and somehow the steady and peaceful gain and growth of the Catholic Church in the last twenty-four years—for I am speaking only of my reckoning—has been very sensible.'

Eighteen months later the old Cardinal makes the last entry in the last of his many journals.

'9th November, 1890. It is more than six months since I wrote in this book. The chief reason is that I have been writing at the bidding of the Bishop of Salford, in another MS. book for my successors.

But there is one thought, I may say fact, that has come before me, and I wish to note it. I remember how often I have said that my chief sacrifice in becoming Catholic was "that I ceased to work for the people of England, and had thenceforward to work for the Irish occupation in England."

Strangely all this is reversed. If I had not become Catholic I could never have worked for the people of England, as in the last year they think I have worked for them.

Anglicanism would have fettered me. The liberty of Truth and of the Church has lifted me above all dependence or limitations. This seems like the latter end of Job, greater than the beginning. I hope it is not the condemnation when all men speak well of me.'

. . . . . .

Think not time is short, as Newman said, for God can make it long.

Archdeacon Manning was forty-three when he gave up an influential position in the Church of England, and the prospect of high preferment. He 'ceased,' so he then thought, 'to work for the people of England'; and on the eve of his reception into the Church he said to his companion in that act of submission: 'Now my career is ended.'

Two years before his death, the Cardinal Archbishop

of Westminster looked back over eighty-one years as he finished his last journal, and wrote: 'This seems like the latter end of Job, greater than the beginning.'

. . . . . .

When a man hath done, then he beginneth.

CHAPTER IV

BASIL WILLIAM MATURIN

THE theory that Newman was driven from the Church of England by the un-Catholic tendencies of the Bishops eighty-five years ago has developed still further among those who believe that Anglo-Catholicism fully represents the pre-Reformation Church. They think that if Newman were alive to-day, reaping the harvest sown by him and his fellow-labourers a hundred years ago, he would find all his desires fulfilled and his dreams a reality in the Church of England as she now has become.

But no one who appreciates the swiftness with which Tractarian ideals permeated Anglican doctrine and practice can accept this theory. The later history of the Movement clearly shows that all Newman had vainly longed to see in the Church of England was to be found in her many years before he died. The children of the first Tractarians grew up in an atmosphere far nearer the Catholicism their fathers hoped to restore to the Anglican Church than that which the new 'Liberal' Anglo-Catholicism provides to-day. Father Maturin's upbringing and the life he led as an Anglican till his conversion, on the eve of his fiftieth birthday, in 1897 prove this so conclusively that the following extracts from his letters have been made in the hope that they may show the true and only reason why the Movement has proved powerless from the very start to keep men from leaving it. That reason is very simple—'one *near* One is too far.'

Few in this generation realise how far modern Anglo-Catholicism has moved from the traditional views held not only by Newman and Keble, but by the 'High Churchmen of the old School' who carried on the torches which the first Tractarians put into their successors' hands. Very few have ever opened a *Monthly Packet*, a magazine which for about fifty years brought Tractarian teaching, set forth by able writers, some of them leaders of the Movement, into many English homes. The novels in which Miss Yonge reflected Keble's training and mirrored the great revival in the Church of England due to the Movement are only now read by a small circle, growing smaller every year, whose mothers and grandmothers were brought up on them. Modern Anglo-Catholic literature is chiefly concerned with the conditions subsequent to 1920, when the 'Congress Movement' sprang into being; and serious students of the progress of the Church of England during the last hundred years are few and far between. So only a small minority of those preparing to celebrate next year's centenary have any idea that the Anglican Church was far more likely to tempt Newman back into her fold during the last twenty years of his life than she would be to keep him in it if he were an Anglo-Catholic to-day.

A notice of Bishop Gore has just appeared in an Anglo-Catholic quarterly which says that 'the Church owes him a great debt for turning the Catholic Movement into modern channels by the part which he played in the production of *Lux Mundi*, a venture which caused great anxiety to Liddon and other "High Churchmen of the old School."' It is hard to suppose that Newman, if still an Anglican, would not have shared that anxiety ; and still harder to imagine his approval of some of the books and articles written during the last few years by leading Anglo-Catholics on fundamental points of doctrine.

In view of this, Lord Irwin's question (already quoted in the study of Newman's conversion which begins this book) seems the last infirmity of a noble mind. His anxiety to be loyal both to the founder of the Movement and also to the Church which that leader found himself bound in conscience to leave, is responsible for the confusion of thought his question shows. It is about as easy to answer as those which were discouraged in our nursery by the counter-question : 'If A. had been B. would C. have been D. ? ' To decide whether or no Newman, ' if he were alive to-day, in the Church of England as she is to-day, would leave her as he did eighty-five years ago ' requires a marvellous exhibition of psychological gymnastics. A Catholic would naturally reply that there is no reason to suppose he would have been more blind, or less obedient, to the Heavenly Vision in 1931 or 1932 than he was in 1845 ; but those, and they are many, who echo Lord Irwin's question see things from a different angle.

It is true that the Church of England now allows the Anglo-Catholic party to teach and practise all that was forbidden to the Tractarians by the Bishops at the time of Newman's conversion. We know from a letter he wrote to Manning, in September 1839, what Newman then considered necessary to make the Church of England into the Church Catholic and Anglican of his dreams. But the letter was written in the halcyon days of the Movement, before the storm of utter disillusionment regarding it which shattered those dreams and finally drove him into the port and happy haven where he found Reality.

And having found it, he learnt how far it transcended his man-made 'figure of the True.' That letter is, however, the probable foundation of the belief that if he were alive now, in a Church where all that he once demanded in vain is taken as a matter of course, he would have lived and died an Anglican.

But the picture of the Church of England shown in Father Maturin's letters between 1871 and his conversion in 1897 is a complete refutation of this theory. They show her to have been at least as near to Newman's ideal during the last twenty years of his life as she is to-day. But she could not hold Father Maturin in 1897, just as she failed to keep Newman in 1845. The reason why both men went is the same; not dissatisfaction with the Church of England, but belief in the Church of Rome. This is proved by Newman's letter to Manning just mentioned, a letter occasioned by Manning's anxiety over the first of his penitents who showed a desire to enter the Church. Newman himself had already met with many similar cases of men who desired to leave the Movement for Rome, though only six years had passed since it began. His sermons on the Catholic 'ideal of a Christian Church' had indeed, as one of his hearers put it, 'awakened a want they could not supply'; and the leaders of the Movement were alarmed at a growing tendency among their followers to find that ideal fulfilled and that want supplied by the Church of Rome.

The passage in which Newman describes his panacea for these unsatisfied longings is repeated here; to show by comparison with what follows how completely it was at his disposal long before he died. But many years before then he had discovered it to be as useless as a panacea always is.

'We must say boldly to the Protestant section of our

Church, "*You* are the cause of this. You must concede, you must conciliate, you must meet the age, you must make the Church of England more efficient, more suitable to the needs of the heart, more equal to the external. Give us more services, more vestments, and decoration in worship, give us monasteries, give us the signs of an apostle, pledges that the Spouse of Christ is among us." Till then you will have continual secessions to Rome.'

The doctrines accepted by 'the Protestant section of our Church' differ so much from those held by the Cowley Fathers that it can hardly be said that the Low Church party 'conceded' the Society of S. John the Evangelist to the Anglican Communion. Nevertheless the Church of England was 'given a monastery' within thirty years of Newman's demands. In 1866 Father R. M. Benson founded in Oxford that community of learned, devout, and holy men to whom their fellow Churchmen, at home and abroad, owe so deep a debt. All the 'pledges' which Newman had sought in 1839 in order to prove the claim of the Church of England to be the Spouse of Christ were to be found amongst the Cowley Fathers a quarter of a century before his death.

Catholics may remember that Bishop Hedley's *Retreat for Religious* contains a generous appreciation of the austere life of devotion he found at Cowley on a visit he had occasion to make there; and all Anglicans who know anything of Father Benson's writings, or of the Cowley Fathers' books and sermons, Missions and Retreats, must surely admit that if the spiritual atmosphere of Cowley could not lure Newman back, nor hold Maturin, in the 'seventies, it is impossible that present-day Anglo-Catholicism would have kept either man back from Rome.

Converts from Anglo-Catholicism are sometimes asked by those they have left 'Why did you go? You had *everything* when you were with us.' Father Maturin's letters show clearly where their mistake lies. For even at Cowley, as he wrote many years later, there was 'a something wanting . . . something needed to give completeness and co-ordination to all the separate truths you believed. The clasp upon the string of pearls that would hold them all together and bind them into one . . . the Unity and the Authority of the Church.'

He grew up with the Oxford Movement; and forms an important link between the first Tractarians amongst whom he was brought up and their Anglo-Catholic successors, many of whom can remember him. His letters are an outstanding instance of 'Plus ça change'; revealing exactly the same need which Newman and Manning and Allies felt under circumstances so different and so far less favoured than his.

No one ever knew the Church of England, at her best, more truly than he. His father, Dr. Maturin, was the Tractarian Vicar of Grangegorman, near Dublin; one of the very few adherents to the Movement which Ireland then contained. Probably on account of the smallness of their numbers, they seem to have escaped the mob violence and the petty ostracisms which were the lot not only of Pusey and Neale, but of their children in the nursery and schoolroom. Born in 1847, two years after Newman became a Catholic, when the principles of the Movement were well established, Father Maturin was, he says, 'brought up from childhood to believe the whole Sacramental system to a large extent as Catholics believe it.' The religious atmosphere of Grangegorman Vicarage was such that out of Dr. Maturin's ten children three of his sons took Anglican Orders, and two of his daughters became Anglican nuns.

Basil William Maturin was ordained deacon in 1870, and became curate to his father's old friend, Dr. Jebb, at Peterstow in Herefordshire. During the following year he went to the Cowley Fathers for a Retreat which completely changed the course of his life, and determined his actions for the next twenty-six years. Though not strictly speaking relevant to this study of his conversion, the following letters are included, as they give such a delightful picture of the relations between Dr. Maturin and his son, and also an impression of the Church of England remoulded to the Tractarian's heart's desire. The Church which produced 'the old Tractarian type in its nobility of character, its high purpose, its stern reality, its clear and logical unworldliness' of which the Maturin family was an example, has nothing to fear from a comparison with 'the Church of England as she is to-day.' Those responsible for the Centenary celebrations would do well to study Tractarian biographies before claiming that a sense of dissatisfaction with the Church of England, due to conditions which the Anglo-Catholic Revival has abolished, was the cause of the conversions of the nineteenth century. For there are still 'continual secessions to Rome'; and dissatisfaction is not and never was the determining cause.

The first letter, in which he announces his intention and asks his father's sanction, runs thus:

'MISSION HOUSE,
COWLEY,
October, 1871.

MY DEAREST PAPA,

I hardly know how to tell you what I am going to write about, or rather to write so as to show you how serious and in earnest I am. I have been in the

Retreat at Cowley for nearly the whole of last week, and, to tell the whole thing out plainly, I want to enter Cowley altogether as one of the Brothers. I have thought, as well as I can remember, almost since I first thought of being ordained, at any rate for some time before I was ordained, of doing it at some time; but did not think I should have come so soon till this last Retreat, when I received a special call. Both Father Benson and Father Grafton, who have had a great deal of experience in people entering the Religious Life, said that they thought I had a call. Father Grafton, whom I really think if you saw you would not doubt, told me he had not the least doubt of it. I told him everything I could think of which I thought might lead him to think I had not; but everything I said only the more strengthened him in his opinion.

I don't mean to say that I told him hoping I might not have it, but I longed for it so much that I was afraid I might hide anything which might tell against me. But everything I said only made him say the more strongly that he had not the least doubt. . . .

So, my dearest papa, I hope and pray you will not, as I'm sure you will not, prevent my going at once. Father Benson would not allow me to enter even as a novice till I had been about three months staying here first. He wishes me, and I need not say I wish myself, to begin immediately after Xmas. . . .

If I were to put it off and to die before I had been able to come, oh, what an awful loss I should have. If I did not come immediately when God called me, He might not call me again, and then I should have lost all I might have gained for ever. I know you will say God would not withdraw His call if I waited His will; but aren't there many instances of people being called once, and when they did not answer immediately they never were called again? And then there are so few men, in the Church of England at least, whom God does call, does it not seem almost cruel to Him for those few not to give themselves up with joy and thankfulness that they should be the ones called by Him to be amongst the hundred and forty-four thousand?

And if He has called me, I have so much of my past to make up for that I could never be too thankful for being selected, because of course I know that, in one sense at least, it is a life of penance. . . .

So you will not ask me to wait another year at Peterstow before I come to try it, for goodness knows what might happen in another year! If I did wait I might have a temptation to some curacy, or something else, to travel abroad, something that I might like very much, and perhaps I should yield to the temptation and so lose all care for coming here. . . .

Don't think that they have put me up to it here, for indeed they haven't. They never breathed a word about it till I spoke to them, and then only answered my questions. . . .

I shall be twenty-five next February, so that I think I ought to know my own mind. As far as I am concerned myself, I should come to-morrow without the very least hesitation. In fact I think—indeed I feel quite certain—I could not help coming here to try it without committing a great sin, so I hope and pray, my dear papa, you will not say anything to prevent me.

If God has called me oughtn't you to feel very happy that all your care of us has been so rewarded by His calling two of us already?'

The date, 1871, and the remark about Father Benson and Father Grafton shows that 'the restoration of the religious life' was no novelty in the

Church of England twenty years before Newman's death.

The next letter gives clear proof of his ideals of clerical unworldliness, and his distrust of his power to attain them as a parish clergyman. He says :

'I just want to tell you exactly all my feelings about it, and then I think I may promise to be guided entirely by your advice—whether to wait or not. For I know right well that all you want is for me to do what is right and what God wishes, and it is so hard for one to be sure oneself that there is not some selfish motive or self-will at the bottom, even when one thinks one is doing it only for God.

The first reason that I am so anxious not to delay is that I know I am not like other people. I am so easily distracted. The least thing in the way of going into society or mixing with other people does me so much harm. So that I hardly ever dine out, or go out anywhere that I do not feel the worse for it. I don't know whether it is a right thing to say ; but what I always think, and have thought of myself, is that I must be either very good, or utterly careless, and I do feel that all the time I am waiting I do not get on as God would have me. I don't know whether it is a conceited thing to say, but it will explain what I mean —I feel that I have the power within me, if it was rightly directed, but that I need direction most dreadfully, and require so much Rule . . . and silence, and to be by myself above all.

I don't mean [that I want to go] because it would be necessarily the highest life at Cowley, but because it would be the higher life for me. And every day I feel more and more certain that it is what God intended for me—instead of getting less anxious, I think I am getting more and more anxious to go there.

Often when I have been out dining, and had a very pleasant evening, when I come away I feel such a longing to be there that I cannot but think it comes from God—especially when it is not altogether because it is what I like myself. That is what makes me feel sure that it is a call from God and not merely an enthusiasm ; for I really don't feel so very enthusiastic about it in myself, only because I feel it is what is for me. . . .'

The following, in reply to his father's wish that he should wait a year before trying his vocation, manifests the complete confidence which existed between father and son ; and his unshakable conviction that he must enter the S.S.J.E.[1]

'One of the chief reasons why I have always thought of entering Cowley is that I have always known and felt that I could not get on in a large town parish, or a parish where there are many gentry. I mean to say that I know it would be the destruction of me to go to such a place, for instance, as Richmond. Although I have been impatient enough in wishing to go there, yet I know I have been most providentially prevented from going. For I know the effect going about and being with people has upon me—it utterly distracts me, and keeps me from thinking, etc. I even feel this for the short time that I go home at Xmas and summer. But then I don't think that such a feeling as this might mean [that I ought] always to stay in a country parish—for I really feel that it does me harm being my own master, as I am here. I feel that I am much too cheeky

[1] The Society of S. John the Evangelist, Cowley, is usually known by its initials ; or as 'the Cowley Fathers.'

in my preaching and teaching, and besides that I know very little about the management of a parish and what to do, so that I am sometimes really at my wits' end. . . .

Mind, I don't look forward with feelings of the most perfect happiness at all to going to Cowley, for I know that I shall have to give up a great deal that I am very fond of—for instance, in a great measure grand services, which they have not there, and society. But there are other feelings which we can hardly explain—feelings that I get when I am alone, I mean, almost, if not altogether quite alone, which leave me when I have any company or pleasure. Even having —— here in the summer, which I enjoyed most tremendously ; I still felt often and often that I should have been much better if I had been alone.

I could not describe all those feelings, but I feel myself almost certain that they are a call from God to leave the world. I did not mention this to Father Grafton.

I am not very sorry that you think I ought to wait, because if you do not think it is neglecting a call from God, I am quite certain it will grow stronger and stronger the longer I wait, and that I may be more prepared when I see that it is God's will I should go.

I am quite certain your letter was an answer to prayer that I might be directed to do what is right. . . .

I felt myself that it would be too great a blessing to think I should go at once. Don't you think that if I wait here another year, and then feel as much as I do now, that I should go, that I ought to try it ?

Do you not think that there is no doubt that the Religious Life is the highest to which one can be called on earth ? I always thought that there was no doubt about it, although God does not always call the best men to it, but those who will serve Him best in it.

And sometimes does He not call men to be very near Himself, because they would not follow Him if they were far off? I do feel so really that I should serve Him so much better there; and as to doing good, must not one do most good by devoting oneself entirely to His service by giving up the world?'

In 1873 he entered the novitiate; and thus began the happy and useful life which was to last for over a quarter of a century. His allusions to Cowley in many of his letters after he became a Catholic, and the friendship with some of the Fathers of the S.S.J.E. which remained unbroken to the end of his life, testify to the complete happiness he found as a member of the Society. From the very first he felt 'perfectly happy' in the life he had chosen, as he tells his father in a letter of 1873.

'I felt more and more certain the longer I waited, having especially your full consent, that it was the right thing for me to do; and from the experience of about six or seven months which I have had of the life, it has quite surpassed what I was prepared for. I have felt so perfectly happy since I have come here, though, of course, one must not rest in that. But I was quite prepared to be miserable for some time at first, which has been very far indeed from being the case.'

Three years later he was sent out to Philadelphia to S. Clement's Church, which was served by the Cowley Fathers. After a time he became Rector, and under his charge the Church 'became a centre of wide spiritual influence not unlike that exercised in London by St. Alban's, Holborn.'[1] He remained there till 1888,

[1] From a notice of him by Bishop Hall, S.S.J.E., Bishop of Vermont, who was in close contact with him during his ministry at S. Clement's.

when doubts as to the Anglican position began to trouble him, and he was recalled to the Mother House at Oxford. Some months were spent at the Cowley Fathers' Mission at Cape Town; but the last nine years of his life as an Anglican were chiefly spent in England taking Missions, giving Retreats, and preaching courses of sermons, in spite of the doubts and perplexities which lay always at the back of his mind.

Very little direct account of what led to his conversion is available. There are no diaries like Manning's or Allies's to draw upon. He made no attempt to edit his correspondence or to supply explanatory notes as Newman and Manning did, and except to Lady Euan Smith just before his reception, he seems to have written few letters about himself at the time when he was gathering strength and grace for the final step. But in the advice he gave to friends who were going through the same struggle, as well as to those who came to him with their problems in later years, there is abundant evidence of what led him to his decision. The comparative lack of contemporary letters is of less moment in his case than in Newman's and Manning's, as there has been no attempt to call his motives in question, nor to create a Maturin legend.

The great value of Father Maturin's own account of his experience lies in his clear, untechnical, almost *lay* expression of the need which drove him to the Church and of the satisfaction of mind and soul which awaited him there. His letters contain a wonderful power to encourage and comfort those who are passing through the same trial. Not only do his arguments smooth away preliminary difficulties, but his memory of the first months after conversion makes what he says a great source of strength and consolation to a convert facing the unknown in his new life. So most of the extracts about to follow are taken from the letters written after he became a Catholic ; and deal as fully with ways of consolidating the position when it had been won as with the methods of attack which carried it.

An Anglican friend throws light on those years in the following passage.

'On his return to England in 1890 he began seven years of extraordinarily widespread, and at the same time continually deepening, influence. It is true there were periods, as his letters reveal, of intense heart-searching and perplexity, robbing him of opportunities of doing even more than he did. However careful he might be, as he ever was, of allowing his difficulties to become known, they could not really be hidden ; and, as he was ever earnest and insistent in declaring in later years, his Society treated him with the most affectionate consideration and sympathy. He was even sent to the Continent and to Rome on one occasion, that at that sacred centre he might seek to find the resolution of his doubts. On that occasion he returned with the resolve to remain where he was.'

The most intimate revelation of his mind on the subject was made in letters to a friend who was in the same state of perplexity and indecision ; and was enabled to enter the Church at almost the same time.

On September 27, 1893, he writes to him :

'I feel for you in all you say about yourself more than you can think. I suppose most—or many—who have had those questions stirred in their minds must also feel "if only I had been more true where I am I should be able to judge more clearly whether it is God's leading or my own fancy." The sense that one has been often so unfaithful, both to the grace and the light one has, must indeed add to the difficulty. Yet surely it may also be a means of grace and restoration —to fight the matter out in the dark when one might have been in the light, accepting the difficulties that are aggravated by unfaithfulness. I do not think one can merely set the matter aside when it has forced itself into one's life, because one feels that one has not been true to what one has. Rather, I feel that the battling out the whole matter may be—whichever side one finally decides—the means of restoration. One cannot allow oneself in spiritual lethargy for any time and rouse oneself out of it without intense pain—this may be God's way of rousing you. I mean, all these doubts, and the facing them, may restore more than you have lost. You remember St. Ignatius' tests when two ways lie before a person and he does not know which is the right one.

(1) Which would you advise another to follow who felt exactly as you know yourself to feel ?

(2) Place the two paths before you and ask, which would lead you more directly to God.

(3) Which do you think you would do if you were to die next day ?

Yet when all is said and done, I find it more easy to advise another than to decide myself ! One's mind gets entangled amidst complications, and I am afraid the will shrinks from action sometimes. You ask me how I feel. It is exactly a year since I was here awaiting the final step, when I meant to go to Beaumont.[1] I believe I tried then to see what was right and to do it ; yet looking back over this year I feel that I made a mistake in not doing then as I had meant to do when I left Oxford. This year has not been a success for me, I am afraid, in the sense in which it ought to

[1] To be received into the Church.

have been. This physical breakdown has kept me back from work, which I should otherwise have taken up, and so, it may be, have put the question aside. I can't but feel it has been providential, and I hope I may be able to come to a final decision before November. There are difficulties, no doubt, on the Roman side, but to me those on the Anglican side are more overwhelming; yet the sense of responsibility, and sometimes the doubt whether one has the right to keep the question open which one had meant to close last November, makes me hesitate.

I have spoken to you quite frankly, and I need not ask you to keep my confidence and not to mention this to anyone. . . . Sometimes it is all as clear to me as daylight that I must not go on ministering where I am, and then again all becomes clouded and I wonder if I allow myself to exaggerate difficulties. I know I have your prayers, as you have mine. God grant us grace neither to hold back nor press forward beyond His leading, but to obey as He speaks.'

Another letter to him on the same subject is dated October 19 of that year:

'I do not think anyone can really sympathise with all the perplexing questions on the Roman subject who has not experienced them. It seems as if one ought to see and act; but at the last moment so many things come before one to make one hesitate and doubt. What I feel is this—if it has come before one quite clearly, clearly enough to make one feel it is one's duty to go, then one ought not to reopen the question or go into it again, but pray for grace to act. The star disappeared just within a few miles of Bethlehem. There must be almost necessarily a great reaction at the last moment when all one's affections and feelings and associations plead with one to stay where one is. But if one has not that clear conviction that one must go, then I believe one ought not to go. Newman speaks, just before he was received, of being *certain*. At the same time I think one ought not to allow oneself to be put off by such a question as Indulgences, etc., any more than one ought to be shaken by some detail of Anglicanism. Keep to the main question. Either the Anglican position is defensible or it is not; if it is not, Rome must be right. How very easy it is to write it all down, and how simple the whole question seems; and yet one knows the intricacies and many side currents that carry one this way and that, till one is driven well-nigh distracted. Do what you believe is most to the glory of God and the good of your own soul, and what seems to you, taking everything into consideration, to be right. I think my course seems more and more clear to me. I hope it may continue so. I am truly thankful for this time of quiet and freedom from work. Yet it is hard to do what all those one loves and reverences must think a fatal mistake and a delusion.'

In the spring of 1894 the pendulum has swung back a little, and he writes from Louvain:

'*May* 23, 1894.

I have been waiting to write until I had something definite, or more definite, to say. I feel now as if the end cannot be very far off. I should not be surprised—unless I get some new light on the subject—if it were next week, but you will, I know, keep this quite to yourself at present. I have such ups and downs, and such times of light and darkness, that I scarcely dare to anticipate what a day may bring forth. I trust my own experience will make me very patient and merciful in judging others in such questions, and very slow to rush into controversy and unsettle anyone else, for there are so many complications and difficulties in the question that it is hard to see clearly what is right. One has so often said : " If I could be convinced of such or such a thing I should go to-morrow." Yet when one is convinced one sees other and other points beyond which make one wait many to-morrows. It is difficult to write, as it is hard to say, much just now—hard to know oneself, and see whether there is not lurking behind all some unconscious self-deception ; indeed one feels as if there were possibilities within oneself that are impossible to fathom. I know you will give me your prayers.'

And in July he tells him :

' At present I am trying to put the whole matter out of my mind and to try if one can get an answer by striving to get nearer to God. Perhaps the straining of the mind is not the best way.'

A little later he sends him another letter :

' I am writing the first possible moment to say that, having done all I feel it possible to do in considering the question, I believe it to be God's will that I should stay where I am, and so I hope that I shall never have to reconsider the question. I wanted to go, and should have been thankful could I have seen my way to going, but when it came to taking the final step I felt that the road was distinctly blocked. I felt, too, that it is possible by constantly going over the same ground to get one's mind into such a condition that it is almost impossible to see clearly. I know, too, that though many questions that are disturbing are not answered, yet God may show me without answering them that one must wait and bear difficulties. I have been through some very terrible times this week ; but I hope, please God, that now I shall feel I have had my answer. It certainly is against my inclinations in many ways, as all my drawings lie the other way.'

Many years later, when at last he could bear to speak of what he had gone through, in order to hearten others under similar circumstances, he wrote these words of encouragement and consolation to someone on the verge of submission.

'. . . Those terrible days before I was received I shall never forget, and every detail is as vivid as it was yesterday, though it was nearly nineteen years ago. I have never been able to understand the mental attitude of people who speak of their reception in a state of exaltation. The more real the English Church has been to you, and all your past experiences in it, the more terrible the wrench. And there is added a kind of uncertainty as to what you will find after you are received, the fear of the unknown—and with me, and probably with you, moments of mental agony, lest through some unknown act of your own you are, after all, making a mistake and doing wrong. I had such feelings up to the last moment, and went through the reception like a stone. I think all this is better and truer, and more spiritual, than being in a state of mental exaltation. You only feel the wrench and the fear and the pains of dying, later you will feel the joy of the Resurrection. An act of the will done with every inclination against it—an unaided act of the will, without the help of a feeling, with all the feelings against it, with no help but conscience, and that even often clouded, is not an easy act ; but it is the assertion of one's freedom, and in a sense a redemptive act, atoning for all the weaker yieldings of the will in the past.

At such a moment one feels utterly alone, and how little help one can get from anyone else! But be assured that no agony of regret for what you are leaving, or shrinking from the unknown future, or mental recoil of any kind, need lead you to any uncertainty that you are right. I believe it all to be the most healthy and proper state of mind for anyone who loves and has loved their religion in the past. You have believed in, and been associated with, all that is best and most beautiful in the English Church. Many of the Cowley Fathers are saints, and most of what they teach is true; but you will find in the Roman Church, in time, something more beautiful, more tender and more human, as well as divine, and something so much broader and larger, that you can only understand it by experiencing it.'

Nothing could better express the dread of loss, the sense of leaving what is truly at its best most beautiful, which makes those who have believed themselves 'always Catholic' hesitate so long. And nothing could be truer or more inspiring than the promise with which the letter ends.

The letters to Lady Euan Smith in the years before his reception throw very little light on his mind at the time. She was under his direction; and he naturally did not wish to unsettle her while he was himself so uncertain. In a letter dated April 17, 1894, he tells her:

'. . . I hope you will not allow yourself to think about or go into the Roman question at present. I am sure no one ought to until it is forced upon them in a way in which they feel it would be wrong to resist. I know there is so much to be said on both sides, and I can say from a large experience that it often only leaves people unsettled and dissatisfied; the question has troubled me for a long time and so far I have not been able to see my way to a decision, but I would give a great deal to keep others from being drawn into the difficulties. I hope you will try to put the question away. I feel it is quite possible it may end either way with me, but I don't feel justified in going on with it until my mind is more settled. I can't tell you how I fear your getting disturbed, and I should feel the responsibility in some way rested with me.'

He was sent to Louvain soon after, so that he might think over the question. He writes to her just before going, and says, 'I may be back again in Oxford within a few weeks, and most thankful I shall be if I find I can come back; it feels like going off into the dark just now.' He seems to have been given leave to stay till he could come to a decision, and to have found it very hard to make one. A fortnight later (May 14) he writes in reply to a question from her:

'. . . You ask me how long I shall stay here. I hope to stay till I see quite clearly what I am to do, which is more difficult to see than you might imagine; but I hope, please God, I may not have to wait in this suspense very much longer, as it is very hard. I hope very much I shall not be here into June; that would be rather terrible to contemplate, but at present I can but wait.'

By the beginning of June he had made up his mind to stay in the Church of England, and tells her:

'. . . Well, I am after all going back to Oxford—I hope to leave here to-morrow. I have had rather a hard time of it here, but I do not regret having come and I hope, please God, to look upon the question now as closed and settled. It has been difficult for me to settle for many reasons, and I have only just decided to return this way.'

But the strain must have been great, and a week after his return to Cowley he tells her that he does not expect to be in Town for some time, or to preach again at present. He feels, he says, as if he must stay quiet and rally himself.

There is no further mention of his difficulties in the letters Lady Euan Smith has had printed till nearly three years later; but in February 1897 he left Cowley, without telling the Community his final destination, as their persuasive arguments had till now overborne him against his better judgement, and he did not feel equal to further discussion. He went to the Euan Smiths' house in London; and then, on February 22, 1897, to Beaumont, where he was received into the Church on March 4. Enquiries were made of Lady Euan Smith by his brother, as the Society knew that he had gone there on leaving Oxford, but she had purposely asked not to be told where he was going so as to be able to say she did not know, if asked.

He wrote, however, from Beaumont, and in answer to the reply she sent to him there he sent the following:

'Beaumont College,
Old Windsor,
3rd March, 1897.

Thank you so much for your kind letter. I was very grateful for it. I did write before I came here to Cowley twice and told them what I was going to do, and I told them that I hoped they would not think it unseemly of me if I did not say where I should go, as I was afraid of letters and the urging to wait, which indeed I have done for long enough. I think they will understand my reason. I sincerely hope so; in truth,

I could not stand the kind of letters I should get. They would simply overwhelm my heart without in any way influencing my head. I shall write, I think, to them and to my sister to-morrow evening, as I am to be received on Friday morning; don't mention this, please, till you hear it from others. . . . I expect I shall have to go up to Town next week for a few hours to get some clothes and to see the Cardinal; I am most anxious to keep out of sight for some time. What ages it seems since last Monday week when I stayed the night with you. I am afraid next week I shall have to prepare myself for a storm! It must be faced some time before long. This letter is outrageously selfish. I hope you won't do anything till you see me. It is not a pleasant state of mind when the question takes possession of one. Indeed, I know of nothing more trying. I have always avoided the subject with you. I did not feel it could be right, as my instincts told me that the question was in your mind.'

As a matter of fact he did not wait till the Friday, for the reasons given in the following letter. She must have told him of a third visit paid her by his brother during which he had elicited from her that Father Maturin was in England, but that where he was she could not disclose to him.

The letter runs:

'Beaumont College,
Old Windsor,
4th March, 1897.

Thank you so much for your letter this morning and for your telegram a short time ago. The fact of the matter was that after your letter this morning I hurried things a bit lest my whereabouts should have leaked out, for I felt I could not face an interview and all that it involved. I have written to my sisters and to Cowley giving my address and telling them that it is all over. I suppose it will get out now; though I should be glad if it could be kept quiet a bit longer. I am very sorry to have given you all the bother of being cross-examined.'

It was sent on March 4, after a telegram announcing that he had just been received that day.

Father Maturin's instincts had told him truly what was in Lady Euan Smith's mind; and the letters he wrote to her between April 25, 1897, when she seems to have written to him definitely about her difficulties, and March 28, 1898, when she too was received, throw much light on his own mind during the struggle only just over. He was in Rome, studying for the Priesthood almost all this time, but wrote very fully to her on the problems which now faced her just as they had confronted him a few months before.

The first letter on the subject says:

'. . . I am sure you are right to take time to think and pray over the whole subject. I can't think how anyone could even try to hurry a person; it must be the work of God, though one must use one's brains and heart. Don't let your mind get entangled, and don't let people talk to you. I believe one can get little help from others; two people equally good seem to see it in absolutely different lights. My feeling used to be—what a solitary thing personality is—how in the great questions of life one is utterly alone—yet surely to have to fight one's way to what one finally believes to be the truth is good for one—bracing and strengthening—even though one's conclusions may be wrong, one must have gained much in the search. It seemed to me the other day, thinking it over, as if the divisions in

Christendom were not altogether evils, as they stir earnest minds and stimulate them to seek, and the search is full of blessing. I am sure one must be very pleasing in God's eyes when He sees one can't be content to let things be, but that one struggles and suffers in the effort to learn what His will for one is. If all life is to be a search, Heaven will be the joyous finding and the revelation that the search itself fitted one for a higher place than if we had not sought. Therefore, while I would gladly spare you all the worry and mental racking that this question involves, I feel sure that it will be a blessing to you in the end, whatever you may eventually feel to be right for you to do.'

She had promised her friend, Bishop Wilkinson, not 'to go into the Roman question for a while'; so when Lady Winifride Elwes, at her wish, asked Father Bampton, S.J., to meet her in May 1897, she told him that she could not avail herself of his help at present. She must have asked other advice on the Anglican side too, as Father Maturin writes on June 28, as follows:

'. . . I think Father P——'s[1] advice to you to put off is very unwise, not to say very wrong. He ought to know that if one has a difficulty it is the only true course to face it and meet it. What it means is, of course, that *he* feels sure you are wrong in having any difficulties and he is putting his convictions in your place. He would not give such advice to a Presbyterian thinking of joining the English Church, because he would think the Presbyterian right. But surely it is wrong in principle to take such a responsibility. I can't see how one can expect God's blessing by shirking responsibility, or that those who give such advice will find that it will bring anything but its own reasonable

[1] One of the Cowley Fathers.

Nemesis. He would not give it on any other question; he gives it because he is convinced you are right to stay where you are; on the same ground anyone might rob another of their noblest acts of sacrifice—no one can see for another. If the English Church uses such weapons, it will surely suffer for it. You are quite at liberty to show him this. I think he is perfectly justified in doing all in his power to keep you from taking what he believes to be a wrong step, but to tell you to put off considering, when your mind is in the state it was when I saw you is, to my thinking, exceedingly wrong and unworthy, and can bring a blessing neither to you nor to him. Cannot God give an answer to an earnest and painstaking search for what one believes to be the truth? Is it God's way to shirk difficulties? Can no solution that brings peace and rest of mind be found? Is one to gain peace by refusing to think? Don't follow such advice, it is not right. I believe it would be better after years of perplexity to come to a decision which one felt convinced was right, even though it should be wrong, than to shirk using one's reason to find out what was God's will. Half the battle of life is to find out what is right; many would have little difficulty in doing it if they knew. I believe that one good thing for which God allows the divisions in Christendom is that it may test those who are in earnest to seek. "To those who *seek* Thee, O how kind." "Thou hast set my heart at liberty because I seek Thy Commandments." I know you better than Father P——, or perhaps most other people, and I certainly care more for you, and I would gladly spare you all the misery of doubt and questioning; but I would not. I care too much for you, to spare you the price that must be paid for knowing what is right and God's Will.'

The long period of uncertainty he had endured, partly due to the natural desire of the S.S.J.E. to disabuse him of what they thought a mistaken impression, made him well able to answer all her misgivings.

On September 27, he says: '. . . I want to send this by to-night's post, so I won't write more, except to say that you will, I know, keep to your promise not to bind yourself by any promise. If I did not know all the contortions and twists in the pathway from England to Rome I might give some weight to your very natural and right fear of personal influence, but I think you would be surprised if you could analyse and see how little I have said to influence you. I believe so strongly that yours is the kind of mind that will never find rest till safely housed and sheltered under the strong and firm roof of Rome.'

The next day he writes again, more fully. Mr. W. was anxious to talk to him about her; and asked Father Maturin to allow him to do so during this visit to England. The letter telling her of this arrangement bears traces of his own recent experience.

'I wrote in haste last night and this morning I find I have to go to Canterbury early to-morrow morning, so I telegraphed asking Mr. W. to come to-night, which I hope he will do.

Of course, I knew that you would feel more or less unconsciously the influence of what he said to you to hold back. It must be so. It is not to the credit of anyone to be unmoved by what is said by those they care for who are worthy of trust. Yet I am not anxious, one must needs go through many fluctuations of feeling, and anyone who is really conscientious must be filled with anxiety lest they should be unconsciously actuated by secondary motives. Yet I feel that your state of mind is so like my own, and that of many others whom I have known who have done as I have done, that I feel as if I *knew* what the end must be. You see things as they *are ;* those devout people in the English Church, who are at peace in it, do not. I used often to wonder if it was my own restlessness that made me unable to see what so many whom I loved saw in the English Church, but I believe it to be really that one gets out of the power of idealizing and sees facts. Some people have to go through a long process of reasoning to reach the knowledge which others appear to gain in intuition. I should say to you—certainly see anyone in the English Church you are advised to see, only I know so well what it means, an endless prolonging of the agony till the mind gets so entangled that it can't see clearly. The arguments that are used may, for a moment, make you feel you ought to pause, though they do not convince you in the least, and often the weight of others' character, making you feel that these people ought to know better than you, and so on. Yet think of the weight, on the Roman side, of learning and of holiness. If one weighs individuals there can be no doubt on which side the scale must fall. It is so easy to come in contact with a few holy men who are strongly convinced of the truth of their cause, and who think they represent the Church. Such men are to be found in every denomination. How true it is, the sense of loneliness ; how little one can get of real help from others in any great decision. The responsibility and the merit must rest with oneself. What is as clear to me as the sun in the Heavens, is folly to my closest friend, but we have to act upon our own convictions, not on others'—there is where the solitariness and the dignity of personality comes in. Even our Lord will not force His way : " Behold, I stand at the door and knock." I feel quite sure in my own mind where you will end, whether in a shorter or a longer time, God knows. For your own sake I hope it may be shorter, but I know you are true and single-minded, and I am quite content to leave you in God's hands. God forbid that I should say a word to hasten you on beyond His leading. "The fierceness of man worketh not the righteousness of God." At this moment a lady is being received who only came to see me on Saturday, but she has been in an upset state for a long time.'

His account of the interview between him and Mr. W. is interesting.

'I saw Mr. W. on Tuesday evening and had to rush off before 7 o'clock on Wednesday, and have not had time to write to you since. I had a long talk with him on the subject in general and you in particular. He was, I thought, quite reasonable about you. He thought you ought to see someone on the English Church side first, though he confessed he did not think it could do much good, on which I assured him that I quite agreed with him. He thought your reading had been one-sided, but I said you had not been reading very much—you had read Staley, and then read a book of the same kind on the other side. All I feel, as I said, is the desire to avoid a long protracted time of worry and anxiety, ending, as I believe it must, in one way. However, I am wholly content to leave you in God's hands and to be guided by Him. "In the multitude of counsellors there is safety." I wonder if it is so in matters of faith! But I believe you will follow whatever God bids you to do.

I liked him very much; that kind of man always makes me feel so ashamed of myself, so much better, and leading a self-denying life such as I could not,

I think he took a large and generous view of the position and felt the difficulties. I hope I didn't scandalise him by speaking too strongly.'

He alludes again to her study of the question from both sides in a letter dated October 13 :

'. . . A clever person said to me the other day, who had just been received : "It surprises me that the English Clergy have studied the subject so very little and yet are prepared to give such very uncompromising advice to those under their care." I truly believe it is so ; ask any of the many who take strong anti-Roman lines what they have read on the subject and you will be amazed at how little, yet surely they have no right to take the strong line they do in such ignorance. No doubt personal influence must have some weight with everyone ; it has all along the world's history, and Truth spreads from one to the other often through the channel of such influence. But God forbid that I should press any influence I may have with you to urge you to think as I do. I may be out of the way any day, but it is, I believe, right to use friendship as a channel to explain or remove misunderstandings which in 99 cases out of 100 are what keeps people back from Rome. Yet surely, I would say, let any other influence, on any other side, have its proper and due weight, too. I trust and believe in you too much to imagine that such a grave question can be to any large extent with you a balancing of counter-influences, but I think it is quite right, for instance, that the presence of Mr. W. and what he may say should take off some of the superficial effect of what I may have said ; and then when all that has happened has done its work, underneath there comes the personal sense of responsibility to God alone and the awful sense of solitude. "I must stand and act as I feel right, if those I love and reverence most think me guilty of a crime." How well I know it, and how I long to be able to show you or anyone the way, as it seems to me clear as the day; but I can't and no one else can. . . . But be sure that whatever you decide will not weigh a feather's weight in my affection for you or respect for your absolute sincerity.'

The experience which enables him to enter into her mind, and his great power to console and strengthen are clearly seen in this letter dated November 14, 1897, from Rome:

'. . . I have seen many go through your state of mind. I have gone through it all myself, and I know there is but one issue, one way out of it. The sun shines behind the clouds and it battles with them till they disperse and scatter, but we can't drive them away, we can but wait and long with tired eyes for its light. So I believe, with you. You can but wait and pray and be ready. If it is the Truth, it is God's revelation to the soul. The wonder is that He gives it to some and not to others. I believe He is giving it to you, but all the agony of mind and misery of heart is a preparation. If it all came clearly to you at once, you might not be fit and ready to receive it. I long for it to be clear to you, and I feel tremendously for you in all this time of anxiety, but I would not have it otherwise; it is best for you, a sifting and a testing, a searching of motives, and a looking into yourself. The man in the Parable saw the treasure, then it was hidden, covered up, and he went and sold all to buy the field that held it. You get a glimpse of all that it might be, then it is hidden—hidden so that it seems as if you never saw—and then one begins to sell all to buy it, to realise the value of Truth, and how hard to see it, and how much it costs! If I could take you by the hand and lead you where I am in a week, it would not be a kindness; the moral struggle is itself the preparation to make all the wonders of the Church your own when you are able to come to the door and beg to be admitted. That that day will come for you this year, next year, or the year after, I have no more doubt than that the sun will shine here in Rome again when the clouds disperse. The moment comes when one not only believes the arguments, feels the force of the claims of Rome, but when one says to oneself: "Now I must go, I should be untrue to myself and my God if I did not," and I think when that moment comes, you will not delay; only keep your mind and heart ready to do whatever God bids you do. Till God bids you rise and go you can't go. Samuel heard God's voice three times before he could understand what He was saying.' (It will be remembered that Manning also looked upon Samuel's threefold call as a lesson to 'wait still upon God' before coming to a similar decision.)

He goes on: 'I believe God is speaking to you now, stirring your soul and rousing your mind. The moment will come when you understand what He says, and no power on earth could lead you after that to doubt it. Don't be disturbed by a man telling you he doesn't believe half the doctrine of the Church; if he doesn't he is not a person whose opinion is worth anything on the subject, that's all. Don't bother your mind with so small a question as indulgences; if you believe in the Church's teaching about everything else, surely you can trust Her about that. Keep to the great question—is Rome right or is the English Church right? They are based on two different principles which are incompatible. Rome says our Lord instituted the Papacy, the English Church says He did not. Rome says the Church can't be divided, the English Church says she can. Rome says it is as important that the Church should teach the truth as that she should minister the Sacraments, the English Church permits her Clergy to teach directly opposite doctrines—that is to me, if possible, the most overwhelming argument against her. If our Lord has revealed the Real Presence, think what it is for those in authority to permit people to be taught that He did not—yet you may be in a high position in the English Church and believe either and teach either. The English Church will not utter a word of protest whichever you teach. A few years ago she would not ordain men who did teach it. She has changed her mind on several subjects of grave importance in my lifetime. How can one trust one's salvation to a guide that is so uncertain ?'

On December 2 he answers her difficulty about Anglican orders thus :

'. . . As to what you say about a practical denial of Anglican orders in joining the Roman Church, it is no doubt true, but no more than it has been since the Reformation. From the first drawing up of the Anglican ordinal the Pope has refused to recognise those ordained by it ; it was the discovery of documents showing this that largely decided the line the Pope took in the Bull. The Bull merely puts into words what has been done in practice since the Reformation—that is, the refusal to recognise Anglican orders. I can't imagine the subject being treated more fairly or more thoroughly than it has been. There is a motto in use in the Church : "In the use of the Sacraments there must be no doubt." No one can, I think, read the history of those 300 years and say the matter is above a doubt ; no one, that is, who holds the Roman doctrine of the Sacrifice. I can't conceive of anyone having any difficulty on the subject who really believes that Rome is the Catholic Church, and if they don't believe that, then they can't come. In fact, the real state of one who does believe Rome to be the Catholic Church is this : The Church says one can't accept Anglican orders, they are at least too uncertain. Personally you believe you have received the Sacraments. One does not demand of you a categorical denial of this, merely a submission to her judgement. Which is most likely to be right ? Have you gone into the question thoroughly as she has ? Has the English Church, which denied it till 50 years ago ? On what ground, except a subjective one, do you feel so certain ?—and it is possible one may be mistaken. Knowing what I do here, I conceive it impossible that Rome could have given another opinion than she did,' and adds a long postscript :

'When Jennie' (his sister) 'says you can't become a Roman Catholic without denying that you have ever received any Sacraments in your life, I don't think she is quite accurate. Of course, one can state things in a way that makes them harder to oneself to accept, and one can think of them in the same way. The way I would put it is this : The Pope's Bull said practically, "It is impossible for the Roman Church to accept Anglican orders ; historically and theologically they are too uncertain. Nothing that has a shadow of doubt can be permitted in the ministration of the Sacraments." And I can't see how one can find much difficulty in accepting that judgement in view of the facts ; at the best I believe the matter full of uncertainty. The English Church proposed to decide whether the Scandinavian Church had orders; the question came up at the Pan-Anglican Synod. In other words she professed to be able to decide whether to her mind there were sufficiently strong reasons in favour of Scandinavian orders for the English Church to recognise them. Doubtless there are many devout Scandinavians who believe they have received Sacraments; but if the Scandinavian Church is to be in communion with other parts of Christendom, those parts must decide whether they can accept her orders. Well, surely, *some* outside authority must be able to say about the English Church what she professes to be able to say about the Scandinavians; and what authority will the English Church accept? A few years ago almost all the Bishops would have agreed with the Pope; in 1833 only two Bishops believed in Apostolic succession; who is to decide? Already two independent bodies—the Church of Utrecht and the Church of Rome—on the *same grounds*, quite independently, decided against the Anglican orders; that is, that they are too doubtful to be accepted. Now English people say the Eastern Church will accept them, but that can only be a matter of opinion. I believe they will never give an opinion at all, as is the Greek custom. If a General Council were appealed to, the English Church couldn't sit in it as she would be on trial, and Rome would outweigh the East in numbers by about two or three to one, so that we know what the judgement of a General Council must be. However, you aren't asked at your reception to deny anything. You have but to accept the Creed of Pope Pius the Fourth. I asked a learned Jesuit yesterday if I was not right in saying that the Pope's Bull practically meant that Anglican orders were too uncertain to be recognised, and he said, "Quite right."'

Three weeks later he writes: '. . . I can understand what many can't—the position of one who intellectually feels no difficulty as to the Truth of Rome, yet morally feels unconvinced that it is God's will, or right, or her duty to go. I can understand it, though I think it is only the entrenchment before the last attack and surrender! I wonder if you would do right to give your mind a whole rest on the subject—say, till Easter—and simply think of it in your prayers by acts of self-oblation; sometimes I think the mind gets so strained by long consideration of one subject that it gets into grooves of thought, and a rest gives it an opportunity for a fresh review of the whole position, though, on the other hand, you may well feel that you must settle the matter once and for ever.'

On January 12, 1898, he sends her a long letter, from which these extracts are taken:

'. . . I feel as if I might say a good deal, but feel so sure you are in God's hands that I would rather leave Him to work it all out His own way. You will see how one would shrink from deliberately disturbing one who believed in the English Church now that you know how difficult a question it is to settle. It seems so very simple until one gets into the thick of it, and yet after all it is simple really. I imagine after one's intellect gets convinced, custom, habit, and association raise such a clamour that the reason for a moment is puzzled and wonders whether all this noise is really its own and whether there are not strong arguments, lurking behind, which one has not faced. I can't myself imagine that you can find yourself settled again and at peace in the English Church, though, whatever the result, I am sure God will bless the earnestness and simplicity of your purpose. I am truly glad you bearded Father G. So many say such outrageous things in perfect ignorance of the whole position, and every word said that is not true hurts the cause in which it is uttered; besides, it is a sin against charity to accuse anyone of acting from unworthy motives. . . .'

'One studies and thinks and asks questions and does one's best to study the question honestly—this is the work of Nature—then God breathes on these facts that you have filled your mind with, and something more than seeing the strength of the arguments comes to pass. They become radiant, convincing, overpowering; both intellect and heart are flooded with light and warmth, and one knows what one ought to do. That is the supernatural response to the efforts of Nature. Till that or something kindred happens, one can do nothing; when it does, one knows what to do. As to going on with your Communions, I should be guided by my conscience. I can readily imagine a person feeling it quite impossible, and I can imagine a person feeling able to go on with them, though I think it would be almost better not, myself. How I wish I could help you more. Don't ask for too much before you come to a conclusion; ask for what you feel is enough to enable you to make a reasonable and responsible judgement, and don't let anyone either hurry you by half an hour or hold you back. When you feel that God demands of you to decide, and has given you enough light to decide by, then decide and stick to it. Try writing down reasons for and against, it may help to clear your mind. On one side put down all the reasons why you should go, and on the other why you should stay, and see which outbalances the other. I do really think it would be a mistake to bring all Father Bampton's arguments to an Anglican; probably you would feel that his answers to Father Bampton's arguments ought to be submitted to Father Bampton again! It would be interminable and would keep you simply on the rack. You are quite capable of forming your judgement as to the value of Father Bampton's arguments yourself; keep yourself, as I am sure you do, before God, and do what you feel right before Him; one is bound to act like a fool or without sufficient advice in the judgement of one side or the other. Above all, when you look the future in the face, ask yourself, "Where shall I find myself freest from any possibility of further unsettlement in the future?" God can't mean you to be constantly undergoing unsettlement of mind.'

A letter of January 27 is full of comfort to those going through the stage he describes, which is for most people in such circumstances probably inevitable.

'. . . I know all you are feeling and all the twists and turns of that seemingly endless road and how at one moment one seems within clear sight of the end, and the next one finds it all seems to lead to a *cul-de-sac*. I used to feel sometimes that it was all so clear that I seemed ready to be received at that moment, and then reaction set in or some other train of thought and all was utter darkness again. Yet the moment will come when you will say to yourself, I believe my time has come, it is God's Will I should go. I would not have you received and then doubts come afterwards; indeed, if they do, you will treat them as directly diabolical. Let me say this: After you are received, quite possibly there will be a reaction of feeling and you will have no sense of happiness; perhaps no assurance you have done right; perhaps, only for a time, disappointment. But this is no sign that you have not done right; on the contrary, I think it is far more healthy than the exaltation some say they have felt. Two of the most enthusiastic Catholics I know had such experiences as I speak of after their reception—one was dismayed with the fear that she had done wrong, and the other, who was not young, was miserable for a time—now I know few more ardent. Indeed, I had no feeling after I was received of exaltation or joy; for a time nothing but fear lest after all I had done wrong. I say all this to encourage, not to discourage, you. You do your best to find out the right course, then you act and leave all the rest to God. "If I perish, I perish"; but you will not perish. A tree often, when transplanted, looks at first as if it were going to wither, till it spreads its roots and sucks its nourishment from the new soil. I hope you won't see anyone else after Father B., it's no use. Can you imagine yourself settling again in the English Church? All acts of faith have a certain risk—leaping out into the darkness—but not till you have heard as an answer to your prayer, "Lord, if it be Thou, bid me come to Thee," "Come." When you have heard that, then you will *know* you ought to go even if the risk be drowning! I am so sorry for what you say about the line Hilda[1] takes, but I suppose it really means that God will test you to the utmost to see if you will act even at the risk of what you love most.'

Three days later: '. . . How easy it is to say, "Give your mind a rest." 'Tis like telling a person suffering from insomnia to go to bed and take a good night's sleep! Yet rest lies at the other side, I hope; at any rate, you will never know till it's all over and a thing of the past how your soul has drawn nearer God in all this, and, after all, truth or falsehood, Rome or

[1] Lady Euan-Smith's daughter.

England, anything and everything, is only of value for this. God allows the way to be long and dark for those who He knows will not rest till they have reached the end, whatever that end may be. Try to let all your prayers be acts of self-oblation to the will of God. Try to get yourself to feel indifferent how it ends, whether in Rome or the English Church, so long as you can only feel sure it is God's will for *you*. It is the greatness of the agony of personality that it has to stand alone and decide for itself. S. Agnes, a child of 14, with all the power of heathen Rome against her, took the line she felt right, and God and that child conquered the world. I know what it is to hear those one respects—whose boots one isn't fit to clean—saying: "You are simply under a delusion," and yet to feel, "I see something that they seem not to see. To me it is clear, I must take my own line, and if I perish, I perish."

What is this mysterious and overpowering spell Rome casts over people, of such different characters and modes of thought? It is too great to be human—it is either diabolical or divine—in truth, I believe it is—to be very poetical!—homesickness. It's the longing for one's true fatherland and the home God has made for all of us on earth, which satisfies and proves its fitness to house and shelter all who enter it.'

The letter of February 14 is full of insight and wise advice:

'It must be fearfully trying for you, all this uncertainty—and yet I am sure that not an hour of it is wasted. God *could* give you in an instant, if He saw fit, a perfectly vivid realisation of what you ought to do. If He withholds it, it is because He sees that the anxiety and waiting is really able to do you more good than the certainty, and if one is growing in self-knowledge and the knowledge of Him, and waiting only to know His will, what matters all else—even if we be kept shivering between the two worlds ? I do not myself think that it is of the least consequence that you should see your way clearly to all the details if you feel clear on the main points. Many minor points you will grow into, and they will only become clear and acceptable in time. I don't think, for instance, that such a question as indulgences ought to hold you back for a moment, if you feel that with all your heart you believe that the Roman Church is the one which our Lord founded, and that in His words to S. Peter He taught that He established the See of Peter as the centre—the necessary centre of Christendom. All else is involved in that—if He intended that to be the centre, He certainly and necessarily pledged Himself to keep it free from error in all matters of doctrine. It was a long time before I saw that clearly, but it seems a necessary and simple Truth if one believes that in those words, "Upon this rock, etc.," He pointed out the centre around which all must gather, or the foundation upon which all must be built. You would not advise a person to put off his Baptism till he could accept and see clearly every detail of the Christian religion ; you would say, "If you believe in our Lord and in the great doctrines of the Creed, come ; all else will follow afterwards." S. Paul must have had many questions unsettled when he was baptised ; indeed, he probably understood nothing except that Christ was God. Do you feel as sure that the Roman is the true Church as S. Paul did, after his vision, that Christ was God ? If you do, all else will follow. At the same time, if there is any detail against which you have strong feelings or clear convictions, I do think it better to have them cleared up. There is, of course, a risk in coming, but that risk, for one who comes rightly, is the risk faith demands. Sufficient certainty to risk all that may need to be risked. . . .

Two questions I think you ought to keep before you. (1) Can you ever settle down in the English Church again? God can't mean you to go on for ever in a system which you distrust. (2) Could you expect the matter to be made more clear to you than it has been before you take the step? Keep clear in your mind the difference between conviction and the constant currents of feeling that come and go, which are often independent of conviction. I mean the mind may get so weary with thinking that a rush of feeling may come sweeping over the soul, seeming to break down all convictions and only leaving one hating the idea of taking the step and disgusted with the whole question—hating for the time Rome and all its ways! I know that state well and was often deluded by it into imagining I didn't believe in Rome; but latterly I was able to keep the two states of mind quite clear and to realise that all the revulsions of feeling really left my convictions untouched. As to waiting six months; I don't know what to say. I don't see how you could go all those months without religion, or how you could return for the Sacraments to the English Church feeling as you do. The sense of not being as ready now as a few weeks ago is really of no account. What it means is that when you were contemplating the step immediately, your will was lashed up to action and your mind had clearly its convictions before it; now, naturally, the will holds back and needs another lash or two, and the freshness of your convictions is not as strongly felt. Look in and you will see that they are in fact just as real and just as living. Yet, when I have said all this, I still feel bound to say you cannot take the step till you feel yourself that the moment has come and that God bids you take it. That personal conviction and personal responsibility makes us all feel in a great crisis how utterly alone each stands and how little really anyone can help us ; but then, when that moment comes, you must act. . . .

No one ever does a hard thing believing it to be right, but the influence goes out from them to others. . . .

If it rested with me to give you the peace and certainty you desire, you should have it by telegraph to-day !—but that is because I care more for alleviating your pain than developing your character, which is what God cares for. It is good to remember that any of us who bear all this trouble well are perhaps paying some of the penalty due to all the sin and sacrilege of the 16th Century, and helping by our patience, more than we can tell, in restoring unity to the Church. Suffering for the sake of what we believe to be the Truth is, at any rate, in its degree a martyrdom, and the blood of the martyrs is the seed of the Church.'

The day before her reception, when still unaware of her decision to act at last, he wrote from Paris :

'. . . How easy it seems and what an agony it is. I remember feeling tides of different sensations rise and pass over me every few moments during those last days, but through it all I had the conviction that if I believed in anything, it was Rome ; that I never could feel that I trusted the English Church again, and that to turn back was to turn back for the sake of my affections not my convictions. And I think it is the same with you. I can see ahead, a year hence, say, when you have settled into your new surroundings and feel at peace, that you will feel that you have got to your true resting-place, and I am sure the more you suffer now the more blessings it will bring you in the end. It is part of the price that must be paid for all the wrong and wickedness of the 16th Century. Remember the promise which certainly will never fail on God's part, "If with all your hearts ye truly seek me, ye shall surely find me." One can't expect to uproot oneself from the surroundings of a life without strong protest from one's heart and one's nature. Those who can take such a step lightly are not likely to gain much from it, nor indeed to have much security for persevering in it. . . . I wouldn't have you delay for a day, as I wouldn't have you hasten by a day. May God lead and order all for His glory and your happiness, and may any influence I have ever consciously or unconsciously had with you, if it has led you to other than God would have, be blotted out of your mind. I often pray that.'

About ten days later he sends this piece of advice, which may help some under similar circumstances :

'. . . Don't be troubled at questions stirring your soul still, it would be a miracle if they didn't ; often crossing the Atlantic some of the roughest weather has been the disturbance after the storm was over !—which poetic allusion means that many heavings of heart and mind go on after the storm has really passed. Put resolutely away any questionings, refuse *absolutely* to open the question ever again, shut and bolt the door if questions try to come back. It's your only chance to get the peace and the joy that will surely come, in a year perhaps ; but you didn't come for peace, you came because you felt it to be *right*—no doubts, fears, worries, made the conviction that led you to take the step less of a reality. Suppose it all came clear as day to you that you had done wrong in coming, I should still cry as long as I had a lung to cry with, "You are deceived, it is the devil's effort to upset you again; the conviction you believed you had compelled you to come, now stay and put out your roots, and look upon everything that would induce you to do otherwise as temptation." It would be so strange, that you might well be afraid, if never a question rose in your mind after all you have been through.'

Among the letters written to other friends[1] from Rome at this time, the following, to one of the Cowley Fathers, gives an interesting account of his new impressions. His correspondent had evidently asked if he would visit the Community during his summer vacation (he was studying for the priesthood at the Canadian College), which he intended to spend in England. He says: 'I don't expect that I shall be in Oxford. I am afraid there are not many there that want to see me now. It's curious to feel oneself shut out from many places where one had many friends a few months ago, but that is quite natural and probably right. At any rate, I am more than repaid by finding myself at home in any church all the world over; and what wonders one finds when one has passed the doors and entered. It is an amazement to me that we in England should live so close to what we are wholly ignorant of—for we are; one has no idea of what it all means till one enters and sees for oneself. It strikes one as being so broad and so obviously true. I wonder where the idea that people generally attribute to Rome of slyness and untruth comes from. I can only imagine it to come from hell, for I can see no faintest token of it. Faith seems perfectly fearless, for it knows it is grounded in reason, and there is a completeness of conviction all

[1] The letters which now follow are all to be found in *Father Maturin. A Memoir*, etc., from which the extracts between pages 327 and 341 have been taken.

around one that is contagious. I think one has but to cross the threshold and enter to find conviction pour in through every sense and faculty. I saw and had the privilege of living amongst the very best of the Church of England, men infinitely better than I ever hope to be, and I thank God for all the holiness and devotion that there is there ; but truly the difference between all that and this is the difference between individual effort and organised life. Amongst savage tribes there is perhaps a greater display of individual courage than in an English regiment, but the savage tribes can't produce anything like one of our regiments.'

He ends with : 'There is toc, none of that almost necessary self-consciousness which springs from the fact that one does and believes differently from others,' meaning, of course, those in the Church of England who belonged to the other two parties, differing, on various grounds, from each other, and from the High Church party of which the Cowley Fathers were members.

In his next letter he says he will go to Oxford after all, and gives ample proof that he did not leave the Church of England from any personal dissatisfaction with his life in it.

'. . . I am so often in thought at Cowley. Someone said to me the other day that it was said I did not feel leaving at all. I often think I am the most callous brute on earth, but I don't think I shall ever cease to love Cowley and all that belongs to it. I say the old prayer every day, and I intend to slip down quietly to Oxford before I leave and prowl about unseen, and, if I can sum up courage, look into the church,' and to another friend he writes at the same time : 'Of course, the final step is full of suffering—indeed, I know of no suffering like it. Near though we seem and are in faith, yet the step is a wrench like death ; but we cannot have the best thing life has to give us without paying a heavy price for it.'

A letter, undated, which was written some years later to someone who had just entered a convent, seems to show traces of what he then went through. It does not seem to refer to his own experience as a novice ; for in the letter quoted on page 333 written after his first six months at Cowley, he wrote : 'I have felt so perfectly happy since I have come here.' At any rate it seems well to include it here, as 'times of darkness, solitude, and trial, when every memory of what you had comes crowding back and calling you to come back' often make the first months after conversion very hard to live through. Father Maturin's bracing, comforting words, though written to meet other needs, exactly meet those times.

'. . . I suppose it would be comparatively easy to give up everything for God, if we at once felt His Love and Presence. But in times of darkness and solitude and trial, when every memory of what you had comes crowding back, and calling to you to come back, and you keep on saying, "No, I shall go on if He leaves me in the darkness for months," then the soul becomes more and more perfected, and all that was amiss in the past gets purged off. God, at those times, is asking you, "Do you love Me enough to leave all and wait for Me, even though I *seem* to ignore you and leave you to yourself," and as you wait in patience you are really saying to Him, "Whom have I in heaven but Thee, and there is none upon earth that I desire in comparison with Thee." The wrench from all you had in the world, and I don't know anyone who had more to give up,

I don't think anyone could have borne better; at least I never saw anyone give up everything more generously and courageously. But the inner wrench, the turning of the whole self to God, and the loosening of the heart from everyone is harder, and there must be, I suppose, for everyone that terrible time of testing when you have given up everything, and seem for the moment to have got nothing. That is purgatory, the intermediate state between earth and heaven, when the heart cries out for love and has nothing to rest upon but God, Who does not seem to care. Every hour that you go through such times of darkness purifies your soul more and more for the Vision and the Love when it comes; and it will come most surely, strengthening and refreshing you and making you more and more certain that God has chosen you for Himself, and counts every tear and heart pang, and is watching you when He seems furthest from you with loving and anxious eyes.'

This passage from a letter dated February 23, 1891, during the period when, as he once put it, the Roman question was never out of his mind for an hour while he was awake, probably reflects those heart-searchings which made his advice in later years so full of insight and so valuable.

'You may be *quite* sure, I think, that God does not reject an offering because it has taken you some time to make up your mind to make it, and whatever the cause of your feeling it does not come from your offering being rejected.

It is, I think, quite natural, that when one has made, or is trying to make, an offering that costs one a good deal, one should feel very cold and loveless, for two reasons:

(1) The reaction after a struggle of the kind often leaves one spiritually numbed and powerless to feel.

(2) The testing of the will, by the withdrawal of all those aids to choice that come through feeling and emotion and love. Some of the greatest acts of life have to be done simply with the reason telling one it's necessary, or conscience with its unimpassioned voice bidding us do what costs us all we love. And then if the will unaided obeys, it's like a lever lifting the whole weight of our being to a higher moral standard. But at such times there's no emotion, no sense of exultation or of triumph, the nature is left, as it were, to recover its footing and to regain breath ; the sense of peace comes later. . . .'

The following extracts are taken from a long series of letters, between 1894 and 1901, to a lady who came back to the Anglican Church (after a lapse into Theism) under his guidance, but never overcame the prejudices which clouded her outlook towards Rome. As she seems to have advanced practically all the usual objections made by those in her position, his clear and patient replies cover much ground. His arguments against the non-Christian Theism which at first attracted her are very plain and convincing, but only those bearing on her objections to Catholicism will be given here.

On October 26, 1894, while he was still an Anglican, he writes :

' . . . It is not enough to feel drawn to Rome, and to feel a dislike to much amongst ourselves. Nothing would justify one's leaving the English Church but a belief that it was no true part of the Church of Christ. If one feels clear about that, there is nothing but to go. If one doesn't think that, I can't see how—however one loves and longs for much that Rome gives—one can go. Of course it is absurd to say it would suit one's temperament, unless by that it is meant that a person of a certain temperament naturally will be led by God to believe Rome alone is right. I think that that seems to be true. This is clear to me, that those who have gone to Rome and been blessed had not a doubt. It was quite clear to them that Rome was alone the true Church. Others, *many*, have loved Rome and wished to go, but have been held back by the feeling that they did not believe Rome alone was true, however beautiful. I wish I could help you more, but I feel that I cannot say much on that question to help anyone. I can only say I have thought more about it than most, and so far I have not felt I could go, but that is little use to others. Don't let your mind get entangled, try to see what God leads you to and act up to the light He gives you. After a time one only gets hopelessly muddled.'

Three years later, a few weeks after his reception he gives an arresting account of the wonderful manner in which conviction of the truth of Catholicism comes, 'not with observation' nor by mere human aid.

He begins :

'*March* 26, 1897.

Thank you for your letter. I do not feel at present that I have any right, or indeed any inclination, to try to influence others one way or the other. My own experience has taught me more and more clearly that no outside influence can really hasten or accomplish God's work—if it is His work, as I believe. If you try to know His will and to prove and test yourself, He will not leave you always in the dark. At the same time one must make use of the guides which He has given us—reason and conscience and feeling. I had felt for a long time mentally clear that Rome only could be the end ;

but then a few weeks ago it came upon me with a clearness and vividness that took possession of me, that I must act *now* or I should go on for ever in doubt and misery. That light never really left me till it had brought me safely to my Bethlehem. I could distinguish as I never could so clearly before the different currents that were acting upon and influencing me—the impossibility of leaving in the midst of work, the wrench, the beginning a new life, and a hundred things. But through all these drifting clouds the star of a clear conviction of what was right shone out and never failed me. Till that conviction comes who can dare to act? I would not give you the very slightest push. I know you are in earnest and you will act in God's time. This I feel sure of. When once one gets that view of the English Church that makes its inconsistencies a vivid reality that can't be explained away, one never can find peace there again. One may patch up one's difficulties for a time, but the patch soon wears off and one's misery returns. I do think that no secondary consideration such as the effect upon others ought to influence you—leave that in God's hands. If you feel convinced that you ought to take the step, go out upon the waters at the risk of drowning and losing all. God will take care of the rest. The act must be done in the dark, but scarcely has one done it than "there springs up a light for the righteous and joyful gladness for such as are true-hearted." If you could see all and arrange all before, you would lose much of the blessing of a blind act of faith. I say all this on the condition that you are clear as to what is right; till you are clear, of course, you can do nothing but wait—if need be till death. . . . I have been staying with Cardinal Vaughan this week, and he has been taking me about to a number of places. Certainly what I have seen this week strengthens one's faith in the supernatural powers in the Church. God forbid that I should underestimate what is so good in the English Church, but this is different.

God bless you and guide you aright.'

In May of the same year he tells her :

'. . . One can't, it is quite true, anticipate God's time. I believe one must have an inner conviction that it is right for one to take the step before it is possible to take it, but that conviction may come by facing the question straight. And always remember God gives us our reason to guide us—the lesser light is still the light where faith is not clear. If all one's reasoning leads in one direction, I think one should ask, " Why, then, do I not follow where it leads ? " There must, indeed, be a shrinking—a fear—perhaps almost a dread, lest after all one is mistaken, and in truth as one steps out of the boat the water under one's feet gives way. . . . Yet our Lord will not readily forsake you if you have gone forth, because you have thought, through the storm of questionings and doubts, that you have heard His voice saying " Come," and when you feel as if all were over with you, you will find His arm about you and you will know you were right, " Oh, thou of little faith, wherefore didst thou doubt."

For my part, I can only wonder that I could have waited so long—the English Church evaporated like a cloud city on my way to Beaumont and has never had any substance since. It is as different from what I am now in as possible, in ways difficult to explain. The atmosphere and tone is different here ; it is broader, wider, with an extraordinary liberty. There is fearlessness in devotion and a certainty in faith, and an unending variety and fullness. . . .

I do not believe I am the typical convert, as I cannot bring myself to be scurrilous towards what I have left, nor perhaps do I run into the extremes that some whom I have known do. But I am afraid Canon —— (to whom I have not written for many years) would be scandalised, and would give me up as irredeemable if I were to tell him—even in well-chosen words—what I really feel as to Rome and the English Church. But why should I hurt anyone's feelings even if they do say of me things that are not true. I don't feel as if my present position needed sharp words to defend it—it is too strong and too great. I believe you will come, yet I should not say a word to hasten you, only this—face the whole question. Stand alone before God in the matter. I know what it is to have to act in a way that those [whom] one advises must think folly, yet God does allow one person to see what another can't, and each has to act as each is led. You will not find—on this side—any ghosts to frighten you when you come, or any secrets to which you are to be initiated. All is clear, open, and straight. I can see nothing which causes the suspicion about untruths in Rome. I can only attribute it directly to the devil; certainly I find nothing of it.'

To her difficulty about Anglican sacraments he says: 'As to what you say about the Sacraments and the possibility of being mistaken, I think this: God deals with His Church as the one organised body which He created. He sanctions its acts, He guides its words. He has created the Sacraments as unfailing channels of grace. But God deals with individuals everywhere, and pours out blessings on all who love and try to serve Him. Therefore there is an abundance of grace poured out on individuals all over the world. If the Church of

England has forfeited her place and rights, then God deals with every individual in her with His fullest love, and if her Sacraments have failed God makes it up to those who believe in her. . . . What one has to do, and what is so hard to do, is to look at the two bodies, the English and Roman Churches, apart from oneself, and ask which is most like a Divine work. One certainly does not love or contend for the truth, as it allows opposite doctrines to be taught—the other certainly does. What *you* believe of the Blessed Sacrament, Confession, etc., you did not get through or from the English Church, nor would you be satisfied with her doctrines if you had to keep to them. I remember when Apostolic succession was a burning question ; it was not half a century ago when few of the bishops believed it. They don't all believe it still. Is it a wonder that they can't get others to believe it ? No one doubts that Rome has it, nor has she ever allowed anyone to question it and remain in her fold. To me for a long time the English Church as an organisation looked more and more human, less and less divine, and Rome more and more divine. Yet all we get, we can only use as a test of truth by seeing if we get it through the organisation. I used to feel that most of what I taught and believed I did not owe to, and I could not thank, the English Church for. I looked to where I got it, and came here to receive all the rest.'

Six months later, September 1897, he answers some objections she has sent him on the subject of Purgatory.

'As to purgatory, all such things as you quote are not of faith—all that is actually of faith is, "There is a Purgatory in which the souls are aided by the Prayers of the Church on earth." That, or words similar, is all that has been defined about it in the Council of Trent.

Any speculation or ideas in regard to the suffering of souls in purgatory, however, does not interfere with the belief that whatever their sufferings their happiness in the midst of it all is greater than any happiness known on earth. They are in intimate union with our Lord and with the Will of God. They would not desire anything but God's Will. They know they are safe, that they cannot sin nor fail soon to see God face to face. We may feel, I think, about the dead, that we can commit them in perfect faith and trust to the Hands of Him Who has proved His love by dying for them. We know that His own desire is the hastening of their admission to His Presence, and that we, by our prayers, can aid in this. What more do we need to know. If they do suffer we are sure His love will bless and comfort them in it.'

On November 11, 1897, he deals more fully with the difficulties regarding the Sacraments which he had tried to remove from her mind in the letter of May 29,

'As to what you say that no one can enter the Church without denying that he has ever received a Sacrament, it is not true *actually*. You are asked to deny nothing nor profess anything except the creed of Pope Pius, which you will find in the Golden Manual. Of course in coming one accepts the Pope's decision, which practically means this: there is not sufficient [certainty of the] validity of English Orders to allow them to be received. An axiom of the Roman Church is: "In regard to Sacraments, there must be nothing that has a doubt." What you say about the possibility of a universal scepticism if one doubted English Orders, that perhaps Roman were not valid either, this seemed to me to be just the opposite of true. Remember the facts. In the year 1833 there were two bishops on the

English Bench who believed in Apostolic succession—in those days everyone would have agreed with the Pope's decision—the English Church has changed her mind on the subject. The bishops at that time, and on, till comparatively a few years ago, did their best to stamp out faith in the priesthood; now they have turned round and say they were wrong. With such changes of teaching there's plenty to make everyone uncertain, and God is not to blame. The English Church *as a whole* has never taught the doctrine of the priesthood, she does not now—she allows numbers to believe the opposite. Therefore it need engender no universal scepticism to feel uncertain about her Sacraments. On the other hand, Rome has confessedly never hesitated as to priesthood and Sacraments, nor will she allow a doubt on the matter. The Sacraments in the English and Roman Churches therefore stand on very different grounds. England has allowed, still allows, their denial. A few years ago she wouldn't allow her people to believe in them—few did, many still don't—a comparatively small body believe in the Sacrifice. . . . When people speak of the awfulness of a doubt about the English priesthood they close their eyes to very recent history and to many present facts. Would you like to receive Communion from Mr. A.'s hands? Yet though he would get furious at being told it, he is as much a priest as Mr. B., and Mr. B. is no more a priest than he. The English Church gives place to both, and allows both to teach.'

She still fails to grasp his meaning, and in another letter, undated, he makes a further attempt to explain.

'. . . Experience is a great thing indeed, and God forbid one should give up the faith based on personal experience; but experience backed by the universal belief of Christendom is more reasonable and beyond the appearance of a doubt. . . . Surely one can feel that faith based on one's own experience, while many of one's co-religionists tell one one is mistaken (and a few years ago all the bishops would have done so), and while the greatest part of Christendom tells one one is mistaken, is a very different and less reasonable faith than a faith based first upon authority and universal experience, and then supported by and strengthened by one's own personal experience. Such is the faith in Roman Sacraments. If in the English Church you were beset with doubts—say as to the Real Presence—you would consult different people, and you would be told by some that there was no such thing as the Real Presence; by others, that your doubts were temptations. You would feel how much was personal and subjective, how little authoritative. If you were a Roman Catholic and had the same doubts you would be told everywhere and by everyone the same truth, altogether independent of personal experience. Surely you can see on what a different foundation the faith in the two Churches rests.'

A year later, October 22, 1898, he answers further questionings, with a note of despair underlying his patient answers:

'. . . What more can I say on the subject of the Church than I have already said? Of course each soul stands alone before God, and has to act as God leads him or her. What is as clear as day to one is full of difficulties to another. Yet it can't be God's Will that one should be constantly examining and questioning the foundations—"Therefore leaving the principles of the doctrine of Christ, let us go on to perfection, not laying again the foundation." Certainly God has given you many blessings so far, but I think such evidences are scarcely safe as tests of the truth of a system. God will bless anyone who is in earnest and ready to suffer for Him, whatever their faith may be. . . . No doubt many who come into the Roman Church do not seem any the better, but it is very difficult to use such things as evidence. A break in middle life is a terrible upsetting no doubt, and it needs a very close fidelity to grace to develop one's soul amidst new surroundings, and there is the danger of resting after a hard battle and a great trial, and a hundred other things. Besides, God doesn't give such evidence of His truth as leaves no possible room for doubt; if everyone who came to Rome advanced forthwith by strides to holiness, no one could doubt. But I don't think one can say that all Presbyterians or Unitarians who enter the English Church show any advance in holiness, though the English Church has certainly far more truth than either of these. One must keep to the point—is Rome or England true? If Rome is true, one must risk everything temporal or spiritual and join her.'

In August 1899 she seems to have reached the stage when the fear of hurting others by becoming a Catholic constitutes a stumbling-block; and he gives her advice which goes fearlessly to the point. As every one is not always so courageous in teaching 'the utmost for the highest' Father Maturin's brave and weighty words are specially valuable to those faced with similar temptations.

'As to what you say about yourself. You know all I feel, and I do not suppose I need say more—of course, in so grave a step one has to consider its effects on those around one, in the sense, but only in the sense, that it ought to make one as sure as one has the right to feel before taking such a step. That is to say it ought to hold one back from any hasty action, but surely no responsibility to anyone else can make fidelity to conscience, or what one believes to be the truth, less binding. There are moments in life when our Lord's words have a very terrible and literal meaning: "He that loveth father or mother more than Me, is not worthy of Me," and the other side of these words in that other saying: "There is no man that hath left house, or parents, or brethren, or wife, or children, for the Kingdom of God's sake, who shall not receive manifold more in this present time, and in the world to come life everlasting."

These words are an encouragement. God will make up to us for any sacrifice made for His sake, even in this world.'

The rest of the letter, indeed of the correspondence, is concerned with the objections which seem so weighty to many outside the Church, yet vanish like smoke when once the threshold has been safely crossed. Her arguments can be guessed from his replies.

'. . . In Rome, no doubt, there is the human side and the narrowness of individuals is often trying—yet one feels the vast difference between the irritating ways of individuals and the actions and utterances of the body. Bring the English Church face to face with its constituted authorities—the Bishops—and no one can doubt what it is. You may get out of it by saying the Bishops are not true to the Prayer Book, but after all that means to your interpretation of the Prayer Book. A book needs an interpreter, and throwing oneself back upon the "undivided Church" as the interpreter of the Prayer Book is only a subtle form of private judgement. How do you know [that] what you believe is what the

Church believed before the Eastern break? Take, for instance, devotion to the Blessed Virgin. How do you know it stopped just where you stop? Only because you are told so, or because your education and feeling tells you to go no further. So in regard to the Papacy. I once thought as you do, now I feel confident I was wrong. Before, I drew the line under the natural guidance of my education and prejudice and the teaching of those I trusted, but in other points I went beyond my instructors—in fact I believed what appealed to me as true—and what so appealed I found in the "Early Church." There must be a guide to whom one bows and submits as divine, and that guide must not be a sublimated form of one's own bias.'

In a letter of October 27, 1899, he tries to prevent her from making 'S. Bartholomew's'[1] bulk larger in her eyes than the question of the truth or untruth of Rome.

'I think what you feel is quite natural, but the question of the truth or untruth of Rome, you must remember, stands upon its own feet, whether St. Bartholomew's[1] stands or falls. If it were undergoing all the trials of a bitter persecution, or if it were in a condition of the most triumphant success Rome is equally true or untrue, and once you are *convinced* she is true, nothing would justify your remaining longer in the English Church—not even to see St. Bartholomew's safe through a crisis, or to avoid being considered as deserting it in the hour of need, nor on the other hand in the hour of victory, and when all the associations with it are dearest. And on the other hand, remember the Bishops' protestantising of the English Church doesn't make Rome right. If all the Bishops were to

[1] The church she attended.

forbid everything you care for and to deny the Real Presence and to force the clergy into submission—all this wouldn't make Rome right, nor justify you in being received, except on the ground that she, and she alone, is the Church of Christ. You must keep the issues clear; in a time of trouble one is apt to get mixed. To lose all faith in the English Church is quite a different act from believing in the Roman Catholic Church; it is a positive, not a negative act. I am sure if you did believe that Rome was the one true Church you would come to her. Keep it, therefore, clearly before your mind that the English Bishops' depriving the English Church of everything you hold dear does not make Rome any more the true Church than she was before. Nor would St. Bartholomew's passing through ever so sore a trial justify your delay to see her safe out of it, if once you did believe Rome's claim to be true. That claim is simple—the necessity of being in union with the See of Peter, the impossibility of a breach in the outward unity, and the claim that it is as necessary to have a voice that speaks with authority as to have hands to minister Sacraments. Again the lives of Roman Catholics may also be below their standard; they may be narrow, worldly, uninteresting and uninterested in works of charity; that does not affect the claims of the Church. The movement of the English Church is sixty years old; the Catholic Church is not under the stimulus of such a movement, she has gone on through the ages. . . . It's natural that an especial earnestness should show itself amongst those just awaking to Sacraments, etc., but all these things are no tests. One thing I know that the Roman Catholic Church produces what Anglicanism can't produce in the great penitential orders—a type of sanctity out of her reach—and, besides, a Priesthood throughout the world who voluntarily give up the happiness of domestic life. Compare not individuals but the broad products of Rome and the English Church in the religious life. Missions abroad, the demands of obedience freely given—the surrender of many plans and ideas—the great ascetic orders—the vast number of convents of men and women, and I think the result speaks for itself.'

On February 1, 1900, he thanks her for some magazines which evidently contained aspersions on the Church, as he says :

' . . . It seems to me that the things said about the Church are like a miasmic mist that ever hangs about her clear and beautiful light—invented by the devil to keep men back. Much the same happened with our Lord Himself and He practically foretold it : "If they have called the Master of the house Beelzebub, how much more shall they call them of His household."

It seems amazing that such things should be believed, but they always bring to me—if I needed it—an additional proof that Rome is the Church of the ages. The same kind of things were said from the first days of Christianity on. They are said about no other body. The unmistakable supernatural power of the Church, like that of our Lord, is attributed to any other rather than the true source, "He casteth out devils by Beelzebub." . . . The constant breath of scandal that hovers around the Church, misrepresenting her ways and doings was one of the great prophecies—the very first, the serpent bruising her heel. Standing within, it seems to me amazing that people should be found to believe such things. Yet it is just what one should expect if the Church is our Lord's Presence on earth.'

In the next letter he replies to further carpings, February 19, 1900:

'I really think you take Mivart's affair to heart far more than it is worth. . . .

I have scarcely seen or heard one paper or one person support him—even the *Record* considered that he was quite rightly treated, and most of the secular papers expressed themselves strongly against what he said—even the *Times*, being unable to support him, has kept a significant silence. What would you have?

If you are shocked at a man saying such outrageous things and calling himself a Catholic, so am I, and I think the sooner he ceases to call himself a Catholic the better. If it is a token of disunion in the Church then I am afraid *that* kind of disunion began soon after the Church's birth and will continue to the end. But no one can deny that it shows that Rome does all she can to protect the Faith, and does it as the Catholic Church always does—by rejecting from her body those who refuse to accept her Creed. I should have thought that the whole incident told very well for Rome, and showed in strong relief the contrast of her methods to those of the English Church where Mivart might have continued a member and said all he liked. The assertion he makes about numbers of good Catholics who go to Communion and deny the Incarnation I confess I simply don't believe. But anyone who does so, does it certainly secretly; and who can prevent anyone going to Communion in a public church? If anyone chooses to commit sacrilege it is only too easily possible. Mivart's letter and article clearly show a mind in rebellion against Faith, and I confess a tone that didn't seem to me straight or true. I think the event has shown how little sympathy he awakened, and I protest against his being quoted as an instance of the antagonism between science and Rome. It's the antagonism between bitterness, ill-temper and pride, and Faith. He has taught *science* all these years unlet and unhindered. He wanted to teach his amazing theology and it was time to stop him. I really can see nothing but the evidence that Rome is watchful for the Faith.'

In May she evidently sent him more controversial matter; as once more he thanks her for 'the magazines' and administers a most courteous snub; so courteous that, to judge by the letters which follow, it had no effect on her.

'*May 7th*, 1900.

. . . I did not read Mivart's article, I am a little tired of him. I don't like his methods, and I profoundly disbelieve his statements. If one turns away from speculations and ill-tempered gossip and looks at facts they are more restful. The church I was at in Scotland has about 4000 at Mass every Sunday, and the Easter Communions were about the same. Another Church I was at in Liverpool out of a population of about 5000 had about 2600 Communions at Easter, and all this is taken in the most matter of fact way; I could scarcely get the numbers out of the priests. Well, if people worship God and go to Communion and Confession in this way I am quite willing to leave the Mivarts and others to have their grumble. "To the poor the Gospel is preached," and these numbers are largely the poor. Let the wise of this world have their say at the congregations in Rome; I should be glad to see some changes in those congregations, but meantime the Church works and saves souls. . . . These are facts, the others are speculations.'

On May 30 he writes : '. . . Why do you listen to all the stories gathered from anywhere about Rome. Of course, if Rome is *essentially* what your friend in Spain describes her, she can present no attraction to you or anyone else, but is to be abhorred. If the Church at that particular place is in a bad way I am very sorry for it, and no doubt the misdoing of Catholics anywhere from St. Paul's time down to to-day does harm. "Through you," he said, "Christ is blasphemed among the Gentiles." So that all the argument deducible from your friend's experience is that the Church in that part of Spain does as much harm as the Church to which St. Paul wrote in the days of the Apostles. If she or anyone else draws sweeping conclusions from Bilbao and says, the Catholic Church is like that all over the Continent, I can only answer that after a good deal of experience from inside it, in Italy, such a conclusion is absolutely untrue. But what have abuses and bad priests and ignorant prejudice got to do with the question whether Rome is the true Church ? . . . One must keep one's mind to the one question—Is Rome or is England the representative of the Church of the Apostles ? All the abuses in the world and all the bad priests and lax morals in the world do not affect that question. My advice to a person who said she was held back by such rumours and scandals was this—Go and live where the Church is at the lowest and scandals are real ; if you cannot keep your faith in Rome in face of all such things you do not really believe in her. Scandals and wrong-doing are indeed terrible evils, and "the corruption of the best is the worst" ; but that corruption was in the Apostolic College itself where one out of the twelve was a thief, and I think it is well we should remember that such a scandal happened under the eyes of our Lord. The holiest and strictest discipline can't keep out corruption. The Apostles were rebuked when they desired to pluck out the tares : "Let both grow together until the harvest." '

His inexhaustible patience enabled him to write two more long letters in February 1901, after which date no more of the correspondence is given.

On the 14th he writes : ' . . . To come to Rome in your present frame of mind would be impossible. Every line you write shows you distrust her, dislike her, and disbelieve in her. Be quite clear that you never could be received with the smallest hope of any peace till all that dwelling upon small defects, or pressing the lives of Catholics into the position of an argument, have passed away. . . . I have heard people speak in a way as if they had found some short cut to Heaven without the trouble of moral effort. But what of that ? Such people may be found everywhere. In Rome, these people lay hold of the least important things and exaggerate them into chief places in their life. In other religions probably the same class of people would give up religion altogether, or take up with the trivialities in them.

As to the Church of England compared with Rome, in its products I can only say, if you will insist on this as the chief test, you must compare justly. Compare the highest in each or the lowest in each, but not an ordinary or commonplace Catholic with the best the English Church has. Take the English Church as a whole and Rome as a whole. The best product of the English Church that I know is such men as Cowley and such women as, say, Lloyd Square. The best product of Rome is the *multitude* of such orders as Carmelite Nuns, Poor Clares, etc., and of men Carthusians, Trappists, etc. Cowley numbers not fifty I should think. The Jesuits in England alone some years ago numbered some six hundred.

. . . Then again, Rome deals with a class that no other religion has anything to do with. She does keep hold of multitudes who do little else in the way of religion than go to Mass on Sunday. These are a class that in other religions would probably never or seldom go to church at all, yet numbers of them die good deaths. Of course, if you compare devout Anglicans with these, they are far superior—but so are devout Methodists or Presbyterians. You speak of the English Church as trying so hard to do right, etc. To my mind she has a fundamental disregard for truth. Her formularies are drawn up with a view to holding those who believe directly opposite doctrines. She has and always does sacrifice truth to keep numbers, and on any controverted question she leaves her children to shift for themselves, and then Anglicans talk of the untruth of Rome!

What I should advise you is to put aside all these questions of comparison; who has knowledge enough to carry out such comparisons, and to keep to the one question—which is true? If our Lord instituted the Papacy, no abuse, or sin, or worldliness can justify its being given up. If *He* instituted it as the centre of unity, then all separated from it are no longer in the Church.'

The last of the series, dated February 17, 1901, begins:

'. . . I am sorry if what I said upset you, yet I am not sorry I said it. I don't think you *could* be received while your mind remains in the state it always has been whenever you have discussed or written on the question to me. How can you commit your soul to the care of a Church whose first and chiefest claim is to be divine, to teach with divine authority, who claims for herself, and for herself alone, all those startling words of our Lord—" If he neglect to hear the Church, let him be unto thee as an heathen man and a Publican." " He that receiveth you receiveth Me," etc., etc.—and yet constantly find fault with small details of her methods and constantly compare to her disparagement those of other communions. Certainly, as Newman says, the Church that has been on earth two thousand years has collected some of the dust of earth upon the skirts of her garment, yet that garment is " of wrought gold." Certainly you will find many of her children formalists and trivial, and in many places you will find that the clergy are not as zealous and enthusiastic as the best of the High Church clergy, who belong to a movement still in its fervour. Unless you come, therefore, with your faith in her so strong that it stands independent of the people you may be thrown with, and even independent of any formalism or lack of zeal amongst the clergy, you would never find the peace you seek. Surely such things as slackness of individuals, or, what is sometimes more trying, the laying stress upon the least important things ought not to be things to dwell upon or to upset—especially for you coming as you do from a Church where the holiest doctrines are denied, and all one's feelings of reverence constantly outraged. You keep yourself from realising all this by practically confining yourself to one parish, and closing your eyes to what is all around you. There are but few churches where you *could* go to Confession, many where your sense of reverence would be shocked if you went to Communion. What are individual carelessnesses, etc., compared to those which eat the very heart out of the English Church. Can you not rise to the fact that you will not get on this side of the grave any religion which has not *something* in it, or in its members, which may jar? You will certainly find none where you have greater width and liberty for your own soul (and consequently for the souls of others) than in Rome. I constantly feel that one has all the heart can long for or the imagination dream of. Yet the liberty tolerates what suits some temperaments and jars on others. Many Italian devotions I should not like, but I am never asked to like, to use, or even personally to endorse them, but why should I not allow to an Italian the liberty he allows me?'

He ends the letter thus: '"To the poor the Gospel is preached." I confess I have neither time nor talents nor sufficient power of historical criticism to be able to prove my faith from history. How can I tell that my mind is not warped in one direction or the other to begin with? Therefore, there must be some other way of getting at the truth, and I think that other way is to take the Church as you and I find it to-day. Here is Rome with the Papacy, so to speak, in possession. She claims that the Papacy is divine. She quotes the words of our Lord which could not be stronger or clearer if He did mean what Rome says He meant. She points to ages of the past in which the holiest of her children submitted and suffered in submitting to the Pope's authority as divine. She bids you look round, wherever the Papacy is not there is just that lack which the Papacy supplies—discipline, unity, freedom from secular interference. She says: "All this works so well and the lack of it causes so much injury to the Church, that one might suppose beforehand that our Lord would not have left us to supply what He could leave supplied, and nothing but the belief that the authority of the Pope is divine would *work*. Men of all countries and ages would not yield except to a divine authority, and this authority is so declared by our Lord in words that are hard to explain otherwise." As I think I said to you the other day—either they mean what they imply, or they mean nothing.'

He refers of course to ' Thou art Peter, and upon this rock I will build My Church,' Matthew xvi., v. 17–19, and goes on to show how impossible it is that ' Our Lord who saw beforehand the history of the Church used them ; knowing they would be misunderstood (if Rome is wrong), and selecting words that certainly were calculated to mislead. . . . Moreover, those who take them literally find that they do produce the effect they imply—a rock of strength, coherence, and unity.'

He points out that just as she would trust an English history written by an Englishman more than one by a French historian, because the Englishman breathes English tradition and in the present has a key to the meaning of the past, it follows, for the same reason, that ' the Church must be the interpreter of her own history.'

The following extracts are taken from a series written to one who had lost her faith in the Church of England and had become an Agnostic, but was later received into the Church and eventually became a Carmelite.

In 1907, when she first came to him with her difficulties, he wrote a letter full of encouragement in which he told her :

' . . . I believe you are now absolutely, so far as I can see, on the right path, the road that ends in faith and light and peace, and that if you keep up the moral effort to live true to all you do believe, however little, you will get what you are in search of—the pearl of great price. But remember the seeker for that pearl has to keep his mind open, and to be ready to part with what he has already purchased when he sees a better. The search prepares the hand and eye to detect any flaw in what has been already purchased, and to recognise the perfect pearl when it is seen. The search is no waste of time, even if it be not crowned with success; for surely everyone who goes out on that quest will find the object of his search in the next world, if not in this. There is all the difference in the world between a person who is always in search for truth and one who is content without it. One thing I should like you to try as soon as you feel it possible, and that is to say any prayers you can, such as the 32nd, or 25th, 27th Psalms. In saying them you can unite yourself with the spiritual longings of earnest souls for the last 2000 years.'

Six months later, June 10, 1908, he writes after what was probably a long interval, as he says:

'I have so often thought of you and wondered how you were getting on. I can sympathise with you so much, as I have been through the same tangle myself. The nearer one gets to the City of God the more intricate and perplexing the many cross-roads and turnings become—till in a moment the road lies out clear and straight, and the City stands out before one's eyes with its wide open gates of welcome. Please God you will see it soon.'

Ten days later he warns her against feeling bound to become an Anglican once more, just because she had been one when she lost her hold on Christianity. He tells her:

'. . . Don't take any step till you feel both spiritually and intellectually clear that you are right. One must—to find a permanent resting-place—feel clear as to the intellectual grounds of one's faith in a system to which one commits oneself. Better to wait *any* time than to act before one knows that one's intellect is not resting on an insecure foundation which in the long run must upset one's faith. I feel for you so much, and understand all you are going through. I have been through so much the same thing myself; but if you are patient a conviction certain, clear, and overpowering will come to you: "This is the way, walk in it." Till you get that conviction you can but wait, and offer your waiting in suffering to God, in atonement for any fault of your own through which you may in the past have lost your faith. . . . You said you felt more strongly the claims of Rome than of the English Church; if so, how can you join the English Church, or rejoin it with mature judgement and deliberate consent? Don't be deceived by the argument that in becoming a Catholic you leave the Church of your baptism. You were baptised in the Church of Christ, the Church He founded; you could not be baptised in anything else. . . .'

She was received before the end of that year, and the last letter of the series is very consoling to those who know what it is to feel 'isolated from religious sympathy,' after leaving the Church to which most of their friends belong, till their roots have taken fresh hold after their transplanting.

'. . . I think the way you have been at once thrown upon yourself, as soon as you became a Catholic, so far from a Church and so isolated from religious sympathy, is in many ways a very good thing, and tests and develops your convictions and your character. It's very hard I know, but I think later on you will not regret it. After all, so far as each one of us is concerned, the Church, with all its organisation and many helps and attractions, exists only to help us to know and love God and to get nearer to Him. Even though you see and feel so little of it around you, you are a citizen of that great City and bear about with you its freedom, its breadth, and its power, and perhaps a person who is very isolated religiously may feel all this more than others, as an Englishman might feel in some other land the greatness of being an Englishman.'

The following extracts are from letters to Anglican clergymen who sought his advice on the Roman problem.

'. . . May I say first of all, that I cannot understand how any one who is *convinced* that the claims of the party to which you belong, and I did belong, cannot be upheld, can remain on with a view to a corporate movement. If ever there is a corporate movement to Rome, it will be due largely to the individuals who have already gone and led the way. But I cannot see exactly what a corporate movement means when it comes to a question of truth and untruth, right and wrong. I suppose people arrive at their convictions in different ways and with different degrees of certainty. But how could you or I go on receiving Communion and ministering in the English Church after we became convinced that any body of Christians not in union with the Holy See is in schism, in order to wait for others? To my mind, there are two states of mind that are apt to be confounded—one is a loss of faith in the possibility of the English Church ever being able to recover itself—a despair of the whole position—the other is an absolute conviction that, quite regardless of anything else, the claims of Rome are right—Rome *is* the Church. Now, no amount of mere Anglican anomalies could justify a man in becoming a Roman Catholic. The only ground is that the Church and Rome are synonymous. And, when a man believes that, how he can possibly stay on in a body which he knows not to be the Church in order to influence others, I cannot understand. It seems to me like a man who has married a divorced woman and lives on with her agitating meantime for the repeal of the divorce laws. Spencer Jones' books are incomprehensible to my mind—a man spending his time and learning in proving the Divine authority of the See of Peter, but not submitting to it. It is like a Presbyterian writing to defend the Divine authority of the Episcopate while remaining a Presbyterian. That a number of people can arrive simultaneously at the same conviction is, I suppose, true; but that people, especially those who teach and minister in a body, should go on ministering with a view to getting others to leave with them is to me incomprehensible. It is unjustifiable in itself, and it is most unfair and disloyal, forgive me for saying it—treacherous to the body to which he belongs. What right has a man to hold a representative position in a body with a view to induce its members to leave it, wearing its livery, owing his position of influence to it, receiving its pay, with the hope of, so far as he is concerned, destroying it?

. . . You ask my advice—it's rather difficult to give as I am ignorant of your state of mind, but I should sum it up in a few words.

(1) If you believe in the Divine Authority of the Papacy and that Our Lord built His Church upon the Episcopate with the See of Peter at its head then make

your submission; if, or as long as, you have doubts on this subject stay where you are.

(2) If you have any belief in the Anglican claims to be part of the Body of Christ stay where you are. The two theories—that the Church can be divided, and that National Churches are autonomous and can reform themselves; and the theory that the Church is a kingdom which is at unity with itself—are absolutely irreconcilable. There is nothing in all nature to uphold the theory that an organism can be inwardly at one and outwardly divided, the flow of the sap through the tree depends upon its outward and visible unity, so of the blood through the body, so of the different members of a Kingdom—destroy the outward unity and the inward ends with it. Grant all that is claimed by Anglicans as to the corruption of the fifteenth and sixteenth centuries, as to the repeated appeals for a General Council which were unheard, as to the harshness of the treatment of England by Rome, or the political influences which directed the policy of the Pope. Grant all that. There is but one way of a member of a body protecting itself from the disease which is contaminating the whole body—heal the body—you can't heal or protect a member of the body by cutting it off. Its life is bound up with the life of the body. If a branch be cut off from a tree and planted and grows it may have a healthier development than the tree, but its life, its history, are no longer that of the parent tree. The history and development of the English and Roman Churches have been on different and independent lines since the separation—what the English Church boasts of, her comprehensiveness, etc., Rome hates. The two bodies have gone each their own way, and their ways are wholly different. Our Lord's prayer for Unity was

"that the *world* may know Thou hast sent Me"—the unconverted ignorant world, the man in the street—and I can't but think that that proverbial person would be astonished if you told him that the English and Roman Church were one, and that their Unity ought to be to him a witness of the Incarnation. But this ignorant and unreligious person somehow does feel the force of the Unity of Rome.

Well that's my advice. I thank God I did not become a Roman Catholic till I was wholly convinced of the claims of the Roman See—now, and ever since, I have as little doubt of it as of the existence of a Church at all. And truly from the time I made up my mind to be received the English Church melted before my eyes and ceased to exist as a Church. "I went by, and lo she was gone; I sought her, and her place could nowhere be found." And I have found in Rome all that the heart can desire.'

Another who consulted him receives the following answer, dated November 1, 1900:

'You know how I sympathise with you. It is an agony to feel entangled in the tortuous labyrinth of this question. I used to feel as if one went round and round, sometimes seeing as clearly as possible the exit, and then finding oneself as much entangled as ever. Often Rome seemed so clearly the only conclusion that I felt, "if it is so clear everyone must see it, and as they don't I must be deceiving myself." And then when the intellectual position seems solved the moral one rises up, and one wonders if men so much better than oneself reject Rome, how can God leave them in the dark and give me the light, etc., etc. You know it all, no doubt. Yet it is not our part to solve the mystery of God's leadings, but to obey as He seems to lead each one of us. I think one thing is good to remember, that when one thinks of the intense goodness and holiness of so many in the English Church whom you and I have known and lived with (such as the Cowley Fathers and numbers of others) who believe most of the Catholic Faith—what they live on is not given them by the English Church, they have got most of it from Rome. If it would be possible to bind them down hard and fast to the Prayer Book and the teaching of the bishops, how many of them could stand it? The Church that they love and profess to obey is an ideal—non-existent, a dream, the Church of 1500 years ago—one that God guided for 500 years and then abandoned! When I analysed the Church of my dreams and of my allegiance as an Anglican, I found it living at my side in the form of Rome. In coming to Rome I felt that I simply transferred myself to where I belonged. I believed practically what I have always believed, with the addition of the divine authority of the Papacy. That kept me back for a long time. I felt once or twice as I stood on the threshold that I did not believe it and so I went back, and I am thankful I did not come while a shadow of a doubt remained on that subject. I have never had a doubt or a question upon it since I came. When one is brought up in the belief that the Papal position is purely ecclesiastical, one interprets facts and writings according to that theory, yet one feels how often one has to strain things to suit the theory. The same things become luminous when one has grasped the fact that our Lord instituted the Papacy as truly as He did the Episcopate, and that the Church legislated as to the way in which both offices should be exercised. . . .

One is not called upon to take so grave a step in a hurry. Even when it all seems clear I think one ought to take time to make sure that this is a lasting conviction—not a passing moment of insight. One's old faith should have a decent burial, as St. Augustine says of Judaism. Be as *sure* as you *can* be ; so sure that whatever you may have to go through afterwards you can't be shaken. The upheaval is terrible—the breaking of old ties and associations—the tearing up one's life by the roots. Many Catholics you will find narrow, ignorant of all you have been interested in in the past, and not much interested in you—a stranger coming from a land they despise. You will feel very lonely ; no one knows the people and the things of your past ; often your heart will feel so torn that you may think it is your intellect that wavers, that is uncertain, and as the heart turns back to its old moorings it may seem as if you acted hastily or without conviction, or with impatience. Therefore you need a sheet-anchor to hold you fast in such stormy times. I felt the hold of that sheet-anchor more than once in the certainty that whatever I might feel I knew that there was nowhere for me to turn. The English Church melted before my eyes before I left it, and never has taken substantial form since. I knew that I had to hold on to the Papacy as divine, and I knew that however trying *some* (by no means all) Catholics might be, I had no doubt that Rome was the Catholic Church. I hope you may see clearly what you ought to do, and may do it. . . . I ought to add that I have had really a wonderfully easy time of it ; things have been made more easy than I could have imagined, but everyone must expect at first a time of inward suffering.'

To a third he writes :

'You have my very deep sympathy in the difficult position in which you find yourself placed. Of course there can be no question that a man is bound to follow his conscience at all costs, however much pain it may bring to those he loves and to himself. But one is certainly justified in testing one's self and making sure that one's convictions are real, and that one is not acting upon impulse. I do not know how long you have felt upset, or the exact nature of your difficulties. You only speak of the attraction of Rome. I believe myself that that attraction is one of the inevitable results of the truth of her claims ; if she is the Body of Christ, His divine Presence upon earth, the result should be precisely what it is, that she should draw out the most devoted love and the bitterest hatred among men, just as Our Lord Himself did, and just as with Our Lord many good and earnest men could be ranked amongst His opposers. But at the same time, such an attraction is not in itself sufficient to justify an educated man in becoming a Catholic. Her appeal is to the head as well as to the heart. It's not enough even to have lost all faith in the Church of England, you must have a positive belief in the claims of Rome. She appeals no doubt, like her Head, to all those who are weary and heavy-laden that she may give them rest, and this rest she does most assuredly give ; but the reason and the intellect must first find some measure of that rest, which comes from the firm belief in her claims and which leaves no lurking doubts as to their justice. I do not know how far you have considered all this, as you do not say. My own belief is, that to any one who knows what her claims are, not what they are supposed to be, and who clears his mind of all conscious or unconscious prejudice her claims are irresistible. After sixteen years of experience, I thank God with all my heart that I became a Catholic, and realise more and more that the Church is the only body that seems to me able to exist in the gathering storms of modern thought, or to guide men safely through them.'

The following passages are on the subject of Anglican Orders.

'*November* 20*th*, 1899.

. . . The English Church always awaits a General Council, so she says. If a General Council were to meet the question of her Orders would have to be gone into before her bishops were allowed a place. Would you—having the same subjective experience as you have had—be prepared to accept her judgment if it were against their validity ? (*A priori* one would suppose that such a decision must be against, as every body, outside herself, who has gone into the question has given it against them : the (Jansenist) Archbishop of Utrecht on almost the same grounds as Rome.) If you would accept such a judgment, then the argument from subjective experiences (which is certainly one to give full weight to) which you now use, yields to the stronger objective one of authority, and your reason for giving them so much weight is really that you do not accept the authority which has condemned English Orders. I suppose you would say, "If a General Council were to meet I should sink all personal objections and be prepared to pledge myself in advance to accept its judgment." If so, then the falling back upon the strength of conviction of the validity of English Orders is merely another way of saying, I do not believe that Rome is the Catholic Church—or, in other words, I do in my heart believe the whole Anglican claim, and in that case what can you do but stay where you are ?

But, on the other hand, if you examine the grounds of your conviction of the validity of Anglican Orders as a "real fact"—as you say—leaving aside for the moment subjective experiences which no one can argue with—on what do they rest? Not on the authority of the English Church as a whole and continuously, for she has always allowed a larger or smaller portion of her ministry categorically to deny them, and, as Gore said the other day, sixty years ago only two bishops on the Bench believed in them. There has never, therefore, been either a unanimous or uninterrupted belief in them in the English hierarchy; it is therefore on the authority of individual scholars and theologians, or as the outcome of your own private studies. I don't suppose that you rely with confidence on the latter as against Rome, so you are thrown back on the authority of individuals. Have you such implicit confidence in, I do not say their scholarship, but in their having the traditional theological ethos as would lead you to accept their judgment in so delicate a matter, as against the traditional methods of Rome? "De sacramentis nihil dubium." There must be a certainty, a doubt in such a question is impossible. Do you then feel such an entire confidence in individual authority in the English Church on this question as to outweigh the decision of Rome, and all the conception you had formed on other grounds of her claim to authority?'

'*April 18th*, 1904.

. . . I can, in the most decided way, assure you that your informant is mistaken in saying he or she ever heard me say I believe in the validity of the Orders of the English Church. It would be impossible for me to be mistaken in this matter, and I would ask you to beg this person to contradict it to whomsoever he or she may have said it. The repetition of such things does much harm in holding people back, and I have been fettered with so many things I have neither said nor thought, that I think the person owes it to the cause of Truth to say, at any rate, that if it was thought I said it, the person is mistaken. As to my own personal conviction. When I made up my mind to be received the question of Orders never troubled me. I never had any doubt on the subject; but in making up my mind to be received I felt that, in a question of that kind, if, as I did, I believed Rome to be the Catholic Church, I could not hesitate to accept her judgment. It never occurred to me to be a question to consider, whether I should get ordained. I did so without scruple or question. To my mind the question is a far larger one than a matter of that kind. Orders do not make a Church, and *the* Church always has claimed and exercised the right of deciding as to the validity of the Orders of any heretical or sectarian body.

As to past experience of Sacraments in the English Church, I answer as I always have done. I do not care to be logical or to define, and I leave it with God, being deeply grateful for all of good—and I cannot measure it—that I did get in the past. If the question were ever reopened in Rome, and if it were decided that more was to be said for Anglican Orders than thought, no one would rejoice more than I; but I feel that it is all a very technical question for skilled theologians and that subjective experiences must not be given undue weight.'

'*July* 4*th*, 1912.

The whole question of Orders, for many years before I became a Catholic, seemed to me a secondary one. What I felt was this. If Rome *is* the Catholic Church, it is for her to decide what is necessary for the conveyance of Holy Orders. If a man is not ready to trust her in such a matter, it is because in his heart he does not believe she *is* the Catholic Church. I felt that I did not trust the judgment of the English Church alone, in anything, though personally I never had any doubt, even when I left, as to my Orders. But I never could conceive of a man who on other grounds believed the Roman claims hesitating to accept and act upon her judgment in such a very technical matter, and I never had a question or a scruple about being ordained after I was received. I do not see how any man could reasonably accept the Roman position, and accepting it, refuse to accept her judgment upon such a point. After all, the question as to what is necessary to convey Holy Orders is a very technical one. The Anglican Church never professed to train their[1] clergy in very technical theology: the Roman Church does. Therefore, *a priori*, I should have been ready to accept the judgment of a Roman theologian before that of an Anglican on so vital a question. Nor should I feel the least disturbed if—say ten years hence—Rome reopened the question and reversed her decision. I should believe I had acted right in accepting her decision at any time; that the whole responsibility rests with her, though I do not think she is ever likely to change her opinions on the subject. . . . It is, I think, the height of unreason to believe that Rome *is* the Catholic Church and not to accept her judgment upon so fundamental a point.'

On August 20, 1912, he writes to the above correspondent:

'. . . For myself, I can truly say that it was what I believed as an Anglican that drove me to Rome—to stay where I was seemed to me to stop short suddenly and unreasonably from the conclusions involved in the

[1] [*sic*] ? her.

premises which I had so far accepted. Even to have the succession, does not make the body which has it the Church or a part of the Church. . . .'

Other letters to lay people who sought his advice contain many useful points. In one (Feb. 23, 1899) he says:

'. . . I can see, I think, and am glad to see the best side of the English Church; it was my lot to live amongst men whose lives were as true and as holy as I believe are to be found anywhere, and certainly, the present movement in the English Church has produced multitudes, amongst the laity, of most devout and pious souls. I never feel tempted to say hard things of the English Church; on the contrary I feel towards her, I think more tenderly than I did when I was in her, as I can now read calmly of the things which jarred upon and irritated me when in the English Church. But, having said all this, it would not be true if I did not add that seeing her as I now do I have not the least remnant of faith in her, as an organisation, or in her claim to be a true part of the Body of Christ. It came to me long ago what an outrage upon Truth, and what a constant dishonour to our Lord, it must be for a body calling herself a Church to allow her clergy to teach as they pleased either that our Lord is or is not present in the Blessed Sacrament. It seemed to me it would be better and more to His honour to insist upon all her clergy denying it than thus treating it, as if it did not matter how one took His words, and the same with Confession and several other things. Such a position seemed to me to be so radically untruthful, dishonest, and a nursery for scepticism. . . . Nor could I accept the common answer which maintained that the Prayer Book taught true doctrines, and if the clergy were not true to the Prayer Book it was not the fault of the English Church. It seemed to me much like saying that a country had most excellent laws in the Statute Books, but was powerless to enforce them. Moreover, of late the bishops have as clearly as possible put themselves in opposition to that party in the English Church to which I belonged, and to which you still belong. Therefore through her legitimate rulers the English Church repudiates the only party in which I for one feel any interest. . . .

No doubt many of the statements in the Prayer Book which looked entirely Protestant *can* be construed in a more Catholic sense, yet to the ordinary mind they do not read so, and I believe they were drawn up intentionally with a view to the possibility of a more Catholic interpretation. This seems to be contrary to the whole spirit of historical Christianity, which ever sought to state accurately and clearly what she believed and to remove all possibility of doubt.

. . . (1) Of course such a step as you are just now suffering from, your confessor and trusted teacher leaving the English Church, must naturally upset you and set you thinking. I believe God often uses such means for leading people. We are all rightly influenced by those we trust. St. Paul's conversion doubtless shook the faith of many in their position as Jews. At the same time, what convinces one may not convince another, and therefore you mustn't let yourself be *unduly* influenced. He may have reasons that do not convince you, and in the turmoil of mind consequent upon his act, you may not be able to judge clearly the force of your convictions. Wait, therefore, till your mind recovers its balance, and till you can see things as they are. He, I am sure, would urge you not to act as he has done, because he has done it. Your convictions must be strong and sure, and able to hold out against any questionings that may hereafter arise in your mind. Each soul in one sense stands alone, and has to answer for its acts before God. Arguments at this moment may appeal to you with greater force than they would at ordinary times—give yourself time to weigh them calmly and with your soul at peace. Truth does not need precipitation—on the contrary, it is calm, strong, eternal, and therefore can take time to work its way.

(2) Remember there are two states of mind often not kept clearly apart as they need to be. It is *one* thing to doubt the English Church, *quite another* to believe in the Roman. All the doubt possible of the English Church doesn't necessarily mean belief in Rome, and without this latter you could not come, you would never have any peace. Rome demands, rightly, an absolute faith in herself; if you have not that, you would be worse off than you are if you came. Therefore, all those things people say so commonly—" Go to Rome (the city) and you'll be cured of any desire to become a Roman Catholic "—I think are quite properly said; for what it really means, I suppose, is, if you do not find the *practice* up to what you expect you'll lose your faith in the system. I should go further and say, if any such arguments weigh with you at all, go to S. America, or anywhere where things are supposed to be at their worst. If irreverence or slovenliness or even badness in the priesthood would weigh with you, you don't believe in the Roman Church. Personally, I can't imagine their weighing with *me* at all. I believe in the Roman Catholic Church from convictions too strong to be moved by any local scandals, however grievous, and I believe if one has faith enough in Rome to become a Roman Catholic that all such arguments

are devoid of the smallest weight. A local scandal would be a very poor reason for leaving the English Church. I left it because my faith in her, as a system, had wholly died out. I became a Roman Catholic because I believed—whatever possible evils might exist in any place—she was the only representative of the Church of the Apostles on earth. By all means, therefore, come to Rome and see all you can see, or go to Spain or S. America, or anywhere you are advised, and if anything you see in any of these places holds you back, it is because you have not faith in the Roman Church strong enough to justify your becoming a Roman Catholic. . . .

(3) You must not gauge it by the sensible effect of the Sacraments. I have myself had no sensible devotion of any kind since I was received, but I should be sorry to put the Sacraments to any such test. I do know and can bear witness that there are forms of life produced in the Roman Church that the English Church does not even dream of—I mean in many of the strict religious orders. I was amazed at what I saw even in London a few weeks after I was received in this respect. This is the real test of the Sacraments—in individual cases the effect of the Sacraments may be modified by the life of the individual; but in the corporate body no one, I think, who knows both the English and Roman Churches, can doubt that the evidence of their reality in Rome is something that the English Church has never produced, and can't produce. That part of the English Church to which you belong has still the fervours of a first beginning—in Rome all these things have been going on for ages, therefore you may even at first be disappointed at not finding a certain kind of fervour such as you have been used to; but if God leads you to take the step, and if

you take it, compelled by your convictions of faith, you will not regret it.'

To another enquirer he writes on November 18, 1908 :

'I sympathise with you very much in your trouble. I went through so much myself for several years before I was received that I know something of what you must be suffering, but this I think I can say without exaggeration, that the question was never out of my mind for an hour while I was awake for ten years or more; very soon after I was received it passed away for good, and since then I have never had a doubt or question. . . .

1. There are two states of mind on the subject that are quite distinct :

(*a*) Loss of faith in the English Church.

(*b*) A firm faith that the Roman Church *is* the Catholic Church founded by Our Lord.

I have known of many who took it for granted that despair of the Church of England necessitated a belief in Rome. This is a mistake. Rome stands upon her own claims—they are positive and distinct ; if you believe in them you can't believe in the English Church, for her claims are quite incompatible with every belief in Anglican claims. But it's quite possible to lose all faith in the English Church and not to accept the claims of Rome.

This, I think, you will see, but you must keep it clearly before your mind. I should most certainly refuse to receive a person who desired to be received *only* on the ground that he had lost all faith in the English Church.

2. You must try also to keep clearly before you the difference between conviction and any feeling of attraction.

I only learnt this after a long experience of the reaction

of the whole mind when facing the step. All the associations and spiritual experiences of a lifetime may rise in loud protest, while conviction remains unchanged. . . .

The star of Bethlehem was no doubt often clouded as the wise men followed its leading, and many a time they must have wondered if they were not deluded. I remember a very short time before I was received being overwhelmed with a deep repugnance against Rome and the whole question, and in the midst of the tumult of the rush of feeling, and association and desire to stay where I was, looking up, and there was the star of conviction clear and steady above all the battling elements within. . . .

3. Again, you speak a great deal of your spiritual state, of its being at a standstill, etc. But the hope of new spiritual awakening is not enough to lead you to take the step you are considering; it is undoubtedly true that if you become a Catholic you will have new and great spiritual helps—indeed, I have felt that there is nothing the soul can want that is not provided for it in the Catholic Church, it is in truth a land flowing with milk and honey. But the shock of change can do harm as well as good—a break in the middle of one's life is a serious thing not devoid of danger; moreover, it may be your lot to find if you become a Catholic that God will plunge you in spiritual darkness. He does do so to many good people. No, you must not let such hopes unduly influence you. . . .

You must act simply upon your conviction; "It is the Truth, and I must obey it, come what will."

I have known of many who have deteriorated by becoming Catholics—that does not affect the question "Is it the Truth?"

You can't make conditions with God. Surely, if you act rightly, God will help you, but if you take the step the result spiritually will depend upon your own earnestness and fidelity.

4. You speak a great deal about the Will of God. " Is it God's Will that I should go or stay where I am ? " This, I think, is misleading. It is a curious kind of distinction that you make between obeying what you believe to be the Truth and the Will of God.

It is simpler to put the question barely to yourself: " Do I believe that the Roman Church is the Church of God, and that her claims are true ? "

That's the whole question. If you do believe it, it's certainly the Will of God that you should act upon it, if you don't—the question is at an end. It seems to me that you make the Will of God a separate factor, to be considered quite apart from the only question that really exists for you : " Is it true ? " I think people sometimes get their minds contorted by separating between the Will of God and acting upon conviction, saying to themselves : " Yes, I believe Rome is right, but at the same time I feel as if it is the Will of God that I should stay where I am." Such an attitude is, of course, self-deception.

To obey the Truth, or what we are convinced is the Truth, *is* to obey the Will of God. And be sure God will give you no special revelation. You must obey in these matters the conclusion of your reason. Reason leads to the Truth. Faith then comes and makes you certain, suffuses the whole nature with unshaken conviction. . . .

You must go out, in some sense, into the darkness if you act on Faith. There is the feeling, perhaps I shall be disappointed, perhaps I shall find things I don't expect. Well, I can only tell you that I should be sorry to keep back anything from you, or to stretch out a hand to help you to come where you would find what would lead you to regret the step afterwards.

I do not plead for a cause that I have espoused, nor am I particularly anxious to proselytise—you are a perfect stranger to me, I only want to help you. If there is any fear of lurking revelations or discoveries after you take the step, tell me what your fears are and I will truly tell you if they have any foundation in reality. I know of nothing. I have discovered nothing. Many individual Catholics are narrow, many ignorant of what is going on outside the Church, many very uninteresting, many do harm by their proselytising campaign. But the Catholic Church *is* the city of God where the soul finds peace and plenty, and there is a spirit of joyousness and a power of dealing with sin that is not even dreamed of outside.'

In answer to another person on the verge of conversion who asked him what had been his own reasons for becoming a Catholic, he writes, February 22, 1902 :

'. . . You asked me what convinced me that the English Church is not a part of the Church Catholic. It is not difficult for me to answer. It was practically two things :

1. Her isolation from the rest of Christendom, of which she claims to be part. No one recognises that claim except a minority of her own children. The English Church as a whole does not make the claim, only the High Church part of it. Moreover, I could not see what guarantee she could give for the truth of what she taught where she differed from the rest of Christendom. She never claimed to be infallible, yet in many points she differs from the rest of Christendom, whether you take that to mean Rome alone or Rome and the Orthodox East. Why should I believe that in any such points of difference she is right and all the rest wrong ?

Why should a few bishops who break away from the

rest of the body be protected from error and say, "We are right, and in these points all others are wrong."

No doubt it might be so in the nature of things, in the Arian troubles the minority were right; but I think we have a right to ask a small fragment making such a claim to prove by miracle or the extraordinary sanctity of its followers that its claim is reasonable. For instance, from the Fourth Lateran Council, 1214, up to, say, 1549, the English Church in union with Rome taught that Transubstantiation was Divine truth. From 1549 to to-day she has taught that Transubstantiation overthroweth the nature of a Sacrament and is plainly contrary to the Word of God. Why should I believe her for the last three hundred years of separation when she contradicts categorically her own teaching in union with Rome of three hundred years before? Moreover, since she changed this doctrine she has practically robbed her people of faith in the Real Presence.

Again, apart from all the rest of Christendom she refuses Unction to the dying, though distinctly commanded by St. James. Again she has deprived all her children of the practical doctrine of the Communion of Saints.

Why should I believe her to be right and all the rest of Christendom wrong? Certainly not because of the fruits of this teaching, for the fruits have been such that every High Churchman to-day deplores and tries to remedy them. . . .

The unity of the Church is necessary for its infallibility—it all holds together: every bishop has the right to interfere with every other bishop if he seems to depart in any way from the Faith, and at the head of all is the Pope. From a mere human point of view, so closely coherent is the whole Church that it would seem impossible that it should drift from the original teaching.

2. My second point was, that on a matter of fact the English Church *can't* teach at all. She allows you to hold most Catholic doctrines, and she allows someone else to hold every Protestant doctrine. . . .

Her clergy can teach what they believe as any other clergy can, but all parties quote the Prayer Book, that is the authority of the English Church, and she will not speak, she will not say which represents her. The only foe she has to fear are her own children, and the only reason because she will not tell them which are her loyal children.

I must not write more. Let me say, however, a word on two points.

(*a*) "Leaving the Church of your baptism."

That is pure nonsense. You were baptised into the Body of Christ—the true Church, whatever it is. If the English Church is the true Church, every Roman Catholic was baptised into it. If Rome, then everyone, everywhere has been baptised into Rome—the *true Church*, whatever it is. If you believe Rome is the true Church, you enter then with heart and reason and faith the Church of your baptism from which heresy and schism hitherto held you back : instead of leaving the Church of your baptism you *enter* it with your own will.

(*b*) The other point is about the exercise of your private judgment.

Your reason and your private judgment were given you amongst other reasons to lead you to the Truth. . . . I consider such an act the highest and noblest act of the private judgment. The wrong exercise of private judgment is for the individual, having entered the Church, to imagine he can test each separate doctrine and reject or accept what commends itself to him. The true exercise is by the use of reason to find out where that Teacher is of whom was said: "He that receiveth you, receiveth Me."'

He writes on a historical point as follows:

'. . . Consider the two Reformations. There were grave abuses no doubt in the sixteenth century—abuses that no doubt had their influence in leading to the Reformation. The English Church claimed the right, apart from the rest of Christendom, to reform herself, and she did so, and you see the result. At the same time Rome reformed herself and got rid of the abuses, while keeping the faith and discipline of the Church intact.

The English Reformation destroyed in the minds of the people the idea of a Church, faith in the Blessed Sacrament, and deprived them practically of confession and absolutely of Holy Unction. The Roman Reformation left the old system intact and swept the abuses away. *Everyone* can see the continuity between the pre-Reformation Church and Rome, only a few prejudiced people can suppose the English Church of to-day to be the representative of the pre-Reformation Church. . . .

To say that England and Rome are one is absurd; the forms of government of the two Churches are different. One is Papal—the Episcopate with the Pope at its head, equally divine in their origin—the other is Episcopal; they are as different forms of government as a monarchy and a republic. America might as well claim to-day continuity with the Colonial States: she ceased to be English and monarchical at the Revolution, and the English Church ceased to be the old Church when she changed her form of government, to say nothing of her doctrine, at the Reformation; but I am afraid I am dogmatising.

Have you read Gairdner's Henry VIII in the *History*

of the English Church, edited by the late Dean of Winchester. Do read it. I feel for you in the throes in which I suffered so long, but I am sure it will end right. Don't hurry yourself by an hour. God will give to your mind a clear and undoubting conviction if He is leading you to the Catholic Church. But as one draws near often the light dies out and leaves one in utter darkness for a time ; the mind clings and turns back to its old mode of thought, and the heart yearns after its old associations and all the memories of many blessings in the past—verily, it's like Peter leaving the shelter of the boat and going out into the storm to follow the Voice that called him.'

The following are taken from letters written to console and strengthen some of those who had, with his help, made up their minds to enter the Catholic Church.

May 27, 1904.

' . . . You may feel assured that He who has led you so far will lead you on to the full light of His Truth. Those resting-places in the past were but temporary, while your mind and heart were being prepared for something vastly larger and fuller.'

June 27, 1904.

' I think you are quite right to go into every question, and leave no ghosts to come later out of dark corners to disturb your peace. There are many questions, of course, that can't be answered, but I always think the answers given by the Church are less unreasonable than those given outside, when she does give an answer, and please don't imagine a difficulty is looked upon by me as trivial if it doesn't happen to be my own difficulty. The greatest difficulties often spring from having to adjust the mind to new intellectual surroundings ; it feels ill at ease in its new home, and is awkward in moving about and cannot settle comfortably on the new resting-places, which later on it delights to lounge and rest upon. The *things* are there and they are seen and known and measured and understood, but the *mind* feels strange and awkward in dealing with them.'

August 13, 1904.

'. . . One wants, above all, to dispel from the minds of intelligent non-Catholics the nightmare that as soon as one becomes a Catholic one is forced to say certain things. Make your friends feel that your mind was never so free or vigorous, that the Catholic Church is not a system of intellectual rigorism, but that the "Truth makes you free."'

November 26, 1906.

'. . . I think there is nothing in the world like mental suffering, and perhaps no mental suffering like that which comes from having to hurt one's friends. But when that is the condition of testing and proving one's love to God, God must surely accept and bless it abundantly. And He will, and when you have settled down in the richer soil and purer air, you'll feel it.'

March 6, 1912.

'. . . I hope your reception will bring you many blessings, but you must not, and I am sure will not, expect to see any immediate results. . . . Tearing oneself from associations with which one had been bound up all one's life, and which hold all one's best and holiest associations, is not an easy step, and one does not grasp all the consolations till one gets a little healed and soothed—that will come in time. Don't look back, never reopen the question, never analyse your motives, but try to throw yourself into your new surroundings and life. Don't let yourself criticise ways that seem to you not to be as good as those you have been used to, and don't be scandalised at the quiet ways, instead of a good deal of the enthusiasm you have had where you were. You are coming into a system that has gone on over 2000 years without a change, that has converted the world, that does not lay itself out for bright services, etc., but has the strength to house and shelter the world against the assaults of unbelief, and I believe no other body has. In a year or two you'll be singing your Te Deum—to-morrow you'll possibly be sore and worried as to whether you have done right; but you have, and it will all come flooding your soul with peace and consolation in time—but wait and be patient, be strong, and put your trust in the Lord and He will bring it to pass.'

June 27, 1914.

'. . . You may perhaps be feeling what I felt when I was where you are—an intense loneliness, and sometimes a wish that someone could understand; and I want specially to say that I feel great sympathy for you and remember you daily in my poor prayers, but you have to fight it out alone. . . .

I should like, if I may, to say one or two things which I learnt in the storm and stress, when I felt as if it was hopeless to expect to be able to come to a definite conclusion one way or the other.

1. There comes a time when there is no use in reading, or indeed in definitely thinking further. Your mind has taken in all it will ever be able to assimilate on the subject; then pray and look up, not in. I should like to give you a passage from Bergson that is very suggestive on this subject. He is speaking of his theory of intuition. He says, "Anyone who has been engaged in literary production knows perfectly well that after long study has been given to the subject, when all documents have been collected, and all sketches made, one thing more is necessary—an effort,

often painful, to set oneself in the heart of the subject and get from it an impulse as profound as possible, when there is nothing more to be done than to follow it. This impulse once received, sets the spirit on a path, where it finds again all the information it had collected and a thousand other details. The impulse develops itself, the further you go on the more is revealed, yet if you turn back to apprehend the impulse you feel behind you, it is hidden from you."

That impulse in questions of faith is, I believe, partly human, partly divine. It's partly the unconscious outcome of digesting and assimilating all you have read and thought, but it is also partly divine—"the spirit of the Lord moving upon the face of the waters" and bringing order out of chaos. But the voice of the Holy Spirit is so gentle, so careful never to intrude upon your liberty, never to compel you to a conclusion, that it is only after the decision has been come to that you realise how much you were led, and how great a part He took in making the issue clear.

2. And therefore you must not look for anything strikingly supernatural. You are to be led to the door of the Truth mainly—as it may seem to you, almost entirely—by the guidance of your reason. Waiting for a call, or to know God's Will as people say often, is sometimes a delusion. God's Will is that a person should be reasonable, should not believe truths which are contradictory, etc.; that a person should be truthful and sincere with his own convictions. There is, indeed, the supernatural illumination of faith that makes a synthesis of all the streams of thought that led in one direction, but that may be the crown of the acts of the labour of the intellect and reason.

3. Do not pay any attention to the reaction of feeling—moments when the whole subject becomes abhorrent to you, and you wonder if it wouldn't be better to leave

it all alone and go back to where you were. This, I believe, is the last fight between heart and head. It may be that in the end, if you make up your mind to be received, you'll have to do it in cold blood, without an emotion, with an aching heart and a weary brain, only knowing that you cannot longer keep any self-respect without doing it. Those who think you are doing wrong will of course, rightly, try to dissuade you, and bring up sometimes quite irrelevant matter as reason to deter you, such as scandals and abuses and so on; but remember that in our Lord's time the state of the Jewish Church was pretty low, when Phariseeism was the predominant influence, yet He said, "Salvation is of the Jews."

The one and only question is, Is Rome right, is she the Church of Christ?—and if by God's grace you enter it, I for one can promise you that you will say, "I was led haltingly and painfully and uncertainly—even at the last I almost went back, but now I know, for I have seen with mine own eyes, and the half was not told me."'

Less than a year after this letter was written, in Lent 1915, Father Maturin went to New York to preach a course of sermons. He booked his return passage in the *Lusitania*, and went down with the ship on May 7, 1915. One of those he helped to save tells us that he was last seen 'striving to keep people calm, giving Absolution to those who asked for it, fastening on life belts, and helping women and children into the boats. . . . Then he stood waiting for the end, quite calm, but as white as a sheet. . . . He put on no life belt. He did not take off his coat. He made no attempt to escape, but simply awaited death.'

* * *

Vixi in fretis, morior in portu.

APPENDIX

Note 1. The italics and parentheses throughout the letters are exactly as found in the original text; except when 'italics mine' follow an italicised phrase or the brackets enclosing the words in parenthesis are square ones. Most of these additions were made by the compilers of the books from which the letters are taken, to supply the omission of words the writer of the letter evidently intended to use. In a few cases, where the modern reader might find the old-fashioned wording difficult to follow, or miss the point of an allusion, the present writer has also made use of parentheses in square brackets, in the hope of supplying what is necessary.

Note 2. *The Donatists.* Bowden's Catholic Dictionary says: 'Schismatics who afterwards became heretics; and held that the validity of the Sacraments depended upon the moral character of the minister, and also that sinners could not be members of the Church. They were first condemned in 313.' Milman tells us: 'The Donatists . . . asserted themselves to be the only elect people of Christ, the only people whose clergy could claim an unbroken apostolical succession, vitiated in all other communities of Christians by the inexpiable crime of Tradition.' *History of Christianity.* (Cf. Article XIX: *Of the Church.* Book of Common Prayer.)

Ward's *Life of Newman* (p. 67) says: 'S. Augustine had replied to the claims of the Donatists to be really Catholics on the ground that they adhered to antiquity by the words *securus judicat orbis terrarum.* The mere appeal to antiquity had been disallowed. For a religious society to belong to the Universal Church it was necessary that the Church should recognise its claim.'

Note 3. *Tract* 90. A letter written on March 8, 1841, by the Rev. J. B. Mozley, clearly shows what Tract 90 contained, and why it so horrified the Evangelical party of which, at that time, almost the whole Anglican Church was composed: 'A new Tract has come out this last week which is beginning to make a sensation. It is on the Articles, and shows that they bear a highly Catholic meaning; and that many doctrines of which the Romanist are corruptions may be held consistently with them. This is no more than what we know as a matter of history, for the Articles were expressly worded with a view to bring in Roman Catholics. But people are astonished and confused at the idea now, as if it was quite new, and they have been so accustomed for a long time to look on the Articles as on a par with the Creed that they think, I suppose, that if they subscribe to them they are bound to hold whatever doctrines are (not positively stated in them, but) merely not condemned. So if they will bear a Tractarian sense they are thereby all of them Tractarian.'

Note 4.

Article XXII. Of Purgatory. The Romish Doctrine concerning Purgatory, Pardons, Worshipping, and Adoration, as well of Images as of Reliques, and also invocation of Saints, is a fond thing vainly invented, and grounded upon no warranty of Scripture, but rather repugnant to the Word of God.

Article XXXI. Of the one Oblation of Christ finished upon the Cross. The Offering of Christ once made is that perfect redemption, propitiation, and satisfaction, for all the sins of the whole world, both original and actual; and there is none other satisfaction for sin, but that alone. Wherefore the sacrifices of Masses, in the which it was commonly said that the Priest did offer Christ for the quick and the dead, to have remission of pain or guilt, were blasphemous fables, and dangerous deceits.